AQA Religious Studies: Philosophy of Religion

AS

Exclusively endorsed by AQA

Anne Jordan
Neil Lockyer
Edwin Tate

Nelson Thornes

Published in 2008 by:
Nelson Thornes Ltd
Delta Place
27 Bath Road
CHELTENHAM
GL53 7TH
United Kingdom

09 10 11 12 / 10 9 8 7 6 5 4 3 2

A catalogue record for this book is available from the British Library

ISBN 978 0 7487 9820 9

Cover photograph: Alamy/Design Pics Inc.
Illustrations by Gordon Lawson; additional illustrations by Hart McLeod
Page make-up by Hart McLeod

Printed and bound in China by 1010 Printing International Ltd

The authors and publisher are grateful to the following for permission to reproduce photographs and other copyright material in this book:
p14 Bettmann/Corbis; p19 Corbis; p31 Mary Evans Picture Library; p36 Hulton-Deutsch Collection/Corbis; p43 Bettmann/Corbis; p48 Mary Evans/Sigmund Freud Copyrights; p59 Bettmann/Corbis; p67 Scott Houston/Corbis; p82 Bettmann/Corbis; p93 Mary Evans Picture Library; p112 David Biagi/Fotolia; p114 Benjamin Lowy/Corbis; p123 Craig Barhorst/ iStockphoto; p128 Vadim Cebaniuc/Fotolia.

Contents

AQA introduction

Nelson Thornes and AQA

Nelson Thornes has worked in collaboration with AQA to ensure that this book offers you the best support for your AS or A level course and helps you to prepare for your exams. The partnership means that you can be confident that the range of learning, teaching and assessment practice materials has been checked by the senior examining team at AQA before formal approval, and is closely matched to the requirements of your specification.

Blended learning

Printed and electronic resources are blended: this means that links between topics and activities between the book and the electronic resources help you to work in the way that best suits you, and enable extra support to be provided online. For example, you can test yourself online and feedback from the test will direct you back to the relevant parts of the book.

Electronic resources are available in a simple-to-use online platform called Nelson Thornes learning space. If your school or college has a licence to use the service, you will be given a password through which you can access the materials through any internet connection.

Icons in this book indicate where there is material online related to that topic. The following icons are used:

🔆 Learning activity

These resources include a variety of interactive and non-interactive activities to support your learning.

✅ Progress tracking

These resources include a variety of tests that you can use to check your knowledge on particular topics (Test yourself) and a range of resources that enable you to analyse and understand examination questions (On your marks…).

🔗 Research support

These resources include WebQuests, in which you are assigned a task and provided with a range of web links to use as source material for research.

🔖 Study skills

These resources support you develop a skill that is key for your course, for example planning essays.

When you see an icon, go to Nelson Thornes learning space at www.nelsonthornes.com/aqagce, enter your access details and select your course. The materials are arranged in the same order as the topics in the book, so you can easily find the resources you need.

How to use this book

This book covers the specification for your course and is arranged in a sequence approved by AQA.

AQA Unit 1C, Philosophy of Religion is covered in the first four chapters of the book. This encompasses: The cosmological argument; Religious experience; Psychology and religion; and Atheism and Post-modernism. AQA Unit 1D, Religion, Philosophy and Science is covered in the next four chapters of the book. This encompasses Abortion; Euthanasia; Religion and the Created or Uncreated World; and Environmental ethics.

Learning objectives

At the beginning of each section you will find a list of learning objectives that contain targets linked to the requirements of the specification.

The features in this book include:

■ Key terms

Terms that you will need to be able to define and understand.

■ Links

These refer you back to other points in the book which consider similar points

■ Think about

Short points for discussion within small groups or your class.

■ Activity

Things for you to do that will reinforce the information you have just learned.

AQA Examiner's tip

Hints from AQA examiners to help you with your study and to prepare for your exam.

AQA Examination-style questions

Questions in the style that you can expect in your exam. AQA examination questions are reproduced by permission of the Assessment and Qualifications Alliance.

Learning outcomes

At the end of each chapter you will find a list of learning outcomes. These remind you what you should know having completed the chapter.

■ Summary of key points

Each unit finishes with summary of key points from the previous four chapters.

■ Web links in the book

Because Nelson Thornes is not responsible for third party content online, there may be some changes to this material that are beyond our control. In order for us to ensure that the links referred to in the book are as up-to-date as possible, each web site is accessible through this Nelson Thornes site: www.nelsonthornes.com/aqagce.

Please let us know at **webadmin@nelsonthornes.com** if you find a link that doesn't work and we will do our best to redirect the link, or to find an alternative site.

Introduction to this book

What is philosophy of religion?

Any definition of the philosophy of religion will be controversial. This is because it is traditionally used and interpreted in very different contexts. In modern times, particularly in Europe and America, the philosophy of religion has meant an analysis of certain elements and concepts of (particularly Western) religions. In the main, this has meant a critical study of Christianity and, to some extent, Judaism.

The questions raised by this study are far too numerous to be listed here, but they include the following:

- Does God exist?
- Can God be experienced?
- Has the impact of psychology on religion been negative?
- Is atheism a real alternative to religion?
- Do miracles occur?
- Is there conflict between science and religion?

All of these questions and more will be discussed in this book.

Why study philosophy of religion?

Socrates (470–399 BC) is regarded by many as the 'Father of Philosophy'. However, he was tried, condemned and executed for his teachings. This was because many of his contemporaries (such as Aristophanes) argued that his method of enquiry was irreligious, as it attempted to understand 'the Divine'.

Despite the physical demise of Socrates, his impact on logical investigation and what would become the philosophy of religion was profound. Indeed, this academic area is of such interest today because of the method of critical enquiry that Socrates, and others, developed.

Many people have suggested that science was the 'new religion' of the 19th century. If this is the case, then surely philosophy is the 'new religion' of the 21st, for exactly the same reasons: that is, it enables an individual to question what he or she is told, and to reach *his or her own conclusions*.

As such, the study of the philosophy of religion develops an enquiring mind, the ability to analyse a point of view, the ability to develop and reason through an argument, and the ability to reach a logical and justified conclusion.

What is involved?

The simple answer to this is *reading* – and lots of it! You will find some primary source material in this book, but mainly summary, comment and evaluation. Therefore, background reading to back up the material here is essential for a full understanding.

At the end of each chapter you will find 'Summary questions'. These questions are typical of questions for AS papers.

The book is written particularly for AS GCE students studying either or both of the AQA Religious Studies Specification units Philosophy of Religion (1C) and/or Religion, Philosophy and Science (1D). The content of each chapter relates to one of the topics within the specification.

Philosophy of Religion

1 The cosmological argument

Learning objectives:

- to understand how far the cosmological argument seeks to prove that God exists

- to understand why religious believers argue that the cosmological argument demonstrates that it is reasonable to believe in God

- to assess the strengths and weakness of the cosmological argument so you can evaluate it as an argument to support religious faith.

The cosmos refers to a complex and orderly system, such as our universe, which is the opposite of chaos

Key terms

Cosmos: the world or universe as a perfect and well-ordered system.

The cosmological argument seeks to prove the existence of God based on the starting point that there is a universe. The argument seeks to prove why there is a universe and a world in which we live rather than nothingness.

The cosmological argument has taken many forms and has been presented in many ways. In each form, the argument focuses on the causes that lead to the existence of things. The argument appears to answer the questions:

- How did the universe begin?
- Why was the universe created?
- Who created the universe?

■ The classical cosmological argument

The cosmological argument is also known as the 'First Cause argument'. It derives the conclusion that God exists from an *a posteriori* premise. The argument is *a posteriori* because it is based on what can be seen in the world and the universe.

The starting point of the argument is observation of our world. These observations show that things move and change. Things are caused to happen as the result of how actions affect them. From our observations we can see that things come into existence and then cease to exist. However, we do not live in an empty universe as there is always something existing in our world rather than nothing. The cosmological argument seeks to prove that the universe (cosmos) and all that is in it has a cause and that cause is God.

> To speak of chance for a universe which presents such a complex organization in its elements, and such a marvellous finality in its life would be equivalent to giving up the search for an explanation of the world as it appears to us. In fact, this would be equivalent to admitting effects without a cause.

> *Pope John Paul II*

The cosmological argument is used to support the existence of **the God of classical theism**, who has **necessary existence**.

Aristotle and the Prime Mover

The ancient Greek philosopher Aristotle (384–322 BC) believed that all movement depends on there being a mover. For Aristotle, movement means more than something travelling from A to B. Movement also includes change, such as growth, melting, cooling and heating. Aristotle argues that behind every movement there must be a chain of events that brought about the movement that we see taking place, and that there was a 'common source' of all substance; in other words something/someone that was responsible for the beginning (at least) of everything. Aristotle argues that this source is an eternal substance, which exists necessarily and is immune to change, decay and death. Aristotle argues that there must have been an 'unmoved mover' who is the ultimate cause of the universe as if there were no ultimate cause to begin the chain of causes and effects then there would be no chain at all. Nothing would have come into existence. Aristotle calls this unmoved mover the Prime Mover.

The Prime Mover causes the movement of other things: not as an **efficient cause**, but as a **final cause**. In other words, the Prime Mover does not start off the movement by giving it some kind of push, but is the purpose, or end, or the *teleos*, of the movement. This is important for Aristotle, because he thought that an efficient cause, giving a push, would be affected itself by the act of pushing. Aristotle believes the Prime Mover causes things to move by attraction in much the same way that a saucer of milk attracts a cat. The milk attracts the cat but cannot be said to be changed in the process! The Prime Mover is perfect and all in this universe desire to be such and are attracted to God because all things desire to share this perfection. For Aristotle the Prime Mover is God.

Aristotle argues that:

- God did not create the universe.
- God did not sustain the universe.
- God did not act in the universe.
- God had no interest in the universe.

God is supremely happy because God contemplates himself. Aristotle considered contemplation to be the highest end, and God, being **supremely perfect**, would have no interest at all in the universe. Instead God thinks about and contemplates his own nature, and since God is supremely perfect this would make God supremely happy.

The universe is in space and time but God is outside space and time. God is spaceless and timeless. God is radically different from anything in the universe.

St Thomas Aquinas (c. 1224–74)

Aquinas's chief work was *Summa Theologica* (Summaries of Theology). Aquinas felt that Aristotle's system of logic and ethics was compatible with Christianity, and often quoted from Aristotle to support his arguments. Aquinas distinguished between the two different routes that an individual could take to God. Although Aquinas acknowledged the superiority of revelation in 'finding' God, he suggested that the same knowledge could eventually be found through human reason.

Aquinas did not accept that the statement 'God exists' is self-evident. He states that it is a proposition that requires demonstration. In the *Summa Theologica* Aquinas developed 'Five Ways' to prove the existence of God, which he called *demonstratio* for the existence of God. Aquinas based his arguments on what could be observed. His observations included that in the universe even inanimate objects move and change. From those observations he reached conclusions about the existence of God.

The first three of his Five Ways form the cosmological argument as a proof of the existence of God. Aquinas accepted that it might not be possible to prove that the cause of the universe is the God of classical theism.

> God's effects ... are enough to prove that God exists, even if they may not be enough to help us comprehend what He is ...

St Thomas Aquinas, Summa Theologica

1.2 The cosmological argument of St Thomas Aquinas

Aquinas's Three Ways that support the cosmological argument are:

- motion or change
- cause
- contingency.

The First Way

The First Way is based on motion. Aquinas was speaking of motion in the broadest sense. Aquinas included not only movement from one place to another, but also movement in the sense of change of quality or quantity. According to Aquinas, an object only moved when an external

Activity

1. Before you read Aquinas's version of the cosmological argument, list the similarities and differences between Aristotle's Prime Mover and the God of classical theism.

   After you have read the section related to Aquinas's cosmological argument look again at your list. Are there any changes you would now make to it?

2. List the conclusions you think Aquinas could have derived from the evidence seen in the world of nature and the movement of the heavenly bodies seen with the naked eye.

3. Now study the Three Ways of Aquinas which form the cosmological argument as proof of the existence of God and consider where there are similarities and differences between your list and Aquinas's findings.

Think about

Aquinas did not accept infinity because he believed that there had to be an adequate explanation for the existence of things. If a chain of movement or causes went back for ever with no beginning then there would be no reason for the existence of the universe.

■ **Key terms**

Infinity: eternity; time without end.

Potentiality: the inherent but undeveloped capabilities and possibilities of someone or something for development or change.

Actuality: a state of being, the reality of something at this moment in time.

force was applied to it. According to Aquinas, this chain of movements or changes cannot go back to **infinity**. There must have been a first mover, or Prime Mover, which itself was unmoved. The Unmoved Mover began the movement in everything without actually being moved. Aquinas argued the Prime Mover is God.

> The first and more manifest way is the argument from motion. It is certain, and evident to our senses, that in the world some things are in motion. Now whatever is moved is moved by another, for nothing can be moved except it is in potentiality to that towards which it is moved; whereas a thing moves inasmuch as it is in act. For motion is nothing else than the reduction of something from **potentiality** to **actuality**, except by something in a state of actuality.

St Thomas Aquinas, Summa Theologica

The need for an external influence

Aquinas continued that objects only changed because some external force had brought about the change. He spoke of things achieving their potential through an external influence. Aquinas used the example of fire making wood hot. Fire when applied to wood changes the wood to achieve its potential to become hot. In order for a thing to change requires actuality; whatever brings the change from potentiality to actuality must itself have achieved the actuality to achieve this change or movement. If it did not, a thing would have to initiate change in itself, which would require that it is both actual and potential at the same time. Aquinas considered this to be a contradiction.

For example, if wood could make itself hot then it would be hot already. Wood cannot be hot to begin with; otherwise, it would not change and become hot. The fact that it is wood is its actuality. The fact that fire can make it hot is its potentiality. In turn, something must have made the fire change and become alight. Each change, therefore, is the result of an earlier change. Aquinas, however, did not accept that there was a series of infinite changes. He concluded that there was a point at which the first movement (or change) occurred, brought about by 'a first mover'. Therefore, according to Aquinas, 'it is necessary to arrive at a first mover, moved by no other; and this everyone understands to be God'.

The Second Way

■ **Link**

Look up the definition of 'efficient cause' on p2.

In Aquinas's Second Way he identified a series of causes and effects in the universe. Aquinas observed that nothing could be the cause of itself, as this would mean that it would have had to exist before it existed. This would be a logical impossibility. Aquinas rejected an infinite series of causes and believed that there must have been a first, uncaused, cause. This first cause started the chain of causes that have caused all events to happen. This first cause was God.

■ **Think about**

How is Aquinas's Second Way related to efficient cause different from the first way linked to motion?

Why do you think that Aquinas uses the term 'effects' rather than 'events'?

> The second way is from the nature of efficient cause. In the world of sensible things we find there is an order of efficient causes. There is no case known (neither is it, indeed, possible) in which a thing is found to be the efficient cause of itself; for so it would be prior to itself, which is impossible. Now in efficient causes it is not possible to go on to infinity, because in all efficient causes following in order, the first is the cause of the intermediate cause, and the intermediate is the cause of the ultimate cause ... Therefore it is necessary to admit a first efficient cause, to which everyone gives the name of God.

St Thomas Aquinas, Summa Theologica

Aquinas's rejection of infinite regress

In order to avoid an infinite regress in his theory of causality (and second proof of God's existence), Thomas Aquinas proposed that there had to be an 'uncaused cause' that began all change in the universe. Aquinas rejected that the motion and change, or the cause and effect, went back to infinity. Aquinas argued that motion/change and cause/effect cannot go on into infinity, because then there would be no first mover, and, consequently, no other mover. According to Aquinas there must be a first mover, which is how we define God, because there cannot be an infinite regression of movers putting objects into motion.

Similarly it is impossible to go on into infinity with efficient causes because of the very definition of efficient causes: the first is the cause of the intermediate cause, which is the cause of the ultimate cause. No matter how many intermediate causes there are, a first and an ultimate cause always exist. The cause cannot be taken away because the effect is removed with it.

To deny infinite regress means that there must be a Being which in itself is an uncaused cause and eternal; a Being which does not depend on anything else for its existence, otherwise this being would have had to have a beginning and therefore have been caused to exist. This means the chain would continue as we would have to ask what was the cause of the Being and what caused that cause and so on. For Aquinas the motion/change and cause/effect starts with a being with necessary existence, and this being is 'what we call God'.

A later philosopher, Gottfried Leibniz (1646–1716), developed an argument for '**a sufficient reason**' which gives additional support to Aquinas's argument for rejecting infinite regress. Leibniz accepted the cosmological argument because he believed that there had to be a sufficient reason for the universe to exist. Leibniz rejected an infinite universe because he did not believe that it was a satisfactory explanation for its existence. He accepted that God was the first, uncaused cause on which everything else depends. He argued as follows:

> Suppose the book of the elements of geometry to have been eternal, one copy having been written down from an earlier one. It is evident that even though a reason can be given for the present book out of a past one, we should never come to a full reason. What is true of the books is also true of the states of the world. If you suppose the world eternal, you will suppose nothing but a succession of states and will not find in any of them a sufficient reason.

Gottfried Leibniz, Theodicy, 1710

> ### Key terms
>
> **Sufficient reason:** an adequate reason that explains the cause of an event, in this case the origin of the universe.
>
> **Contingency:** an event or condition that depends on something else, which may or may not happen. Things do not contain the reason for their own existence, but depend on external causes. Objects around us exist but they could just as easily not exist.

The Third Way

Aquinas's Third Way relates to the argument that something must have started off the universe. This is based on the fact that everything that begins to exist has a cause. The universe began to exist and therefore the universe must have a cause. This means that Aquinas is examining not only the cause of the universe but also all the contingent matter in the universe.

Based on this fact that the universe came into existence and that things in the universe come in and out of existence, Aquinas considered the possibility of infinite time. If time is infinite then there must have been a time when nothing existed. This is because of **contingency**; the very fact that things are contingent means that they cannot continue forever.

If there were a time when nothing existed then there would still be nothing, as nothing can bring itself into existence. Therefore the cause of the universe must be external to it and must always have existed. There must have been a 'necessary being', to bring everything else in to existence. Aquinas argued that this 'necessary being' was God. He concluded that if God did not exist then nothing would exist.

> The third way is taken from possibility and necessity, and runs thus. We find in nature things that are possible to be and not to be, since they are found to be generated, and to be corrupted, and consequently, it is possible for them to be and not to be. But it is impossible for these always to exist, for that which can not-be at the same time is not. Therefore if everything can not-be, then at one time there was nothing in existence. Now if this were true, even now there would be nothing in existence because that which does not exist begins to exist through something already existing. Therefore, if at one time nothing was in existence, it would have been impossible for anything to have begun to exist; and even now nothing would be in existence – which is – absurd … therefore we cannot but admit the existence of some being having of itself its own necessity, and not receiving it from another, but rather causing in other their necessity. This all men speak of as God.

St Thomas Aquinas, *Summa Theologica*

Aquinas is arguing that everything in this world has a finite and conditioned existence that is dependent for its existence on an infinite, unconditioned cause which is understood by definition to be God. Every cause in the chain of causes is dependent on God for existence. Aquinas is arguing that a necessary being is required for the existence of things. Some scholars have criticised Aquinas's argument, asking why did there have to be a time when nothing existed? Surely it could be possible to have infinite regression without a time when nothing existed. This problem is overcome if it is accepted that Aquinas is talking about an **ontological** cause and not a **temporal** cause. In other words a first cause on which everything else depends and continues to depend for its existence.

On pp7–8 the contingency argument of Frederick Copleston is considered. Copleston draws attention to the fact that there are two types of causes: '*cause in fieri*', which is a cause leading to things becoming what they are, but, having started the process, is no longer involved; and '*cause in esse*', in which not only is there a cause that brings a thing into being but that cause must be sustained for that thing to continue. For Aquinas and Copleston, God's existence is necessary to sustain the existence of everything else. If God did not exist then neither would His creation exist. This is why for Aquinas there cannot be infinite regression because without this first cause which in itself is uncaused then there is no explanation for our existence.

💡 Challenges to the cosmological argument

Not all philosophers agree with Aquinas that the universe was caused and sustained by God or even that there is evidence that the universe has a beginning.

David Hume

David Hume (1711–76) believed that all knowledge and ideas, however complex, can be reduced to some experience that our senses have

---

■ Think about

Aquinas argued that it is not possible for a Being to be explained by nothing; there has to be a reason for the existence of things. Human beings are caused by other contingent beings. How therefore would Aquinas explain the existence of necessary beings?

■ Activity

Write a 500–600-word explanation of Aquinas's version of the cosmological argument.

■ Key terms

Ontological: ontology is the branch of metaphysics dealing with the nature of being.

Temporal: relates to worldly rather than spiritual matters.

■ Activity

An example of causation *in fieri* is a boat builder who, having watched the successful launching of the boat he has constructed, walks away. It is left to the purchaser to care for it. *In esse* may be compared to electricity lighting a bulb that illuminates a room. The illumination of the room continues as long as the electricity makes the light bulb work. If the electricity supply is interrupted then the bulb will not light up and the room will become dark.

Make your own list of examples of *cause in fieri* and *cause in esse*.

provided. Hume's examination of people's mode of thinking led him to conclude that humans think that they know a great deal more about the external world than is warranted. Hume argued that the mistake humans make is to allow imagination to make a connection between cause and effect. For Hume, therefore, Aquinas is wrong in making a connection between cause and effect. Aquinas has observed cause and effect around him and the existence of the universe. His error, Hume is arguing, is to join those two events together when they are in fact two separate events. It is just the habit of the mind that has made the connection between the two events; it is **induction**. It is not therefore proof for God causing the universe to exist.

In *Dialogues Concerning Natural Religion* (1779), Hume asked why we must conclude that the universe had to have a beginning. 'How can anything that exists from eternity have a cause, since that relation implies a priority in time and in a beginning of existence?' Even if the universe did begin, Hume continued, it does not mean that anything caused it to come into existence.

Hume argued that as we have no direct experience of the creation of universes we could not speak meaningfully about the creation of the universe. Hume did not believe that there was either sufficient evidence to prove the cause of the universe or even that the universe was caused.

Immanuel Kant

The German philosopher Immanuel Kant (1724–1804) examined the argument of the existence of a supreme Being as a first cause of the universe. He argued that the idea that every event must have a first cause only applied to the world of sense experience. It cannot apply to something we have not experienced. Kant did not accept any justification for the conclusion that God caused the universe to begin. Kant would not accept it as valid to extend the knowledge we do possess to questions that transcend our experience. God would be a causal being outside space and time as we understand it. Therefore, it would be impossible for people to have any knowledge of what God created or of God himself.

Bertrand Russell

The British philosopher Bertrand Russell (1872–1970) introduced the expression **philosophical logic**. This referred to a process in which key philosophical questions were re-worded in mathematical terms. This resulted in Russell's work being presented as such. The reason why Russell felt this to be necessary was because of the fact that normal (that is, 'everyday') language can be extremely misleading. Fundamentally, his argument was that every word stands for something. He believed that words were often used without the user knowing what they stood for – or, in some cases, without standing for anything! As an example, he cited the uses of the word 'is'.

This led to the development of the **fallacy of composition**, which is falsely ascribing the properties of the parts of a whole to the whole. For example, when applied to the cosmological argument it would be making a statement such as: 'Objects within the universe were created. Therefore the universe was created.'

 Radio debate between Copleston and Russell

In 1947 there was a debate on BBC radio between the Jesuit priest and professor of the History of Philosophy at Heythrop College F. C.

■ **Think about**

Copleston's argument is based on the premise that everything can be explained. Is this a valid statement or do you think that Russell was right to reject the demand for a total explanation as required by Copleston?

Copleston (1907–94) and Bertrand Russell. These two philosophers had opposing views about the origin of the universe. Copleston supported the cosmological argument as evidence for the existence of God, whereas Russell opposed it.

The debate focused on the 'principle of sufficient reason', which Copleston supported:

> Cause is a kind of sufficient reason. Only contingent beings can have a cause. God is His own sufficient reason; and he is not cause of Himself. By sufficient reason in the full sense I mean an explanation adequate for the existence of some particular being.

BBC radio broadcast, 1947

AQA Examiner's tip

In the exam, take your time and pace yourself. The exam will give you enough time to read and analyse the question, and to plan your answer before you start to write it. Make sure you have understood what it is asking, and then plan both your answer and your use of time.

Russell rejected the idea of contingency and that there was a necessary being, God, on which all things depend. God as a necessary being would have to be in a special category of His own. Russell raised the question of where this special category comes from, and why should such a category should be accepted. Russell argued that a 'necessary being' has no meaning. To which Copleston replied that the very fact that Russsell was talking about God in this way demonstrated that he (Russell) understood the meaning of a 'necessary being'. The two philosophers could not agree and Russell concluded that Copleston was making a fallacy of composition; just because humans have a mother it does not mean that the universe had to have a mother. The universe does not have to have a beginning. It could always have been there and that was brute fact. As Russell stated: 'I should say that the universe is just there, and that's all.'

One of the major objections to the cosmological argument is the suggestion that infinity is impossible and that the universe had a beginning. Many philosophers point out that Aquinas and Copleston contradict themselves when they reject the possibility of the infinite. Aquinas and Copleston denied the infinite and yet argue that God is infinite. Supporters of the argument point out that God is unique and the laws of nature do not apply to God.

■ **Activity**

Write a 500–600-word essay discussing Russell's statement 'I should say that the universe is just there, and that's all'.

Russell is supporting the possibility of infinite regress. His arguments count against not only Copleston but also Aquinas. He does not agree with the two philosophers that the universe must have had a beginning otherwise there is no adequate explanation for its existence. Russell argues that there may be no reason for the existence of the universe. It has always existed and that is a 'brute fact' that has to be accepted.

💡 Scientific theories and Aquinas's cosmological argument

Scientific theories about the origins of the universe have been used to support and to reject aspects of Aquinas's cosmological argument for the existence of God.

Anthony Kenny

The British philosopher Anthony Kenny (1931–) presents an argument that undermines Aquinas's First Way related to motion and change. In *The Five Ways* (1965), Kenny said that Aquinas's principle that nothing moves itself goes against the fact that people and animals move themselves. He continued that Newton's first law of motion, in which movement can be explained by a body's own inertia from previous motion, disproves Aquinas's argument. It is possible for objects to have uniform motion as well as being in a state of rest. Kenny says that Newton's law 'wrecks the argument of the First Way. For at any given time the rectilinear uniform motion of a body can be explained by the principle of inertia in terms of the body's own previous motion without appeal to any other agent'.

Many philosophers have countered Kenny's argument by pointing out that 'motion' for Aquinas meant any kind of change of state. A human could be at rest but still undergoing change; for example ageing or changes in blood pressure.

🔢 The steady-state theory

The steady-state theory counts against Aquinas's Third Way related to contingency and necessary existence, by suggesting that the universe is eternal. This theory provides a scientific explanation that would undermine the cosmological argument as it denies a beginning to the universe. Until recently, scientists have accepted the theory that energy cannot be created and that therefore the universe will always weigh the same and the energy within the universe will simply be redistributed. The acceptance of the uniformity of the universe led to the theory that it should look much the same not only from the same place but also at any point in time. This is the steady-state theory. It is the opposite view to **Creationism** since it teaches that there is no beginning or end to the universe, that the universe has always been there and that its appearance does not change with time. The old stars are mixed in with new ones. So although the universe is expanding, i.e. its galaxies are moving apart, the theory states new galaxies have to be created to fill in the gaps left by old galaxies. The continuous creation of new particles of matter is at a rate that is automatically adjusted by the cosmological expansion. This is at a steady rate and always the same. 'The universe is a huge self-regulating, self-sustaining mechanism, with the capacity to self-organise ad infinitum.' (*The Cosmic Blueprint*, Paul Davies, p154.) The idea was originally put forward by Herman Bondi, Tommy Gold and Fred Hoyle in the 1940s. Bondi and Gold worked on the theory from a philosophical point of view whereas Hoyle tried to put it on a scientific footing. The steady-state theory has generally been rejected in favour of the **Big Bang** theory.

🔢 The Big Bang theory

This theory provides a scientific theory to explain the beginning of the universe. Both supporters of the cosmological argument, and those who deny it, use the Big Bang theory as a proof for or against the existence of God. Scientific observation has confirmed that there was a beginning to the universe, and has provided further evidence that the universe developed a structure very early in its history.

The Big Bang theory is a challenge to the cosmological argument only if it is accepted as a rival theory to the cosmological argument. If the Big Bang is considered to be a spontaneous random event without reason or cause then Aquinas's assertion that God is mover and cause of the universe is undermined. On the other hand if it is accepted that there must be a reason why the Big Bang happened, and that once the universe began to evolve there seems to have been a sustainer of the universe that ensured it developed and continued, then the Big Bang theory gives support to a belief in the God of classical theism.

Key terms

Creationism: the belief that the universe and living organisms originate from specific acts of divine creation, as in the biblical account, rather than by natural processes such as evolution.

Big Bang: a scientific theory to explain the origin of the universe. The Big Bang is considered to have occurred when a single, extremely condensed state of matter exploded. The universe was formed from the gases created by the explosion. Those scientists who accept the Big Bang theory regard it as the moment at which time began.

Think about

■ What problems would acceptance of the steady-state theory raise for a believer in the God of classical theism?

■ Is it possible for a religious believer to accept scientific theories about the origin of the universe and the cosmological argument?

Link

Read Chapter 7: The design argument. How does the design argument give additional support to the cosmological argument as evidence for the existence of God?

■ Key terms

Kalam: an Arabic term which means to 'argue' or 'discuss'. The Muslim scholars al-Kindi (9th century CE) and al Ghazali (1058–1111) developed the *kalam* argument to explain God's creation of the universe. The *kalam* argument is cosmological because it seeks to prove that God was the first cause of the universe.

Actual infinite: set theory. It refers to sets or collections of things with an infinite number of members. It is not growing towards infinity, because it is infinite already. A part within an actually infinite set is equal to the whole set because it is infinite. For example, in an actually infinite set of numbered books in a library, a count of the even numbered books is equal to a count of all the books. Some philosophers argue that actual infinite numbers cannot exist. This is because whether you add to, or subtract from, an actual infinite number, it would always remain the same number – infinity. An actual infinite is 'complete' at all times, and philosophers regard this as illogical.

Potential infinite: exists if it is always possible to add one more to a series of things or events. It is possible to think of the future as a potential infinite, because more events are always being added to history.

Ex nihilo: derived from Latin, meaning 'out of nothing'.

■ The *kalam* cosmological argument

William Lane Craig

The American philosopher William Lane Craig (1949–) developed a modern version of the argument in his book, *The **Kalam** Cosmological Argument* (1979). The first part of the argument states the following:

- The present would not exist in an **actual infinite** universe, because successive additions cannot be added to an actual infinite.
- The present does exist, as the result of a chronological series of past events.
- The universe must be finite.
- A finite universe had a beginning.
- Whatever began to exist had a cause, as things cannot cause themselves.
- Therefore the universe had a first cause of its existence.
- This first cause was God.

Craig argued that if the universe did not have a beginning, then the past must consist of a series of events that is *actually infinite* and not merely **potentially infinite**. Craig cannot accept this idea because it would mean that past events form a collection of events; in which, for example, there would be just as many wars as there would be all other events together.

Craig concluded that:

- The history of the universe was formed by one event following on after another event – this is successive addition.
- A collection formed by successive addition cannot be actually infinite.
- Therefore the universe must have had a beginning in time.

> Since everything that begins to exist has a cause of its existence, and since the universe began to exist, we conclude, therefore, the universe has a cause of its existence ... Transcending the entire universe there exists a cause which brought the universe into being ... But even more: we may plausibly argue that the cause of the universe is a personal being ... If the universe began to exist, and if the universe is caused, then the cause of the universe must be a personal being who freely chooses to create the world ... the kalam cosmological argument leads to a personal Creator of the universe.
>
> *William Lane Craig*, The Kalam Cosmological Argument, 1979

The second part of the *kalam* argument seeks to prove God as the personal Creator of the universe. If the universe had a beginning, then this beginning was either caused or uncaused.

Either it was a natural occurrence or a choice was made to bring the universe into existence. Supporters of the *kalam* argument argue that since the rules of nature did not exist before the beginning of the universe, the universe cannot be the result of natural causes. Craig concluded that 'if the universe began to exist, and if the universe is caused, then the cause of the universe must be a personal being who freely chooses to create the world'.

The argument depends on the belief that God created the universe *ex nihilo*. If the universe was created out of nothing, then the beginning of the universe was the beginning of time. There must have been a personal agent existing outside time to start the process of creation, an agent who willed the universe into existence.

■ Think about

How is Craig's *kalam* version of the cosmological argument similar to Aquinas's argument from contingency and necessary existence?

How successful is the cosmological argument?

A number of arguments have been levelled against the cosmological argument that those who support it have to counter. The key strengths of the cosmological argument may be summarised as:

- as an *a posteriori* argument it is based on experience and this is a strength. As everyone has experience of cause and effect then they are able to understand the belief in the universe as having a first cause for themselves.
- the Big Bang theory has provided scientific support for the argument as it demonstrates that the universe has a beginning and therefore the universe is not infinite.
- scientists who accept the Big Bang theory cannot explain what caused the big bang.
- as we are able to measure time, this would suggest a beginning to the universe. If we were in an actual infinite universe we would not be able to measure time.
- people can see for themselves that the universe exists and this is further support for the argument that things that exist are caused to exist and that cause is God.
- Richard Swinburne suggests that it is the simplest explanation of why there is something rather than nothing.
- the argument satisfies the need to find a cause of the universe and the origins of everything within the universe.

Link

Look at Chapter 8, pp122–133, to find out more about quantum mechanics.

Look up the meaning of atheist and agnostic in Chapter 4, p51.

The value of the cosmological argument for religious faith

When considering any of the arguments presented as evidence for the existence of God, it is necessary to think whether or not the argument would convert an atheist or an agnostic to believe in God. Would the arguments put forward by Aquinas in his Three Ways be sufficient evidence for the existence of God if there was not already faith in God?

Natural theology is the name given to the use of reasoned argument to provide a basis in reason for believing in God. It could be argued that the cosmological argument would provide such a basis. When added to the other arguments for the existence of God then the reasons for believing in God are strengthened. However, philosophers such as Russell denied that whatever evidence was presented the existence of God can neither be proven or disproven.

Therefore, according to Russell, arguments for the existence of God have no value. Religious believers would not agree. Such arguments simply support their already existing belief in God. They have faith that God exists. This view has become known as **fideism**, which argues that faith cannot be tested by using rational enquiry. Faith is something that a believer has that accepts that the teachings of the religion are true and because of their beliefs then they will look at the universe and see cause and effect, motion and change and accept that it was brought into existence by God. The atheist, on the other hand, may be inclined to see the universe as the result of random chance.

It is necessary when considering the value of the arguments for the existence of God that for a believer, faith is more than believing that God exists. It involves believing in God which includes trust in God, commitment to God and following a particular lifestyle.

Key terms

Natural theology: knowledge of God which is obtained by reason alone, without the aid of revelation.

Fideism: an idea that religious beliefs cannot be justified by rational means, only through faith.

■ Conclusion

Some philosophers argue that even if there was a first cause of the universe, there is no proof it is the God of classical theism. The first cause could be anything. Hume argued that the first cause if there was one could be the material, physical world rather than God. The material world as its own cause is just as satisfactory explanation as God.

One of the major objections to the argument is the suggestion that infinity is impossible and that the universe had a beginning. Many philosophers point out that Aquinas and Craig contradict themselves when they reject the possibility of the infinite. Both Aquinas and Craig deny the infinite and yet argue that God is infinite.

Supports of the argument point out that God is unique and that the laws of nature do not apply to God. The evidence for the Big Bang theory does give support to a beginning to the universe and therefore greater weight to the cosmological argument's basic premise that the universe had a beginning. Recently Quentin Smith has argued against the *Kalam* version of the cosmological argument. Smith uses quantum mechanics to demonstrate the possibility of things existing without direct cause. The universe may have had a beginning, but there is no reason to think that beginning was caused by God.

Whether or not this beginning was caused by God becomes very much a matter of faith. It may be that the cosmological argument supports what the individual already believes and will not convert a non-believer into accepting the existence of God.

Davies takes the position that the cosmological argument cannot stand alone as a proof for the existence of God, and would have to be supported by other evidence. The design argument might be further evidence to establish the existence of God.

> As an argument for a first cause of all existing things the cosmological argument seems a reasonable one. But it does not by itself establish the existence of God with all the properties sometimes ascribed to him.
>
> *Brian Davies*, *The Introduction to Philosophy of Religion*, 1990

Now that you have read this chapter you should be able to:

■ define words associated with the cosmological argument

■ summarise Aquinas's version of the cosmological argument

■ question how far the cosmological argument proves that God exists or show that it is reasonable to believe in God

■ assess the strengths and weaknesses of the cosmological argument

■ evaluate the value of the cosmological argument for religious faith.

2 Religious experience

Learning objectives:

- to understand the variety of religious experience including visions, conversion and mystical experiences

- to understand the argument for the existence of God from religious experience

- to understand the challenges to religious experience from philosophy and science

- to evaluate whether or not a religious experience can show that God exists

- to evaluate whether or not it is necessary to have a religious experience in order to be able to understand what a religious experience is

- to assess whether the challenges to religious experience from philosophy and science are successful.

Key terms

Empiricism: the philosophical theory that all knowledge is derived from experience. Experience always means sensory experience, i.e. experience that depends on one or more of the five senses.

Genuine: by using this term we are not implying that the experience has definitely come from God. We are suggesting that there is nothing to imply that it has been contrived by an individual or individuals (perhaps pursuing his or her own agendas).

Arguably, the proof we rely on most of all in the 21st century is our own experience. If we have seen, heard or experienced something, we accept the 'truth' of whatever that may be (rightly or wrongly). Advocates of this approach would perhaps find the family of arguments we will consider in this chapter the most appealing in suggesting that God exists.

Activity

Write down five statements that you believe to be true, as a direct result of your own experience, or the experiences of other people.

a   Try to work out whether you would be as happy to believe the statement if you had not had the experience, or heard about it from someone else.

b   What evidence would be needed to make you accept the statement?

The term 'religious experience' can conjure up a wide and diverse series of images. We might assume that it can mean anything from saying a prayer, to attending a service at a place of worship, to 'hearing the voice of God'. However, our understanding of the term is important in investigating the concept.

Activity

Write a sentence to express how you would interpret the term 'religious experience'.

If your definition incorporates the idea of personal involvement in any form of prayer, reflection, worship or meditation, then you are focusing in the right direction. However, for our purposes it is important to have a more definitive answer.

What is religious experience?

- A religious experience is a non-**empirical** occurrence, and may be perceived as supernatural.

- It can be described as a 'mental event' which is undergone by an individual, and of which that person is aware.

- Such an experience can be spontaneous, or it may be brought about as a result of intensive training and self-discipline.

- Recipients of religious experiences usually say that what has happened to them has 'drawn them into' a deeper knowledge or awareness of God.

- It is very important to remember that the experience itself is not a substitute for the Divine, but a vehicle that is used to bring people closer to the Divine.

- The experience that each individual has is absolutely unique and cannot be shared with anyone.

- Finally, **genuine** religious experiences seem to be encouraging; they do not condemn the individual, but help them to live a better life, or help others, for example.

■ Characteristics of religious experience

There is an infinite number of different religious experiences, as each one is unique, but there have been attempts to classify them based largely upon the results of the experience. The main classifications of religious experience are:

■ visions

■ conversion

■ mystical experiences.

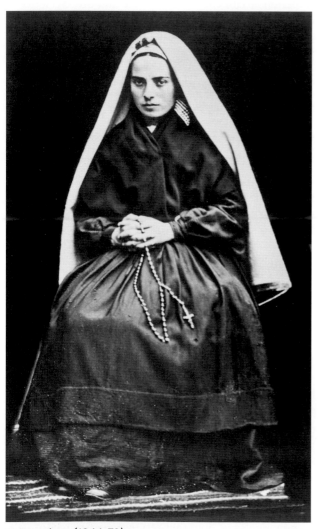

St Bernadette (1844–79)

🔆 Visions

A religious vision occurs when an individual believes that they have seen or heard something supernatural or a supernatural being. There are three ways in which the individual may experience a vision:

■ An intellectual vision brings knowledge and understanding such as a revelation from God.

■ An imaginary vision where something that strengthens faith is seen with the mind's eye such as Jacob's vision of a ladder to heaven (Genesis 28:10–22).

■ A corporeal vision is where the figure is externally present such as St Bernadette's visions of the Virgin Mary.

An example of visionary experience is St Bernadette. When she was 14 years old Bernadette had visions of the Virgin Mary over several months. At first the figure she saw did not speak to her but later Bernadette was given instructions by 'The Immaculate Conception' (The Virgin Mary), that the spring water at Lourdes had healing powers and that a chapel was to be built on the site.

Sometimes dreams are considered by individuals to have been visions. For example in Matthew's Gospel Joseph is warned in a dream to take Mary and Jesus to Egypt to protect them from Herod.

In terms of visions Julian of Norwich, the 14–15th century mystic, is a particularly good example of someone who received visions. In *The Revelations of Divine Love*, she recounted one vivid experience:

And he showed me more, a little thing, the size of a hazelnut, on the palm of my hand, round like a ball. I looked at it thoughtfully and wondered, 'What is this?' And the answer came, 'It is all that is made'. I marvelled that it continued to exist and did not suddenly disintegrate it was so small. And again my mind supplied the answer, 'It exists, both now and forever, because God loves it. In short, everything owes its existence to the love of God.'

Julian of Norwich, *The Revelations of Divine Love*

Numinosity

Many testimonies from those claiming to have had a religious experience refer to a sense of being in the presence of an awesome power, yet feeling distinctly separate from it. The word given to describe this feeling is **numinous**. While many regard numinosity as a feature of religious experience, some classify it as a 'type' in its own right and contrast it with mystical experience.

The German theologian Rudolph Otto (1869–1937) used the term 'numinous' in *The Idea of the Holy* (1936), in referring to being in the presence of an awesome power. He suggested that religion must derive from a being that is totally separate from this world. It is in the presence of such a being that numinosity is experienced. Otto claimed that many of the visions recorded in the Bible, such as Moses' vision of the burning bush, are experience of the numinous. Other scholars argue that Otto is wrong in describing visions as numinous because they involve a much more direct encounter with God. Moses spoke to God when he approached the burning bush.

🔦 Conversion

A vision often results in a conversion. This is when the effects of a religious experience are life-changing. The term 'conversion', in the sense of religious experience, refers explicitly to 'regeneration', and an assurance of the 'truth of the Divine'. The result of a conversion on a personal level is usually a greater understanding of faith. 'Religious conversion' is the process that leads to the adoption of a religious attitude or way of life. These effects can be permanent or temporary.

For instance, you should already be familiar with the story of the conversion of St Paul, as mentioned in the activity on p14. Here, we have Paul (also known as Saul) hearing the voice of Jesus – 'Saul, Saul, why do you persecute me?' This is followed by a declaration that the speaker is 'The risen Christ'.

After this vision on the road to Damascus, Paul converted to Christianity. Paul spent the rest of his life spreading the Christian message and is believed, according to Christian tradition, to have died a martyr's death in Rome.

Types of conversion

There are basically two forms of mental occurrence which lead to a difference in the conversion process:

■ A conscious and voluntary experience – volitional type.

■ An involuntary and unconscious experience – self-surrender type.

The volitional type features a gradual change and consists of the slow development of new moral and spiritual habits. It may be the case that the

Think about

Consider these examples of visions and any other examples you know about. What could be their causes if they are not genuine visions from God?

Key terms

Numinous: the feeling of the 'holy' and includes awe, fascination, religious awareness and the smallness of self.

Activity

The name change from Saul to Paul is significant to show the conversion of Saul/Paul to Christianity. Names in New Testament times were very significant. The name itself carried meaning. Jesus' name means 'God is salvation'. The given name was often linked to the father's name or the place of birth to provide further information about a person. For example, Jesus was Jesus bar Joseph (son of Joseph) and Saul/Paul was Saul of Tarsus to explain that he came from Tarsus in Greece. Paul is called Saul when he first appears in the New Testament: at a time when he was a Jew following the traditions of the Jewish faith. After his conversion to Christianity, he is known as Paul. This is a Gentile (non-Jew) name and was probably chosen to show that he has become a Christian and 'a teacher of the Gentiles in faith and truth' (1 Timothy 2:7).

Find out the meaning of your given name. Do you think that this name matches your personality?

person suddenly 'becomes aware' of the change one day. The subconscious effects are more evident, however, in the self-surrender type.

For the American philosopher William James (1842–1910), the concept of conversion by self-surrender can be illustrated by the expression 'man's extremity is God's opportunity'. What is also evident is that even in the most voluntary forms of conversion, there has to be some element of self-surrender. It would appear that one can only go so far in bringing about conversion; after a certain stage it must be left to 'other forces'. Edwin D. Starbuck maintains that quite often a person must stop 'trying' to change; only then will conversion occur naturally.

Features of conversion

As a rule, there are two things in the mind of the candidate for conversion:

■ The present 'wrongness' in their life – their sins, perhaps – that they want to change.

■ The positive changes they wish to make.

Recently, there has been much interest in the concept of sudden conversion experiences, leading to the assertion that all religious believers probably had undergone such an occurrence. While a majority of conversions are clearly gradual, the sudden experience would appear to be the most significant and profound, as far as its effects are concerned. It often affects people who had no religious faith whatsoever before the experience. In turn, what is most significant about the gradual conversion is the process involved. It would appear that to begin with a person rejects any notion of religious faith, for whatever reason. He or she then reaches a position in which some elements seem acceptable. This continues until such time as there is a 'climax', at which point complete conversion occurs. This process is a vehicle with which the most complicated series of objections to the faith can be resolved. The process can often result in some of the most passionate and fundamentalist advocates of a given religious group.

Examples of conversions

Religious conversion is likely to include a change in belief on religious topics, which in turn leads to changes in the motivation for one's behaviour within the social environment. As a result, it is appropriate to speak of **intellectual**, **moral** or **social conversions**.

Intellectual conversions involve conflicts between two systems of thought. The result of the conflict is often that the new one is 'true' and the old one is 'false'. It can either be to, or from, a religious system of thought, or from one religion to another.

An example of moral conversion can be found in the story of 'Swearing Tom', as told by the British academic Robert H. Thouless (1894–1984):

> For 17 years, 'Tom' lived a most profane and godless life, until one day he entered a church and heard a preacher say that even the most wicked of men could undergo a change of heart, if they prayed to God. Tom left the church and went home, ignoring the public house for a change, and prayed using the words the preacher had used. Sure enough, a change took place and soon his name was changed from 'Swearing Tom' to 'Praying Tom' – a name he went by until his death.

Activity

Using the internet and the library find out about the conversion of John Henry Newman from the Anglican Church to the Catholic Church.

Write an account of the reasons for Newman's conversion and the effect of his conversion on his life and work.

Key terms

Intellectual conversions: a change in the way of thinking about something.

Moral conversions: a change in behaviour so that the individual does what is thought to be right.

Social conversions: acceptance of a different way of life or worship.

Tom's story illustrates a moral conversion – it does not revolve around a system of thought, as the intellectual one does, but around one's lifestyle.

The American psychologist James H. Leuba (1868–1946) clearly views religious life as almost purely moral. He defines the religious sense as:

> The feeling of unwholeness, of moral imperfection of sin, to use the technical word, accompanied by the yearning after the peace of unity ... The word 'religion' is getting more and more to signify the conglomerate of desires and emotions springing from the sense of sin and its release.
>
> *J. H. Leuba*, 'Studies in the Psychology of Religious Phenomenon',
> *The American Journal of Psychology, vol vii, 1896*

Indeed, Leuba gives a series of examples in which sin ranges from drunkenness to spiritual pride.

An example of a sudden social conversion is St Paul on the road to Damascus. Indeed, it is this idea of a conversion taking place slowly in the subconscious, followed by a rapid and sudden conscious experience, that William James calls 'subconscious incubation'.

William James's conclusions about religious conversion are as follows:

■ Sudden conversion is very real to those who have had the experience. They feel that the process has been 'performed' upon them. God causes the conversion.

■ For Methodists, salvation is not truly received unless they have been through a crisis of the sort which is involved in conversion.

■ Those having a sudden conversion feel it to be a miracle rather than a natural process.

■ Even when James saw conversion as being a natural process, he maintained that it was inspired by the Divine.

How permanent is conversion?

In many cases the person experiencing sudden conversion may know very little about what they have come to believe and testify in! Their knowledge may amount to little more than what they have read in a series of leaflets, or what they have heard from a local preacher. As such, there is far more chance of their deciding at some future point that there are inherent problems in what the preacher has told them, or that there are flaws in the literature they have based their 'new outlook' upon.

🔮 Mystical experiences

Mystical experiences are experiences where the recipient feels a sense of 'union' with the **Divine**.

Mysticism involves the spiritual recognition of truths beyond normal understanding.

It has been suggested that there are several features that accompany the experiences which enable their recognition:

■ Knowledge of the 'ultimate reality' is gained. This is knowledge that is normally hidden from the human intellect.

■ A sense of freedom from the limitations of time, space and the human ego is experienced.

■ **Think about**

Gradual conversion is always more likely to be permanent than sudden conversion. This is probably because a slower procedure is more likely to be thorough. For example, a well-planned essay will always be more thorough than a quickly scribbled effort!

■ **Key terms**

Mystical experience: a direct and intimate experience of God.

Divine: used here to mean a perfect being that is all-powerful and is not comparable to anything human. Such a being is usually referred to as 'God'.

■ A sense of 'oneness' or unity with the Divine is experienced.

■ A sense of bliss or serenity is experienced.

Mysticism is seen as the closest that a human can ever come to actually meeting the Divine.

William James is, arguably, the most famous commentator on religious experience. To evaluate the significance of his work as evidence for the existence of God, it is important to understand his aims and perspective. James was an American doctor (Harvard graduate), not a theologian. He had a deep interest in philosophy, and an equally profound interest and specialism in psychology. His famous work *The Varieties of Religious Experience* (1902) was originally a series of lectures (The Gifford Lectures) given at Edinburgh University at the beginning of the 20th century.

Four characteristics of mystical experiences

James recognised that the term 'mystical' is used in a wide variety of contexts, but suggested that using it to refer to 'any person who believes in thought-transference or spirit-return' is far too ambiguous. Therefore, in *The Varieties of Religious Experience*, he offers four characteristics which he claims will enable us to identify mystical experiences: ineffability, noetic quality, transiency and passivity. These characteristics require detailed consideration.

Ineffability

James suggested that **ineffability** is the most easily recognisable characteristic of mystical experience. This is despite the fact that it is inherently negative. As mentioned earlier, religious experiences are *private* events; the recipient goes through certain sensations that are beyond verbal description – they are unutterable.

With religious experiences there is awareness that there is something to be described, but no way of doing so. St Teresa of Avila stated, 'I wish I could give a description of at least the smallest part of what I learned, but, when I try to discover a way of doing so, I find it impossible ...'

Sometimes descriptions are offered, but these tend to be meaningless to the listener who has no experience of such occurrences. For example:

the dissolution of the personal ego

or

a sense of peace and sacredness.

According to R. A. Gilbert, in *The Elements of Mysticism* (1991), such phrases 'serve to illustrate the extreme difficulty of discussing non-empirical concepts solely in terms of the intellect'.

As the British poet Alfred Tennyson (1809–92) wrote in a letter about religious experience, 'I am ashamed of my feeble description. Have I not said that the state is utterly beyond words?' In conclusion, one might suggest that one cannot truly understand what is beyond one's own experience.

Activity

Try writing down a description/ definition of one of the following, as though you were explaining it to someone who had never experienced it:

■ being in love

■ the taste of an onion.

Is this an easy task? Why/why not?

Key terms

Ineffability: the experience cannot be communicated in normal speech.

A unique experience that cannot be shared. Buzz Aldrin on the Moon

Noetic quality

Despite mystical experiences being classed as 'ineffable', recipients are quick to point out that they do provide insights into unobtainable truths – although not through the intellect. Rather, knowledge is grasped through intuition and perception.

The noetic quality of a religious experience, therefore, brings intuitive understanding and realisation of the truth. Throughout her 'shewings' of divine love, Julian of Norwich had noetic experiences, one of which is described as follows:

> Also in this He shewed me a little thing, the quantity of an hazel-nut, in the palm of my hand; and it was as round as a ball. I looked thereupon with eye of my understanding, and thought: What may this be? And it was answered generally thus: It is all that is made. I marvelled how it might last, for methought it might suddenly have fallen to naught for little[ness]. And I was answered in my understanding: It lasteth, and ever shall [last] for that God loveth it. And so All-thing hath the Being by the love of God.

Transiency

It would appear that most religious experiences last between a few minutes and about two hours and may be difficult to remember. The following is a typical description of a mystical experience that is life changing but does not last long:

> How grand the sight was that was displayed before me as the day broke in its splendour…I was ravished with the beauty of the world. I'd never known such exaltation and such a transcendent joy. I had a strange sensation, a tingling that arose in my feet and travelled up to my head, and I felt as though I were suddenly released from

my body and as pure spirit partook of a loveliness I had never conceived. I had a sense that a knowledge more than human possessed me, so that everything that had been confused was clear and everything that had perplexed me was explained. I was so happy that it was pain and I struggled to release myself from it, for I felt that if it lasted a moment longer I should die; and yet it was such rapture that I was ready to die rather than forego it. How can I tell you what I felt? No words can tell the ecstasy of my bliss. When I came to myself I was exhausted and trembling.

W. Somerset Maugham, The Razor's Edge, 1944

Passivity

This final aspect as outlined by William James suggests that while undergoing the experience, one 'loses control' to a more powerful being, namely God, and is overwhelmed. St John of the Cross describes this passivity in one of the stanzas of his mystical work *The Dark Night of the Soul*:

> I abandoned and forgot myself,
>
> laying my face on my Beloved;
>
> all things ceased; I went out from myself,
>
> leaving my cares
>
> forgotten among the lilies.

However, the significance and effects of the experience are out of proportion to its physical duration. The effects of this loss of control include individuals assuming entirely different personalities, writing or drawing certain prophetic visions or messages with the opposite hand to normal, or speaking in a completely different voice or language. This leads one to the conclusion that although many people try to control the experiences, they are in fact beyond human control.

St Paul describes such an experience:

> I knew a man in Christ above fourteen years ago, (whether in the body, I cannot tell; or whether out of the body, I cannot tell: God knoweth;) such an one caught up to the third heaven. And I knew such a man, (whether in the body, or out of the body, I cannot tell: God knoweth;) How that he was caught up into paradise, and heard unspeakable words, which it is not lawful for a man to utter.

2 Corinthians 12:2-4

Types of mysticism

F. C. Happold (1893–1971) sought not to establish a set of criteria to identify mystical experiences as James had, but to provide some sort of context in which to think about and discuss them. In *Mysticism: A Study and an Anthology* (1963), he suggests that we can divide mysticism, 'for convenience', into two types:

- ■ the mysticism of love and union
- ■ the mysticism of knowledge and understanding.

■ **Key terms**

Passivity: refers to the fact that the religious experience occurs without any action on the part of the recipient.

The mysticism of love and union

This, Happold suggests, is the longing to escape from loneliness and the feeling of being 'separate'. To look at it from the opposite perspective, it requires some sort of union (or, depending on your theological perspective, re-union) with God or nature and a loss of self. In the words of Saint Augustine:

> Thou hast made us for thyself, O God, and our hearts are restless till they rest in Thee.

F. C. Happold, Mysticism: A Study and an Anthology, 1963

Happold believes that two urges that govern all of us are the desire for separation (i.e. the need to be an individual) and the desire to be part of something bigger than ourselves (i.e. the need to be accepted in some way). Obviously these two urges are constantly in conflict with one another. Happold believes that these urges have their origin in the fact that we are in some way sharers in what we could call 'the Divine Life'. This suggests that, despite our need to be individuals, we are always trying to get back to God – hence the desire to be part of something bigger than ourselves. In the words of Happold:

> He (mankind) feels himself to be a pilgrim of eternity, a creature in time but a citizen of a timeless world.

F.C. Happold, Mysticism: A Study and an Anthology, 1963

The mysticism of knowledge and understanding

Happold says that people have another 'urge' which is inherent in all of us. We need to try to find out the 'secret of the universe' ('the meaning of life', in other words). Importantly, he says that we do not seek this in sections, but want to know 'the whole story', as it were. The way that we can look for answers to such an ultimate question is through experiential knowledge of God.

Happold points out that philosophers often play games of 'conceptual counters'. By this he is referring to deductive arguments and logic. The point about experiential knowledge of God is that it is intuitive. In James's terms, this suggests 'noetic quality'. As Nicholas of Cusa wrote in *De Docta ignorantia*:

> I was led in the learning that is ignorance to grasp the incomprehensible; and this I was able to achieve not by way of comprehension but by transcending those perennial truths that can be reached by reason.

Nicholas of Cusa, De Docta Ignorantia [Of Learned Ignorance], 1440

Aspects of mysical experience

Further to his separation of mystical experience into two types, Happold says that there are three aspects of mystical experience:

- soul-mysticism
- nature-mysticism
- God-mysticism.

Think about

What do you think Happold means by the phrases 'a pilgrim of eternity' and 'a citizen of a timeless world'?

Think about

What form would such experiential knowledge of God take?

Think about

The phrase 'I was led in the learning that is ignorance to grasp the incomprehensible' appears to be a complete contradiction in terms. Using William James's idea of 'noetic quality', can you explain what Nicholas of Cusa meant?

Soul-mysticism

Soul-mysticism does not deal with the concept of union with God as such (in fact the existence of God is not actually considered). Rather, it sees the soul as something that is hidden or, to use Otto's terminology, numinous. Mystical experience in this context, therefore, is the idea of finding the soul and, therefore, complete self-fulfilment. As Happold says:

> The chief object of man is the quest for his own self and of right knowledge about it.

F. C. Happold, Mysticism: A Study and an Anthology, 1963

Obviously, this form of mysticism does not deal with the God of classical theism, although it does relate to certain Buddhist and Hindu philosophies (the concept of Brahman, for example).

For most Christians, God is both **transcendent** and **immanent**.

Nature-mysticism

Nature-mysticism is found in the belief that God is immanent. He is everywhere, and can therefore be 'united with' in many aspects of nature. Happold suggests that the poets Wordsworth and Shelley expressed this idea well:

> A motion and a spirit, that impels
> all thinking things, all objects of all thought,
> and rolls through all things.

*from Tintern Abbey by **Wordsworth**, 1798*

and

> That Light whose smile kindles the universe,
> that Beauty in which all things work and move

*from Adonais by **Shelley**, 1821*

God-mysticism

God-mysticism is the contention that the souls of humankind desire to return to their 'immortal and infinite Ground, which is God'. There are suggestions that mystical union with God requires the human soul to be 'deified' – it almost becomes God while retaining its own identity. This is something that Sufi Muslims seek through their various forms of worship.

■ Religious experience as an argument for the existence of God

Many people are more likely to believe something if it has been experienced. In religious terms the significance of this was summed up in the 18th century by Jonathan Edwards (1703–58) in *Treatise on Religious Affections* (1746):

> There is not one grace of the Spirit of God, of the existence of which … Christian practice is not the most decisive evidence.
> The degree in which our experience is productive in practice shows the degree in which our evidence is spiritual and divine.

■ Key terms

Transcendent: God is separate and superior to the physical material world. God is outside space and time.

Immanence: God is active in the world.

Nature-mysticism: observing the beauty or vastness of Nature triggers a mystical experience.

God-mysticism: meditating on the attributes of God and the desire to be one with God triggers a mystical experience.

■ Activities

1 Try to find out about the Hindu concept of Brahman. How does this idea relate to Happold's explanation of soul-mysticism?

2 Find out about the concepts of 'pantheism' and 'panentheism'. How might Happold's idea of nature-mysticism be explained with reference to these concepts?

3 'I have had a religious experience.'

Write a 500–600-word examination of what this claim may mean for a religious believer who claims to have had a vision, conversion or mystical experience.

In other words, our experience of God is the best evidence we have that God exists. Furthermore, the evidence for our experiences is not empirical or logical, but 'spiritual and divine'. Obviously, there are problems with accepting such a view, and these will be considered later in the chapter.

⚡ Existential and value judgements

In the first of his Gifford lectures, William James distinguished between **existential judgements** and **value judgements**.

He went on to suggest that value judgments could also be considered as spiritual judgements, as they involve our personal interpretation. The distinction between existential and value/spiritual judgements is extremely important when considering religious experience, as we are essentially asking two questions:

1 what happened?
2 what does it mean?

James was aware that many people in the late 19th/early 20th century were happy to dismiss alleged religious experiences as the product of a 'faulty' mind. This is a view that remains popular today, of course. Instead of rejecting this view, James accepted it – but saw no obvious problem with it. He spoke of 'religion and neurosis' as perfectly compatible and, to a degree, necessary partners. He said:

> In the natural sciences and industrial arts it never occurs to anyone to try to refute opinions by showing up their author's neurotic constitution.

James also quotes Dr H. M. Maudsley (1835–1918) in defence of his argument:

> What right have we to believe Nature (which could be read in context as 'God') under any obligation to do her work by complete minds only? She may find an incomplete mind a more suitable instrument for a particular purpose.

Dr H. M. Maudsley in William James's Natural Causes and Supernatural Seemings, 1886

In a later lecture, entitled 'The Reality of the Unseen', James considers many testimonies of people who have claimed to have had religious experiences. It is the sheer certainty of these testimonies that is most compelling. Here are a couple of examples:

> God surrounds me like the physical atmosphere. He is closer to me than my own breath. In him literally I live and have my being.

> I have the sense of presence, strong, and at the same time soothing, which hovers over me. Sometimes it seems to enwrap me with sustaining arms.

William James, The Varieties of Religious Experience, 1902

Some would question both the nature of these 'experiences' and any attempt to use them as evidence for the existence of God. Again, James is quick to defend their credibility:

■ Key terms

Existential judgement: a 'primary' question, and is concerned with the nature of something – how it came into existence, what it does and of what it is made.

Value judgement: a 'secondary' question, and is concerned with the meaning, importance and significance of something.

Medical materialism: to try to explain mystical experiences through a medical cause such as epilepsy.

■ Think about

What does James mean when he argues that we do not refute opinions in the natural sciences and industrial arts by showing up the author's neurotic constitution? What is he saying about how we should view someone's claim that they have had a religious experience?

Medical materialism is an approach to medical science that seeks to classify everything in physical terms. How do you think that a 'medical materialist' would explain the experience of St Paul on his journey to Damascus?

■ Link

It may help you to remind yourself of the distinction between an existential judgement and a value judgement in the 'Key terms' box above.

Think about

Consider any powerful emotion, like love, hate, joy or jealousy. These feelings are often quite irrational/illogical.

Do we accept the reality and results of these feelings? Why do you think that this is, or is not, the case?

How can such a consideration help us in our assessment of religious experience as evidence for the existence of God?

Could it be that God is no more than 'a feeling'?

These feelings of reality ... are as convincing to those who have them as any direct sensible experiences can be, and they are, as a rule, much more convincing than results established by mere logic ever are.

William James, The Varieties of Religious Experience, 1902

What about induced experiences?

Obviously, some of the experiences we have considered so far could be confused with the effects of consuming alcohol and/or drugs. James recognised this fact:

The drunken consciousness is one bit of the mystic consciousness, and our total opinion of it must find its place in our opinion of that larger whole.

William James, The Varieties of Religious Experience, 1902

In conclusion, it seems apparent that mystical experiences are states of consciousness, which are either spontaneous or induced. While 'under the influence', mystics feel a greater depth of understanding. Although this understanding may be lost as the influence fades, a sense of profound feeling is retained. No matter what ties may connect different people who have these experiences – social, cultural or religious – their experiences are unique.

The conclusions of William James

In turning to James's conclusions, we can find out how he saw people's religious experiences as potential 'evidence' for the existence of God.

Having considered the experiences of many people, like those above, James suggested that the religious life centred on the following beliefs:

- The world we see around us is part of something much bigger (something spiritual), which we consider to be very important.
- Union with that spiritual 'something' is our ultimate purpose.
- Communication/prayer with that higher, spiritual thing is something which produces real effects, and enables real work to be done.

He also said that religious experience (in many forms) chiefly produced the following results:

- A new enthusiasm for life, often leading to profound and significant changes.
- A sense of peace and security, and of great love for others.

The significant thing about all these ideas is James's emphasis on the reality of the experiences and their effects.

Other areas of James's conclusions dealt with some of the common objections to the use of religious experience as an argument for the existence of God.

Many religions exist

Many people argue that the existence of many different religions in the world is evidence that religious experiences are not authentic. It would appear that those who encounter these experiences portray the 'Being' revealed to them quite differently. In some cases it is clearly the God of their respective faith. For example, **stigmata** are linked to Jesus, whereas Muhammad experienced the message of Allah. In other cases it would

Think about

If someone said to you 'I know God exists, because I've met Him', you might be suspicious as to the validity of the claim! What questions might arise in your mind to make you feel suspicious?

Key terms

Stigmata: unexplained markings on a person's body that correspond to the wounds of Christ.

appear to be a deity quite distinct from the God of formal or organised religion. For some, it is simply the force of nature.

James completely rejects this objection:

> I do not see how it is possible that creatures (people) in such different positions (places and cultures) and with such different powers … should have exactly the same functions and the same duties. No two of us have the same difficulties, nor should we be expected to work out identical solutions.

William James, The Varieties of Religious Experience, 1902

■ Think about

What do you think James is saying here about the existence of different religions in the world? What are the objections to this for the 'problem' outlined above?

Religious experience is like emotion

In addition to the different religions in existence, people have also pointed out that religious experience is very like emotion – it is a personal response, which means that any form of empirical testing is useless. James issues two arguments that could be used to counter this in different ways.

Firstly, he sees no problem with the fact that religious experience can be considered as emotion. He suggests that, in fact, it is only the theories of religions that distinguish between them; the feelings and the conduct inspired by those feelings are remarkably similar:

> The feelings on the one hand and the conduct on the other are almost the same for Stoic, Christian and Buddhist saints, are practically indistinguishable in their lives.

William James, The Varieties of Religious Experience, 1902

As emotion/feeling is an integral part of religion it is therefore perfectly reasonable to accept it as 'evidence' in this regard.

In his second approach, James tries to counter the idea that one cannot be scientific when considering religion. He suggests that one can investigate 'The Science of Religion' by considering different hypotheses. Regardless of which religion we might look at, James believed that we would always find two, universal areas:

■ a certain 'uneasiness' (i.e. the feeling that there is something wrong with us)

■ the solution to this (i.e. the way in which we can be saved from this wrongness).

James argues that the way we find this solution is that we become conscious of a being that is 'higher' than us. He goes on to suggest that this 'higher' being might be thought of (in psychological terms) as our subconscious self, as this is an area we know so little about. As the English essayist Frederic Myers (1843–1901) suggested:

> Each of us is in reality an abiding psychical entity, far more extensive than he knows – an individuality which can never express itself completely through any corporeal manifestation.

Frederic Myers, quoted in William James' The Varieties of Religious Experience, 1902

James claimed that the 'doorway' to this higher being/higher self was religious experience, in the form of mysticism, prayer and conversion. Significantly, he pointed out that there could be no doubt (even scientifically) that some of the effects of this alleged involvement of the higher being in peoples' lives were real. He then concluded:

> That which produces effects within another reality must be termed a reality itself, so I feel as if we had no excuse for calling the unseen or mystical world unreal.

William James, The Varieties of Religious Experience, 1902

In other words, the cause of the experiences which people seem to have and are undoubtedly affected by is real; if that cause is believed to be God, then God exists. This does not prove the God of classical theism, but just God in the sense of the source of the religious experience.

Finally, James noted that things that are true tend to lead to 'consistency, stability and flowing human intercourse'. Put another way, if something is real and true it is likely to improve a person's life, whereas that which is false is more likely to restrict and damage a person's life. Significantly, James noted that those who claimed to have had religious experiences seemed to be generally more fulfilled and purposeful in their understanding of the world and their place in it, than those who subscribed to atheist theories.

■ Challenges to religious experience

In examining James's views, we have considered the possibility of using people's testimony of their religious experiences to postulate God's existence. However, if we considered alternative explanations as to what these experiences are, we may find such evidence much more difficult to gather.

In this section we will consider the work of:

- Sigmund Freud (1856–1939)
- V.S. Ramachandran (1951–)
- Michael Persinger (1945–).

💡 Sigmund Freud

Sigmund Freud was an Austrian psychiatrist who founded the psychoanalytic school of psychology. To understand why Freud would dismiss testimonies of religious experiences as evidence for the existence of God, it is essential to understand his ideas about religion in general.

Fundamentally, Freud believed that people were completely material. In other words, if we could understand everything there is to understand about the physical/biological side of life, we would fully understand human beings. What is significant about this approach is that it ignores our metaphysical existence – i.e. it rules out the possibility of 'the soul'. Also, he suggested that the urge some people felt towards religion was no more than psychological obsession. It has been suggested that a number of factors led to Freud's approach: his experiences of anti-Semitism as a Jew; his experiences of the Catholic rituals he observed as a child, when taken by his guardian to church; and, most particularly, the emphasis placed on the material nature of human existence during his education and early professional career.

■ Think about

How might an atheist interpret the testimony of someone who had claimed to have had a religious experience?

■ Link

Read Chapter 3 pp36–42 and make notes on Freud's ideas on religion.

■ Activity

Using your notes list the reasons why Freud rejected religious experience as evidence for the existence of God.

Freud saw religious experiences as, essentially, illusions. More particularly, he believed that they were projections of the ultimate, oldest and most profound ideas that people had. For example, if someone claimed to have been 'on the cross' with Jesus, a Christian who was happy to accept the authenticity of mystical experiences might have no problem in accepting that claim at face value. Freud, on the other hand, would claim that the recipient of this experience was simply projecting his or her ultimate beliefs about suffering, helplessness and separation, along with salvation, hope and desire to be reunited with one's parent (in this case portrayed as God).

As Freud was not even concerned with the truth of religious claims, he would obviously dismiss any attempt to use such experiences as objective evidence for the existence of an ultimate creator and sustainer.

V. S. Ramachandran

Ramachandran is a neurologist best known for his work in the fields of behavioural neurology and psychophysics. He carried out extensive research related to temporal lobe epilepsy from which he has concluded that there is important evidence linking the temporal lobes to religious experience. He has set up an experiment to compare the brains of people with and without temporal lobe epilepsy. He decided to measure his patients' changes in skin resistance, essentially measuring how much they sweated when they looked at different types of imagery. What Professor Ramachandran discovered to his surprise was that when the temporal lobe patients were shown any type of religious imagery, their bodies produced a dramatic change in their skin resistance, much greater than people not suffering from the condition. The professor has concluded from his research that famous religious figures such as St Paul could also have been people who had the condition.

> So what we suggested was, there are certain circuits within the temporal lobes which have been selectively activated. Their activity is selectively heightened in these patients, and somehow the activity of these specific neural circuits is more conducive to religious belief and mystical belief. It makes them more prone to religious belief.

V.S. Ramachandran, God on The Brain, BBC Horizon programme, 2003

Ramachandran is not unwilling to accept that it may be that God exists and has placed the temporal lobe within the brain as a means of communication with humans.

> What is beyond doubt is that the origins of religion are even more complex than had been thought. The science of neurotheology has revealed that it is too simplistic to see religion as either spiritually inspired or the result of social conditioning. What it shows is that for some reason our brains have developed specific structures that help us believe in God. Remarkably it seems whether God exists or not, the way our brains have developed, we will go on believing.

V. S. Ramachandran, God on The Brain, BBC Horizon programme, 2003

💡 Michael Persinger

Michael Persinger is a **cognitive neuroscience** researcher who agrees that the temporal lobes have a significant role in religious experiences, and argues that religious experiences are no more than the brain responding to external stimuli. Persinger claims that by stimulating the temporal

Think about

Voltaire said, 'If God did not exist, it would be necessary for man to invent him.'

How far do Freud's views on religious experience appear to agree with this statement?

Activity

Using the library and internet research, find out about Ellen White, one of the principal founders of the Seventh Day Adventist Church. Ellen White had a head injury, long after which she had unique visionary experiences that gave guidance to the movement in what they understood to be a supernatural way. Why might some scientists challenge her visions as genuine religious experiences?

AQA Examiner's tip

Don't forget the three Rs. Your aim is to produce an examination answer which is Right, Relevant and Readable. If you don't say what you mean, or mix up your facts, or waffle, or produce work that the examiner can't read, then you will be wasting both time and effort.

Key terms

Cognitive neuroscience: neuroscience studies the nervous system, and cognitive neuroscience is the branch of neuroscience that studies the biological foundations of mental phenomena such as religious experiences.

lobes with a unique machine he can artificially induce in almost anyone a moment that feels just like a genuine religious experience. Persinger has developed a helmet which produces weak magnetic fields across the hemispheres of the brain, specifically the temporal lobe.

Over 900 people who have taken part in the experiments claim to have had some form of 'religious' experience. It is thought that this happens because when under the influence of the helmet, the brain is deprived of the self-stimulation and sensory input that is required for it to define itself as being distinct from the rest of the world; the brain 'defaults' to a sense of infinity. The sense of self expands to fill whatever the brain can sense, and what it senses is the world, so the experience of the self simply expands to fill the perception of the world itself. One experiences becoming 'one with the universe'. However, as soon as the electromagnetic field is turned off then the experiences cease.

Persinger's experiments have led two researchers, Andrew Newberg and Eugene D'Aquili, to use a brain-scanning technique called SPECT (Single Photon Emission Computed Tomography) to determine how these experiences arise. The researchers have produced images of the brains of Tibetan Buddhists during meditation and scanned the brain of a Catholic nun, after 45 minutes of deep prayer, to determine what centres were active and what centres were not.

The results show that in both cases, the superior parietal lobe, the centre that processes information about space, time and the orientation of the body in space, is suppressed, and is almost totally quiet, while the pre-frontal cortex that controls attention is highly stimulated. The result is that any sense of time, space or being in the world is suppressed along with the activity in the superior parietal lobe. And not feeling 'in the world' leads to an 'other-worldly' experience. So it is not surprising that those who have this experience describe it as being in the 'spiritual realms'.

Persinger has been able to reproduce this by electrically suppressing activity in the superior parietal lobe using his helmet, and when he performed this experiment on Tibetan monks and the Franciscan nun, they all reported that the experience was identical to what they experienced in their own meditative practice.

■ Problems of verifying religious experience

The difficulties of assessing the authenticity of religious experience include:

- As we have seen, individuals rather than groups undergo these experiences. As a result, we only have one person's testimony as to what has happened. For example, St Bernadette testified that the Virgin Mary had spoken to her. Witnesses to the experience stated that they did not see or hear the Virgin Mary and only saw Bernadette talking to an 'unseen' someone.

- Religious experience is very like emotion – it is a personal response, which means that any form of empirical testing is useless.

- It would appear that those who encounter these experiences portray the Being revealed to them quite differently. In some cases it is clearly the God of their respective faith. In other cases it would appear to be a deity quite distinct from the God of formal or organised religion. For some, it is simply the force of nature.

- In many cases, drugs or alcohol can produce very similar effects to a religious experience. In *The Varieties of Religious Experience* (1902),

■ Think about

Persinger, Newberg and D'Aquili have found that feelings similar to a religious experience can result from the shutting down of communications between the temporal lobes, or the suppression of activity in the superior parietal lobe. Does this mean that religious experiences must be rejected as evidence of the existence of God?

■ Think about

Would you reject a person's claim that he/she had had a vision if you knew that the person had been taking drugs or drinking heavily? What would be your reasons for rejecting the claim?

James refers to experiments using nitrous oxide and anaesthetics. He suggests that, when mixed sufficiently with air, these substances 'stimulate the mystical consciousness in an extraordinary degree'.

The objective/subjective distinction

Consider the following two statements about the same person:

> Kierkegaard was a philosopher.

> Kierkegaard was a great philosopher.

The key difference between these two statements illustrates the objective/subjective distinction.

The first statement is clearly objective – that is, it is open to testing. It can be empirically verified or falsified and shared.

The second statement is clearly subjective – that Kierkegaard was a great philosopher is a private decision. It may be the case that there is something in his work that I find inspiring and brilliant, but it is a decision based on a personal conviction. The fact that you or anybody else might agree is irrelevant to the conviction.

As has been demonstrated throughout this chapter, religious experiences are regarded as subjective because no objective criteria can be applied to them in order to judge their merit, authenticity or anything else.

This presents us with three areas worthy of consideration:

■ A subjective experience cannot be offered as 'scientific'; that is, as empirical or intellectual proof. This is basically because experiences happen to people, and will always be open to interpretation. However, the apparent lack of uniformity between different reports of religious experience does not render them all 'incorrect' or 'inauthentic'. The consequence of all the experiences being different and none being necessarily inauthentic is that Kierkegaard was right – there is no 'objective' way of reaching God.

■ Surely anything as abstract from 'everyday life' as a religious experience can be deceptive. It may be the case that whatever experience takes place is perceived as religious by the recipient. In particular, this would apply to situations in which the recipient claims to have actually seen God. Such a conviction raises considerable theological problems, as even the Scriptures do not feature any physical appearances by God. There are two suggestions as to how such audiovisual experiences could occur:

  1 Psychopathological – the recipient suffers from a medical condition.

  2 The mind can 'misjudge' experiences under extreme conditions (for example, mirages in the desert).

■ Many would suggest that conversion is a form of religious experience that can be verified fairly easily, because the results are readily observed. On the other hand, conversion could be put down to psychological causes, not divine intervention; that is, a person might undergo a conversion because it meets his or her psychological needs as an individual. This idea was supported by Freud, who suggested that conversion was a 'reaction to a hostile world', in which insecure people reach out to God as a father figure who can provide them with love and comfort. Voltaire was of a similar mind when he commented that 'If God did not exist, it would be necessary to invent him'.

Activity

Try to construct your own examples of objective and subjective statements about the same issue.

Is there any overlap? Why, or why not, might this be?

Activity

Look at the way in which God is physically represented in the following 'appearances' in the Bible:

■ to Adam (Genesis 3)

■ to Abraham (Genesis 17)

■ to Moses (Exodus 3).

List the problems these appearances might raise in relation to the claim 'I have seen God'?

Think about

What similarities can you see between Voltaire's statement, 'If God did not exist, it would be necessary to invent him,' and Freud's views on religious experience?

What problems might arise if we assert that things are only 'true' if they correspond with certain earthly facts?

You may wish to consider what the word 'fact' actually means.

Key terms

Correspondence theory: tries to verify the statement (theory) by seeing if it matches (corresponds) to the known facts.

Coherence theory: tries to verify the statement (theory) by seeing if it agrees with other truths that have been proved already.

Pragmatic theory: tries to verify the statement (theory) in practical terms through any benefits gained from the experience.

However, some philosophers feel that approaches such as these are simply attempts to reduce the phenomenon of conversion and/or religious experience into its most basic components, so as to dispute its authenticity.

An evaluation of the argument

The study of philosophy highlights the fact that there are many ways of considering what the 'truth' in a given situation might be. Indeed, the very concept of 'truth' can soon become extremely diverse. With this in mind, we must accept that evaluating any argument involves a search for a theory or theories of truth. In this case there are several theories that could be applied.

The **correspondence theory** asks whether or not a particular statement corresponds to something in the 'real world'. For example, if one is told that the Earth is flat, one could undertake various scientific tests that focus on a specific hypothesis to check this out. However, it is not quite so straightforward when dealing with a statement about God. We cannot exactly contact God, to find out if a person claimed to have been 'contacted' last Thursday is telling the truth! As a result, this theory is not appropriate to prove the truth of a religious experience, and therefore the existence of God from such experience.

The **coherence theory** evaluates the truth of statements by relating them to other proven truths within a given system of thought. If an inconsistency should be discovered, it is either deemed untrue or the system is suitably modified to remove the problem. In extreme cases the entire system may have to be abandoned. For example, if we are told that Spiderman actually exists, but do not actually see him, we can apply the coherence theory. We would consider whether the concept of a human being climbing walls without assistance is consistent with what we know of humans generally. Obviously it is not consistent. Therefore, we can either dismiss the statement about 'Spidey', or suitably adjust our system of understanding human beings to include those who can climb walls, and so on. Of course, the problem with such a theory is that there may be a large number of 'sets' of cohering statements, each with a reasonable claim to be 'telling the truth' about the world or anything in it.

To apply the theory to religious experience, one would have to ask whether:

■ whatever description of the experience is given, and

■ the effects and/or consequences of the experience were consistent with our system of understanding pertaining to God.

A genuinely religious experience should develop a deeper knowledge and awareness of God – it should not result in something or someone else as a substitute for God.

The difference between religious experiences as examples, and the example pertaining to Spiderman, is that if the experience of God seems inconsistent we would not know whether to dismiss the statement or the initial system of understanding about God.

The **pragmatic theory** focuses on the consequences of accepting the experience; the 'truth' of a statement is seen purely in practical terms. Therefore, acceptance of a religious experience would have to produce beneficial results. But how could clearly beneficial results prove the experience to be authentic and therefore from God? The answer lies in the notion that truth is always life-enhancing, in some way or other, whereas delusion will always be, ultimately, life-diminishing.

Consequently, religious experience would have to be found to be life-enhancing to be worthy of our credence. Many of the philosophers from the so-called 'pragmatic' school of thinking would support this attempt to ascertain the truth. For William James, true beliefs 'lead to consistency, stability and flowing human intercourse'. The American philosopher John Dewey (1859–1952) states that all inquiries into the truth start with a 'problematic situation'. If the inquiry is successful, the result will be a 'determined and unified' situation, which will enable a person to act on this truth.

> ## Activity
>
> Consider, for example, cult leaders who demand adoration and praise befitting a deity from their followers. Find out about some of the more famous examples, such as the group led by David Koresh in Texas.

Authoritarianism

Many people have either claimed or been given great status as the result of having (or claiming to have had) religious experiences. In this section, two examples are considered – Padre Pio and the recipients of the 'Toronto Blessing'.

Stigmata

Historically, those who have undergone religious experiences have often been the focus of attention, adoration and, sometimes, even worship. An example of such a following relates to the Italian priest, Padre Pio (1887–1968). Both during his life and since his death, he has had a worldwide following because of his stigmata (the reproduction of the wounds of Christ on the Cross). However, although it is recognised that people who undergo religious experiences do carry, according to James, 'a curious sense of authority' regarding the afterlife, no one can really claim authority on the grounds of religious experience. This is not to suggest that Pio did, as his following seems to have been the result of an accumulative religious fervour.

Padre Pio

Shared experiences

But what about when an experience appears to be shared by many people? As we have already established, the experiences themselves are unique, but the effects, it would seem, can be shared.

On 10 January 1994, a bizarre phenomenon is reported to have occurred at the Toronto Airport Vineyard Church. The phenomenon, which has since been referred to as the 'Toronto Blessing', is said to have been an 'outpouring of the Holy Spirit'. While individual testimonies of the experience may differ, the descriptions of the effects by witnesses are strikingly similar.

The 'blessing' occurred during a sermon by Pastor Randy Clark. Another senior Pastor, John Arnott, described what he saw:

> When Randy Clark preached at the Airport Vineyard ... almost 80 per cent of the people were on the floor ... It was like an explosion. We saw people literally being knocked off their feet by the Spirit of God ... Others shook and jerked. Some danced, some laughed. Some lay on the floor as if dead for hours. People cried and shouted.

> ## Activity
>
> Using the internet and the library, find out about the religious experiences of individuals such as St Augustine of Hippo, Julian of Norwich, St Francis of Assisi, Richard Rolle of Hampole and John Wesley. What evidence is there to support their experiences and why might others reject the experiences as deriving from God?

The first time that this experience is said to have occurred was in 1979. The recipient was South African minister Rodney Howard-Browne. He is considered to be the 'father' of what is referred to as 'Holy Laughter'. Apparently, it was during a sermon in which the minister asked God to 'touch me' or he would 'come up there and touch you'!

The general effects of this particular type of experience are:

■ Falling in the Holy Spirit – where people fall to the ground, as they can no longer remain standing in the 'presence of God'. Some refer to being stuck to the floor by 'Holy Ghost Glue'.

■ Shaking – part of or the whole of the body shakes 'under the power of God'.

■ Weeping – this is said to be the result of repentance for one's sins or feeling the burden of souls not yet saved.

■ Laughter – this 'Holy Laughter' is said to occur when the Holy Spirit comes into a person's life. Those who believe this to be a genuine form of religious experience say that laughter is an expression of the joy experienced. It is, perhaps unsurprisingly, the most controversial element of the experience.

The interesting thing about the 'Toronto Blessing' is that it is a corporate experience – that is, it appears to be undergone by many people at the same time. Since January 1994, it is said to have occurred to many Christians all around the world.

If people were to exclaim 'I have had a religious experience so YOU must believe in God' one could, and arguably should, object because:

■ As has been made very clear already, the experience cannot be corroborated empirically. This means that claiming authority on the basis of an alleged experience is highly susceptible to abuse from those seeking personal adoration or gratification.

■ Partly as a result of the above point, it would appear that no one has ever been able to derive a meaningful statement from such an experience. For example, if the experience is so individual, how can your vision bear any relevance to my life?

■ The way in which you interpret the experience may be entirely erroneous. What basis is this, then, for claiming authority?

■ Richard Swinburne's cumulative approach

Richard Swinburne develops an argument for the existence of God based on religious experience (among a series of other arguments) in his book *The Existence of God* (1991). His basic conclusion is, as he puts it, 'On our total evidence theism is more probable than not'. It is important to note that in reaching this conclusion, he does not solely consider arguments based on religious experience, but a number of approaches including the 'cosmological', 'design' and 'moral' arguments. When considering Swinburne's approach, it is clear that he places great significance on looking at all the arguments together; in other words, he favours a cumulative approach.

Swinburne's definition of religious experience

Swinburne's argument begins with a definition of what he believes a 'religious experience' to be:

> For our present purposes it will be useful to define it as an experience which seems ... to the subject to be an experience of God (either of his just being there, or doing or bringing about something) or of some other supernatural thing.

Richard Swinburne, The Existence of God, 1991

This is a very important definition, as many people have rejected the testimony of religious experiences on the basis that they have not actually featured 'God', but an angel, a messenger or other religious figure (a saint such as the Virgin Mary, for example). If we accept the definition put forward by Swinburne here, we must accept the involvement of such beings under the category of 'some other supernatural being'.

After defining religious experience, Swinburne's argument effectively takes the form of two areas: the **principle of credulity** dealing with the 'four key challenges'; and, the **principle of testimony**.

The principle of credulity

The principle of credulity is summarised by Swinburne as follows:

> If it seems to a subject that X is present, then probably X is present; what one seems to perceive probably is so.

Richard Swinburne, The Existence of God, 1991

In other words, what we perceive is usually the case.

Many of those who have routinely rejected religious experience have done so on the grounds of scepticism. That is, they have responded to such claims by effectively saying 'I don't believe what you are saying', or 'I believe you have mistakenly interpreted the experience you have had'. As mentioned at the beginning of this chapter, the 21st century demands everything to be 'proved' (empirically) before it can even be considered, in most cases. The principle of credulity completely reverses this trend, effectively saying: 'This is what I experienced, and you must believe me unless you can prove otherwise.'

The four key challenges

Swinburne accepts that there are arguments against the authenticity/reliability of religious experiences, and the next area of his argument attempts to deal with such criticisms. The criticisms are well summarised by Caroline Franks Davis in *The Evidential Force of Religious Experience* (1999). In a sense, the criticisms are 'limitations' of the principle of credulity. They are:

- The circumstances in which the experience occurred generally produce unreliable results (e.g. intoxication from drugs or alcohol), or the recipient of the experience is unreliable (e.g. a notorious pathological liar).
- The recipient of the experience did not have the ability to interpret the experience (e.g. if the recipient is very young or has some sort of barrier to general understanding).

■ It is possible to show that whatever/whoever the recipient is claiming to have experienced was not there.

■ It is possible to show that whatever/whoever the recipient is claiming to have experienced was there, but was not involved in/responsible for the experience.

Obviously, the first two criticisms can be countered by arguments put forward by William James. The second two seem, at first, to be fairly sound objections; if we can show that God was not present, then any claim to the contrary is obviously wrong. Similarly, if we can show that God was present but was not involved in the experience, then again we could object. However, the (perhaps unique) problem with religious experiences is that we cannot simply 'check with God' to see if God was/was not present or involved in an alleged experience.

So far, Swinburne's argument has examined why we should accept the perceptions of other people, and how the criticisms of this idea can be dealt with. The next section deals with how we consider people's testimonies (i.e. what people tell us).

The principle of testimony

Swinburne's principle of testimony deals with this issue. Here, Swinburne appeals to a basic rational and verifiable idea – that people usually tell the truth. This may seem an unconvincing, even dangerous assumption to make, but it is probably fair to say that 'we usually believe to have occurred what other people tell us that they perceived occurring', as Swinburne puts it. Again, he accepts that there will be 'special considerations' which may reject this principle. Such considerations would be, as with the principle of credulity, the existence of positive grounds for rejecting what we are being told.

As mentioned at the start of the section, Swinburne's argument is a cumulative approach. In considering the three areas of his argument cumulatively, we might deal with the claim 'I know God exists because I've met him' in the following way:

The principle of credulity suggests that I should accept your perception of your experience, unless I can a) question it on the grounds of any of the four challenges above, or b) demonstrate positive grounds showing it to be mistaken.

The principle of testimony suggests that I should accept your statement of what you experienced unless I can demonstrate positive grounds showing it to be mistaken.

■ Can the finite experience the infinite?

If the God of classical theism is beyond human understanding then many philosophers have argued, 'How is it possible for humans to experience God?' Immanuel Kant argued that it is not possible for finite humans to experience an infinite God. This is because humans (i.e. the finite) can only experience the world as it appears to them through their five senses. (Kant calls this the **phenomenal world**, in contrast to the **noumenal world** which is the world as it really is in itself.) The five senses can only detect objects that are within space and time. Since God is not an object in space and time, humans are denied the experience.

A believer who accepts religious experiences as genuine would argue that for God anything is possible, and therefore the infinite God is able to communicate with finite beings.

■ Activity

Try to list what factors would persuade you to believe something someone was telling you, and what factors might lead you to believe he/she was lying. You might consider some of the following areas:

■ the content of the statement
■ the language used
■ the body language used
■ what you know of the person
■ what you know of the alleged event.

■ Link

Remind yourself of the attributes of the God of classical theism in Chapter 1 p2.

■ Key terms

Phenomenal world: is what is known through the appearance of something.

Noumenal world: is what is known by the mind rather than the senses.

Conclusion

The key advantage to this group of arguments for the existence of God is that it relates to people in a much more direct way than some of the other traditional families of arguments. As such, the approach is much more accessible and, to a degree, understandable. The key disadvantage is that we are dealing with something akin to emotion, not something empirical and therefore verifiable. Perhaps the most persuasive element of the entire approach is Swinburne's insistence that while it may be possible to isolate each element of 'proof' offered and find problems with it, such elements have far greater cumulative worth. Atheist philosopher Anthony Flew (1923–), who was keen to dismiss the cumulative approach, said: 'If one leaky bucket will not hold water that is no reason to think that ten can.' Caroline Franks Davis agreed, but pointed out that it may be possible to arrange the buckets inside each other so that the holes do not overlap. In other words, while individual arguments regarding religious experience may be flawed, it is possible to take elements from each and to end up with a fairly powerful argument for God's existence.

It would seem that religious experience as an 'argument for the existence of God' is only applicable for the individual concerned. As with all philosophical arguments that attempt to prove the existence of God, this argument may well do much to strengthen the existing faith of the believer. This is a point highlighted by C. S. Evans, who suggested that if believers are filled with the need for dependence on a higher being, they will probably be drawn towards the cosmological argument. If, on the other hand, they are particularly moved by the concept of order in the universe, they will probably be drawn to the teleological (design) argument, and so on.

The implication of this for the argument based on religious experience is that a believer who recognises the importance of God's involvement in human affairs will accept it as affirming their faith. William James points out that any criticism of the faith of a believer who has undergone such an experience will be completely in vain.

However, it is perhaps appropriate to conclude that the argument is probably of value to the non-believer only in as much as it points to another area of human life that might involve a divine being. As we have seen, there is no clear answer to the question of whether one can demonstrate God's existence as a result of religious experience.

Now that you have read this chapter you should be able to:

- define words associated with religious experience
- describe examples of different types of religious experiences
- examine whether it is necessary to have a religious experience in order to be able to understand what a religious experience is
- question how far religious experiences show that God probably exists
- assess the success of the challenges to religious experience from philosophy and science.

Think about

Look at the examination-style questions on p77. In Question 2 you are asked to consider whether or not religious experience is convincing evidence for the existence of God. In order to answer this question successfully you need to consider for whom would such experiences be convincing – for example a religious believer?

In part 2 of the essay question you need to consider whether or not religious experiences are genuine. In order to answer this question successfully you need to consider:

- What would be the reasons for challenging religious experiences – alternative explanations that could include natural explanations, philosophical explanations and the problems of verifying the experience?

- How successful are the challenges to religious experience?

Remember to support your points with specific examples.

3 Psychology and religion

Learning objectives:

- to understand the main features of Freud's and Jung's interpretations of religion

- to understand why these views might challenge religious belief and how religion might respond to this challenge

- to evaluate whether God has been explained away by psychology

- to evaluate the strengths and weaknesses of the psychological views of religion

- to examine the relationship between religion and mental health.

Key terms

Psychology: The scientific study of the mind, mental processes, consciousness and behaviour.

Illusion: the term here does not mean a false or mistaken belief but one that is based on fulfilment. An illusion is a belief derived from human wishes.

Wish fulfilment: the secret hope of our greatest longings satisfied.

Neurosis: a psychological disorder. In Freudian psychology – an imbalance of the forces of the id, ego and superego.

Collective neurosis: a neurotic illness that afflicts all people.

The challenges of psychology to religious belief

The **psychology** of religion examines the relationship between the human mind and religious belief. The conclusions drawn can be potentially very threatening to religious faith. Freud and Jung, for example, offer a psychological explanation for religion, suggesting that the God worshipped by believers is first and foremost a construct of the human mind. This clearly challenges religious believers who see God as an objective reality whose existence can be proved by logical or empirical means. For example the God of classical theism is understood to be the omnipotent creator of the world, rather than a human creation of the believer's mind.

Sigmund Freud (1856–1939)

Freud's theory of religion

Freud believed that as an **illusion**, religion is based on **wish fulfilment**. He believed that in certain circumstances the human mind will create beliefs and images to satisfy its most basic longings and desires. Religion is created by the mind to help us overcome:

- inner psychological conflict (religion being seen as a **collective neurosis**)
- the conflict between our natures and civilisation
- helplessness and fear of natural forces.

To describe religion as an illusion is not to say that it is necessarily false, but that it answers people's inner needs. Whether or not an illusion is true depends on whether its claims are grounded in hard evidence or merely invented by the mind. Freud believed that all religious beliefs were created by the mind to fulfil its three main desires.

Religion as an aid to overcome inner psychological conflict

This forms the main body of Freud's work on religion. Freud argued that:

- religion is a collective neurosis (a form of neurotic illness)
- it stems from the **unconscious mind**
- it results from incompletely repressed traumatic memories
- the trauma is invariably sexual in nature
- therefore religion is an illusion resulting from sexual difficulties.

Freud believed that the construction of the mind and the development of the human personality led to deep inner conflicts, invariably sexual in nature. The mind's solution to such trauma is to lock it away in the unconscious mind. Such 'locking away' is unsuccessful, and the trauma re-emerges later in the form of religion.

As a collective neurosis, religion is a neurotic illness that afflicts all people. A neurosis involves physical symptoms (pain, compulsive behaviour, etc.) which – unlike a broken leg, for example – have no physical cause, but are rooted in the mind. Hysteria, obsessions, anxieties and phobias are all neurotic symptoms.

Freud's work with patients suffering from hysteria led him to conclude that as well as conscious areas, the mind also contains unconscious parts which we cannot normally access. Meanwhile, his work on hypnosis and studies of dreams led Freud to realise that the unconscious mind comprises a vast store of information about events which we consider long forgotten.

Freud's work with his patients demonstrated that unpleasant memories which are trapped in the unconscious can surface later in the form of neurotic and hysterical behaviour. This is often in the form of compulsive-obsessional disorders, such as compulsive hand washing.

Freud made the link between religion and neurosis when he noticed close similarities between the behaviour of his patients in relation to the source of their obsession and religious people in relation to the object of their worship. He noticed, for example, that both involve highly specific ritual behaviour. In both cases, this behaviour is filled with symbolic meaning for its followers, while appearing completely meaningless to the uninitiated. In both cases, failure to perform a particular act results in severe guilt, which is inexplicable to others, and in both cases the object of attention is regarded with ambivalence.

From this, Freud concluded that religion itself was a neurosis, caused, as in the case of other hysterias, by traumas deep within the **psyche**. The central and perhaps most startling feature of Freud's argument was his belief that the trauma in question was invariably sexual in nature:

> At the bottom of every case of hysteria there are one or more occurrences of premature sexual experience, occurrences which belong to the earliest years of childhood.

Sigmund Freud, The Aetiology of Hysteria, 1896

Think about

You may have a desperate desire that England will win the World Cup again. If you believe that this will happen, then by Freud's definition your belief is an illusion. But there is no reason why this illusion should not be true.

Key terms

Unconscious mind: contains basic drives, such as breathing and forgotten memories. The conscious mind contains our present thoughts and accessible memories.

Psyche: the technical term for the mind. The term is understood to include all the conscious and unconscious components of the mind.

■ **Key terms**

Libido: the psyche's drive to achieve satisfaction. It includes the sexual drive.

Repression: in Freudian psychology – unwanted or taboo thoughts, desires, fears and anxieties that get banished into the unconscious.

Libido and repression

This was because, for Freud, the sexual drive or **libido** was the body's most basic urge and, as such, the one most capable of causing psychological problems within the development of the individual.

For Freud, the libido involves far more than the desire to have sex. It represents the body's general, subconscious desire for satisfaction stemming from the unconscious. In babies, for example, the libido centres on the mouth, and the desire to suckle from the mother. This changes as the child develops and is gradually transformed to the mature desire among adults to reproduce.

The trauma lying behind neurotic behaviour results from problems in the sexual development of the child. The major problem concerns what Freud termed the Oedipus Complex. Whereas the suckling child was used to having its mother's sole attention, when the libido is transferred to the sexual organ, there is an already present rival in the form of the father. The acute feelings of jealousy and hatred lead to the desire to kill the father. Combined with the great respect and fear previously felt for the father, this results in a deeply traumatic sense of guilt. This desire to possess the mother and the ambivalence towards the father is the Oedipus Complex. Freud goes on to say: 'In the conditions of our civilisation it is invariably doomed to a frightening end.' Unable to carry out his wishes, the child **represses** the conflict and the guilt deep into the unconscious mind.

The mechanism of repression, however, is only partially effective. While the repressed desires and guilt may appear to be long forgotten, the mind continues to struggle to prevent them from re-emerging into the conscious. As a result, they are channelled out in the form of neurotic symptoms. One of these symptoms is religion, which, for Freud, was the 'universal obsessional neurosis of humanity' that 'arose out of the Oedipus Complex, out of the relation to the father' (*The Future of an Illusion*, 1927).

Support for Freud's theory of religion

Freud's arguments caused uproar when they became known. To some, they were deeply offensive; to others, merely bizarre. As the father of psychoanalysis, however, Freud was a respected figure in various branches of psychology and his considerable work with patients claimed to provide support for his theories. We shall now consider the evidence upon which Freud's claims rest.

If Freud's theories are to be accepted, two things at least must be established:

- that the Oedipus Complex is a universal sexual trauma
- that buried trauma can reappear in the form of religion.

Support for the Oedipus Complex

Freud used the work of Charles Darwin to speculate that in primitive societies, the social unit was the 'primal horde'. Hordes were groups of people arranged around a single dominant male who had total authority over the group and held claim over all the females. Over time, the resentment of the younger males grew until they grouped together to kill the dominant male. This resulted in ambivalent feelings towards him: hatred on the one hand, combined with veneration on the other. The strength of these feelings was so great that he became idolised and transformed into the totem of the group.

■ Link

Look at Chapter 6: Creation, pp97–99, and Chapter 7, The design argument, p109–121, and find out about Darwin's evolutionary theory.

This shows that the Oedipus Complex is not simply a personal trauma, but one that has affected all societies at a historical level. It helps to explain why religion is universal as a collective neurosis and why the concept of God is such a powerful one, because it stems also from a historical experience that still affects us. Freud believed in some kind of psychological mechanism whereby guilt for the original crime is passed on genetically.

How does religion result from a buried trauma?

Freud provided a complicated argument to show that the natural reaction of the psyche was to control feelings of guilt by transferring it away from itself and on to surrounding objects and people.

Freud provided five major case studies to illustrate the effects of the Oedipus Complex. One of them, *The Wolf Man*, concerned a young man, Sergei Pankejeff, who had a phobia of animals. After much hypnosis, Freud traced the phobia back to the time when the young Pankejeff witnessed sexual acts between his parents. Freud reasoned that over time, the repressed trauma resulted in the fear of wolves and of God.

Animism

The first stage of the development is **animism**. Freud believed that, when suffering from extreme guilt, the mind's defence mechanism was to create idols (or totems). This involves investing stones, trees or animals with spirits. Having done this, the mind can redirect the feelings of guilt on to the idol and can make amends through prayer and sacrifice, for example. The mind is therefore able to control the feelings of guilt.

In effect, the idol or totem is a transformation of the father. And just as the father was regarded with ambivalence, so too is the totem. Freud's case studies (such as *The Wolf Man*) demonstrate that people suffering from the Oedipus Complex frequently transfer their fear onto animals. Freud draws further historical support from the primal horde. He observed that as veneration of the father grew, the veneration was transferred on to a totem animal. The totem became the symbol of identity of the group. The **ambivalence**, however, remained – while it was generally forbidden to harm the animal in any way, once a year there would be a ritual killing and eating of the totem animal.

Development into religion

The second stage of the development is into religion. As time passed, the animist emphasis on the totem proved unsatisfactory. As longing for the father grew, so did his reputation. Eventually he took on divine significance and became transformed into the gods of religions. Freud points out that the gods of religions are regarded with the same ambivalence as was the original father figure, proving that there is a connection. A favourite example concerned the Christian God who, generally speaking, is treated with great reverence. Every now and then, however, he is ceremonially killed and eaten in the Communion Feast. This example provides an exact link with the animist ritual killing of the totem.

Religion is therefore an illusion created by the mind to help us come to terms with the powerfully ambivalent emotions suffered during sexual development. It is a means of resolving this inner conflict.

> ### Key terms
>
> **Animism:** the belief that natural phenomena such as animals, rocks, trees, thunder or celestial bodies have life or divinity.
>
> **Ambivalence:** simultaneously experiencing opposing or conflicting emotions, attitudes, ideas or wishes toward a person or situation.

Religion as an illusion

Freud demonstrated how the nature of our society is in conflict with our most basic desires. We have seen one such conflict, in the form of the Oedipal desire to kill the father and possess the mother.

Were conflicts like the Oedipus Complex allowed to be acted out, society would not be able to operate. Society depends upon structure and order; those who have responsibility to govern must have authority and this will inevitably conflict with the desires of each individual.

Religion provides a reason to submit to authority. It explains our suffering in terms of the need to obey an omnipotent God. It promises reward for suffering in the afterlife and makes society bearable.

Religion therefore provides the necessary motivation for **sublimation** to occur. The most natural outlet being forbidden, it forces our libidos into other areas. Having sufficiently motivated the believer, it provides ample scope for sublimation in fields such as religious art, music or charity work.

Religion as an illusion to help us overcome fear of natural forces

The natural human response to being confronted by natural forces – including death – is one of panic and helplessness at our defencelessness and solitude. Religion helps by creating the belief that the natural forces are not impersonal, and that we are not powerless, for through religious devotion we believe we can control them:

> Everything that happens in the world is an expression of the intentions of an intelligence superior to us, which in the end, though its ways and byways are difficult to follow, orders everything for the best – that is, it makes it enjoyable for us.

> *Sigmund Freud, Civilisation and its Discontents, 1930*

Religious belief is a reaction against helplessness, providing adults with a father figure who can protect, just as the father protected the child. To the 'strange, superior' powers of nature, the adult 'lends … the features belonging to the figure of his father; he creates for himself the gods'. Religion fulfils our wishes for someone to look after us in a harsh world. For God is the ultimate ideal of a father, being all-loving, all-powerful and totally dependable, giving people the confidence that the future is safe in his hands.

Freud's conclusion about the value of religion

At the outset we explained that Freud does not provide any logical proof against the possibility of religion. He admitted that his arguments prove nothing, since God could exist objectively anyway. In practice, however, he pointed out that beliefs that are derived from basic psychological needs turn out to be false. The beliefs of obsessional neurotics, for example, invariably have no grounding in fact. Freud therefore argued that in the absence of any other evidence for religion, we are justified in concluding that it is false. He goes on to support a complete rejection of all things religious. Towards the end of *The Future of an Illusion* Freud creates a conversation with an opponent to his beliefs about religion. This opponent raises two points on the importance of religion.

First, without religion, civilisation would turn into anarchy:

> If men are taught that there is no almighty and all-just God, no divine
> world order and no future life, they will feel exempt from all obligation
> to obey the precepts of civilisation. Everyone will follow his asocial,
> egoistical instincts ... and chaos will come again.

Sigmund Freud, The Future of an Illusion, 1927

Second, depriving people of religion seems needlessly cruel: 'Countless
people find their one consolation in religious doctrines and can only bear
life with their help.'

In his reply, Freud admitted that religion has performed 'great services
for civilisation'. He also accepted that if religion were entirely positive it
would indeed be cruel to deprive people of it, illusion though it may be.
He went on to argue, however, that religion is not in fact beneficial. It
does not prevent people from rebelling against the restrictions of society.
Many believers, moreover, abuse religion for their own purpose to justify
social immoralities. He gave the example of penance: 'One sinned, and
then one made a sacrifice, and then one was free to sin once more.'
Religion has all too often been used as a tool against the oppressed, to
keep them oppressed. Freud argued that we have been 'overrating its
necessity for mankind'.

Freud's suggested alternative is to replace religion with a scientific,
rational understanding of the world. This, he argued, would make people
more willing to obey the demands of civilisation because they would see
them as being for their own personal good. He believed it possible that
humans can be educated to make their unruly passions subservient to
their wills. Although many would see this as unrealistic, Freud argued
that the pain of removing religion would be more than justified by the
benefits.

A critical appraisal of Freud's work

We cannot deny that Freud had a brilliant intellect, nor that he had a
great influence on the Western understanding of the mind. There are few
today, however, who accept his theories wholesale. For as Michael Palmer
argues, in *Freud and Jung on Religion*: 'almost all the evidence that Freud
presents has been discredited in one way or another.' The following areas
in particular have been attacked:

- The historical and anthropological evidence regarding the primal horde.
- The psychological evidence regarding the Oedipus Complex.
- Freud's dependence on a narrow selection of evidence.
- Freud's conclusion that religion should be overthrown.

Anthropological evidence for the primal horde

The whole theory of the horde was based on Darwin's mere speculations.
It is not now accepted that people were grouped exclusively in hordes.
Instead, it is likely that there was much greater variety. Not all societies
had totem objects, whom they worshipped, and there is no evidence for
the ambivalent attitude towards the totems which was demonstrated
by the totem meal; the British anthropologist E. E. Evans-Pritchard
(1902–73) doubts that this ever happened. The idea that guilt is handed
down from generation to generation has likewise been discredited.

> **Activity**
>
> Write a 500–600-word essay on
> Freud's understanding of religion
> Include the following main areas:
> wish fulfilment, collective neurosis
> and the Oedipus Complex.

> **Link**
>
> Look back at pp38–42 to see the
> link between Freud's conclusions
> regarding the primal horde and
> historical and anthropological
> evidence regarding the primal horde.

This criticism damages Freud's claim that religion is guilt-based because it removes the major source of guilt. The primal crime never happened and could not transmit guilt even if it did. It also weakens the Oedipus Complex theory, since the primal crime was an important illustration of its effect on society.

Psychological evidence for the Oedipus Complex

The major critic of Freud's theory of the Oedipus Complex is Bronislaw Malinowski, in his book *Sex and Repression*. Freud needed the complex to be universal for it to be the cause of all religion, and needed it to be caused by our natures for it to precede religion and be the cause of it. Malinowski attacked both these points. First, he pointed to the Trobriand race, where the role of the father is more that of a weak nurse. In this race there is no evidence of the Complex. Their religion, therefore, must have originated elsewhere. Second, looking at the animal world, he found nothing inherent in the nature of animals that could cause such a complex. The role of both father and mother is one of support. Malinowski argued instead that the Complex is caused by the strict rules of religion – rather than being the cause of them.

This attack on the Oedipus Complex leads to the conclusion that sexual guilt is not in fact the cause of religion. As a result, Freud's attack on religion does not contain the force it was once believed to have.

A narrow selection of evidence

Freud's theories relied on the importance of the father figure, which is developed by the mind into the male God of Judaism or Christianity. They therefore failed to take account of religions based upon female deities, such as the Egyptian Isis cult, or religions which do not have any single dominant object of worship, such as Buddhism. They also failed to take account of societies like the Trobriand race, where the father plays an insignificant role in the development of the child. In societies such as these, religion could not be attributed to the tensions with the father, since no such tensions occurred.

Freud can therefore be criticised for constructing a theory to explain the societies and religions with which he was familiar, and ignoring those of others. In a similar way, we can criticise the way he generalised the results of his five case studies, assuming that the Oedipus Complex that he detected at work in those instances was in fact at work everywhere.

An unjustifiably negative view of religion

The British psychoanalyst Donald Winnicott (1896–1971), for example, has argued that religion is an essential buffer between the mind and external reality. Religion is useful in that it helps humans adapt to their environment by providing a source of comfort and familiarity. The role and value of religion are similar therefore to those of art and music.

Finally, Ana-Maria Rizzuto argued that religion is no more of an illusion than science. Both disciplines require us to interpret data and impose order on the world. Freud's assumption that science has the sole claim to the truth is unacceptable. Rizzuto has therefore argued that Freud has not so much removed the illusion of religion but, rather, replaced religion with an illusion.

Activity

Write a 500–600-word written response to the statement 'Freud's understanding of religion presents a convincing challenge to religious belief'.

 Jung's theory of religion

The Swiss psychiatrist Carl Gustav Jung (1875–1961) spent part of his life working alongside Freud. The first conversation the two had together is reported to have lasted over 13 hours. Yet although Jung was at first influenced by Freud, this did not prevent him from pursuing his own ideas. These ultimately led him to reject many of Freud's conclusions, and especially those concerning religion. Although he accepted that religion was a psychological phenomenon, he objected to Freud's conclusion that:

- Religion is a neurosis caused by sexual trauma.
- Religion is a dangerous entity, to be exposed and overthrown.

Jung replaced Freud's conclusions with the following observations:

- Religion, as an expression of the collective unconscious, is a natural process.
- It stems from the archetypes within the unconscious mind.
- It performs the function of harmonising the psyche.
- As such, it is a beneficial phenomenon.
- The removal of religion would lead to psychological problems.

Carl Jung (1875–1961)

The background to Jung's work

Jung's theory of religion stems from his own unique understanding of psychology. Two features of this are essential in order to understand Jung's work:

- Jung's concept of neuroses and the libido
- Jung's concept of the mind.

Jung's concept of the unconscious mind

Jung's work with patients suffering from schizophrenia led him to reject Freud's view that neuroses were caused by repressed sexuality, for although schizophrenia was a neurosis, it had no obvious sexual component. He concluded that the complete loss of self awareness schizophrenics demonstrate is something far greater than mere sexual disturbance. He was also unconvinced by Freud's view that a baby's suckling was a sexual act. From these observations he concluded that even if religion were a neurosis, it could not be traced back to a sexual trauma. He also concluded that the libido, as the cause of neuroses which affect the whole personality, was something more complicated than a mere sexual drive.

Jung viewed the libido as the source of **psychic energy**. If its flow was interrupted, neuroses would result.

The rejection of the sexual basis of the libido constitutes Jung's greatest split from Freud.

Link

Look back at pp36 and 38 to remind yourself of the meaning of neurosis and libido.

AQA Examiner's tip

Questions are likely to make use of the technical terms that appear in the specification, for example: 'collective unconscious' and 'collective neurosis'. Make sure you know them and that you can link them to the right psychologist. You can help yourself by creating your own 'glossary of terms'.

Key terms

Psychic energy: or psychological energy, is an energy by which the work of the personality is performed.

Jung's concept of the mind

Jung noted how people who were dreaming or suffering from psychic disorders were often preoccupied with similar ideas and images. The schizophrenic Miss Miller, for example, had a dream comparing her desire for God with a moth's desire for light. Jung noted how this parallel between God and light can be found in countless religious traditions. The Aztec preoccupation with the sun and the Christian view of Jesus as the 'Light of the World' are two examples.

To account for the similarities in mental images, Jung postulated a further division of the unconscious mind, into the **personal unconscious** and the **collective unconscious**.

The collective unconscious is the oldest part of the mind. It contains the blueprints for a whole range of ideas and images. According to this theory, the fantasy of Miss Miller and the likeness drawn by religions between light and the deity are all derived from this collective unconscious. Each one of us is born with the tendency to conceive similar kinds of primordial images. One effect of this tendency is that similar images will be produced in dreams. Jung believed that the God concept is one of these primordial images, God being an expression of the collective unconscious. This explains why many of our ideas about God will be shared with other people.

Jung's concept of the archetypes

Jung gave the technical name **archetype** to the part of the psyche which creates these images.

One of the reasons why Jung's concept of the archetypes has come under fire is because it has sometimes been misunderstood. Jung was not saying that the experiences of our ancestors are somehow handed down to us in the form of a set of mental pictures with which we are born. He was saying that the mind contains structures which, when combined with the knowledge gained through our experiences, construct uniform images. In Jung's words – in his book *Symbols of Transformation* – it is not 'a question of inherited ideas, but of a functional disposition to produce the same, or very similar, ideas.'

Jung's archetypes include the persona, shadow, animus, anima, God and Self.

The **persona** represents one's public image. The word is, obviously, related to the words 'person' and 'personality', and comes from a Latin word for mask. So the persona is the mask you put on before you show yourself to the outside world. The persona is the tendency to put up a front to cover our true natures for the benefit of society. This front could be a 'good impression' to be what is expected of us by others or it could be a 'false impression' to manipulate other people's opinions and behaviours. Sometimes the persona can be mistaken, even by ourselves, for our true nature causing us to believe we really are what we pretend to be!

The shadow denotes the disposition to portray the darker sides of our characters that we tend to deny in ourselves and to project on to others. As we move deeper into the dark side of our personality personal identity begins to be lost and individuals experience the chaos of getting closer to the material structure of psychic life. This may be manifested through a wealth of images. These include the image of 'woods' or 'wildernesses'. The shadow is the easiest of the archetypes for most people to experience.

The animus and anima represent the psyche's tendency to express its opposite sexual side. The animus represents the masculine side of the

■ Key terms

Personal unconscious: contains the forgotten memories of the individual.

Collective unconscious: in Jungian psychology it refers to that part of a person's unconscious that is common to all human beings.

Archetypes: can be seen as 'image generators'. They are distinct from the actual images they generate.

Persona: the aspect of someone's character presented to others; the Latin origin is, literally, a 'mask'.

■ Activity

With the other members of your group, identify any similarities in the types of thing you have dreamt about. Many people, for example, have dreamt that they were being chased by something.

If there are any common features, how would you account for them?

■ Think about

Consider the difference between the hunger drive and the desire to eat chocolate.

You are born with a disposition to feel hungry. You are not born with the innate knowledge of chocolate.

Through the experiences of your life, however, the feeling of hunger combines with your knowledge of food and manifests itself in the desire for a particular food.

female and the anima represents the feminine side of the male. The anima may appear as an exotic dancing girl or a weathered old hag – the form generally reflects either the condition or the needs of our soul presently. The animus may appear as an exotic, sensual, young man, or as an old grouch.

The possible result is in dreams, the persona may manifest itself in images of being trapped inside a heavy coat of armour, or appearing at a party in a disguise. The shadow may reveal itself in the form of personifications of evil; for example, Satan or monsters. The animus may generate images of heroes or wise men while anima images include goddesses, seductresses and fictional heroines. The God and Self archetypes are examined in more detail in the following sections.

God as an archetype

Jung claimed that our images of God are themselves archetypal. In other words, each of us is born with the tendency to generate religious images of gods, angels and other religious phenomena. The same principles apply here as with the other archetypes. That is, the actual images we have of God are picked up through our own experiences in the world. The disposition to generate them is, however, innate. For example, the Christian concept of Jesus/God is just one manifestation of the archetypal tendency to develop an image of a perfect, all-powerful being.

Jung's term 'the God within' refers to his view that God is an inner psychological experience. To explain the meaning of this term, you would need to describe Jung's theories of collective unconscious and archetypes, explaining that, as an archetype, God is an expression of the collective unconscious.

Jung's definitions of the words 'religion' and 'religious' rely on Rudolf Otto's understanding of the religious or numinous experience.

Jung did not believe, however, that to describe God as an archetype was in any way to play down the validity or importance of religious belief. On the contrary, he believed that an experience of the God-archetype constituted a genuine religious experience according to Rudolf Otto's definition of the term. Such an experience is simply one which the subject receives 'independent of his will'. It is no more or less significant an experience whether it comes from an objectively existing God or a hidden level of the mind. Either way, it is 'due to a cause external to the individual' and is an 'invisible presence that causes a peculiar alteration of consciousness'. The God-archetype, like all archetypes, is ineffable since it comes from a part of the mind about which nothing concrete may be known. Jung therefore believed that an experience of any archetype would count as a religious experience because all the archetypes are equally ineffable.

Link

Look back at Chapter 2 pp15 and 18 to remind yourself of the meaning of 'numinous' and 'ineffable'.

Jung's conclusion

If belief in God stems from structural components of the psyche, does this mean that God does or does not exist? The answer is similar to Freud's. That is, there is no proof either way. Jung states:

> We simply do not know the ultimate derivation of the archetype any more than we know the origin of the psyche. The competence of psychology as an empirical science only goes so far as to establish, on the basis of comparative research, whether for instance the imprint found in the psyche can or cannot be termed a 'God-image'. Nothing positive or negative has thus been asserted about the possible existence of any God.

C. G. Jung, Psychology and Alchemy, 1944

All that can be asserted is that God, and the whole entity of religion, exists as a psychic reality; that is, to those who experience the effects of the archetypes, God is real. However, nothing can be proved about his existence or nature outside the mind.

Here, then, we have a point of similarity between the approaches of Jung and Freud. What Jung makes of his conclusion, however, is completely different. For whereas Freud thought that religion was a neurotic illness and a dangerous illusion that needed to be overthrown, Jung argued that it performs the role of maintaining the balance of the mind and prevents neuroses through an innate process known as individuation.

The process of individuation

To explain the process of **individuation**, we need briefly to return to Jung's concept of the libido. The libido, we recall, can be described as a flow of psychic energy. To maintain health, all the features of the personality need to be integrated. For example, there needs to be a balance between the conscious mind and the unconscious. There also needs to be a balance among the different archetypes. It is the failure to maintain this balance that is the main cause of mental disorder and neurotic illness. For example, someone who has an excess of mental energy concentrated on the unconscious will appear disconnected from their surroundings, since they will be aware chiefly of the images generated by the unconscious.

Jung argued that whereas the first part of a person's life involves a coming to terms with the outer environment and its challenges – through work, friendships and relationships – the emphasis in the second part, from middle age onwards, is to come to terms with one's own personality. Faced with declining opportunities, energies and possibly health, the individual must find new purpose and meaning in life through assimilating into one's conscious mind the numerous unconscious components. Although ultimately beneficial, it can be difficult, because it involves accepting parts of one's personality which one may prefer to leave undiscovered.

Individuation and its relationship with religion

We have established the importance of the individuation process. All that remains is to explain what it has to do with religion. Here, two points need to be made.

First, individuation as an innate process is one which is governed by the archetype known as the self. More precisely, the self is the innate disposition to become whole. According to Jung's understanding of religious experience, any process or attitude that is governed by archetypes may be termed religious. Upon this basis, individuation is a religious process.

Second, Jung argued that the self aids the process of individuation by generating images of wholeness. The most famous example of these images is the **mandala**, or balancing circles. Another major example, however, is the religious images of God. Jung claimed that the images created by the God-archetype are one and the same as those images created by the Self-archetype. It makes sense, therefore, to say that it is through religious images that the personality achieves its goal of integration. In Jung's words, 'The symbols of divinity coincide with those of the self: what, on the one side, appears as a psychological experience, signifying psychic wholeness, expresses on the other side the idea of God.'

■ **Key terms**

Individuation: the process by which individuals integrate the conscious and unconscious parts of their personality. It results in a psychologically balanced personality, through the acceptance of the various archetypes into the conscious mind. The process may also be called integration.

■ **Think about**

Given that the 'persona' is the archetype which governs the covering up of one's true nature, what sort of behaviour would you expect from someone whose libido was channelled excessively in this direction?

■ **Think about**

Consider, for example, the archetype of the 'shadow'. What benefits to one's own personality and one's behaviour could there be in coming to terms with the unpleasant, darker features of one's own nature? For example, think about how knowledge of your own weaknesses could help you to relate to others who also have such flaws.

■ **Key terms**

Mandala or magic circle: design based on a perfectly balanced circle, the centre of which is emphasised. This design is traditionally understood to represent balance and wholeness.

As a result of this, Jung said that the religious images are used by the mind to individuate the personality. The value of religion now becomes clear. For if one rejects religion, one is at the same time rejecting a substantial part of the individuation mechanism. Those who reject religion are less likely to individuate successfully, and therefore more likely to experience neurosis as a result of the remaining psychological tension. For this reason, Jung concluded that religion is a valuable entity.

A critical appraisal of Jung's work

Although Jung's theories are perhaps less sensational than those of Freud, they have nonetheless been seriously criticised, and not merely by supporters of Freud. The criticism has centred upon four main areas:

- Jung's methodology
- the theory of the archetypes
- Jung's concept of religious experience
- the role of religion within individuation.

Jung's methodology

Jung has been criticised for his view that we can never know whether God exists. This view rests upon his assumption that nothing can be known of any entity outside the psychic world. For example, we can never know whether a religious experience is real or merely created by the mind. This assumption, however, has been questioned. Scientists, for example, base their conclusions on empirical evidence, without worrying that their data are just figments of their imagination. It can be argued that a religious experience should be treated in the same way, and that if there is empirical evidence to support it we should accept it as genuine.

Jung's theory of the archetypes

Jung's theory of archetypes has also been criticised. It is argued that this theory is simply not required to explain the 'evidence' – namely, the common tendency to construct uniform images. Geza Roheim, for example, states that since all humans share broadly the same experiences, it is hardly surprising that we develop myths along similar lines. The common experiences of birth and dependence upon parents and the Sun explain, for example, common ideas about rebirth, parent gods and sun gods. It has also been pointed out that the fact that many religious myths, such as the Mesopotamian legends, respond to the social concerns of a particular community, makes it hard to accept that they come from an impulse that is common to the whole of mankind. On these grounds it is argued that Jung is not justified in postulating an archetypal 'instinct for God' from the evidence that people believe in God.

A further point which rendered Jung's concept of the archetypes less acceptable is the fact that many people do not believe in God. Jung's answer to this criticism was that atheism itself is a form of religion. Again, however, we see Jung's reluctance to allow empirical evidence to count against his theory; faced with the simple fact that many people are not religious, he twists this to his advantage. By manipulating any unfavourable evidence in his favour, he effectively makes his theory unfalsifiable. It becomes a necessary truth, but without justification.

Activity

Write a 500–600-word essay on Jung's understanding of religion. Include the following main areas: collective unconscious, archetypes and individuation.

Jung's concept of religious experience

Jung's theory of religious experience is often criticised. Martin Buber, for example, is not convinced that an experience which stems from the mind, and as such is in no way external to the subject, can properly be termed religious. In particular, Jung's argument that any archetypal image may be described as religious has come under fire. The problem is that if a vision of being trapped in armour is as religious as a vision of God, Jung has failed to preserve the uniqueness of religious experience. He has also failed to explain why this type of experience is so distinctive in the mind of the subject.

The relationship between religion and mental health

For the same reason, the definition of individuation as a religious process may be questioned. If it is governed by the Self-archetype, then it may be argued that it has nothing to do with God. The image of Christ, for example, is only significant for Jung inasmuch as it is a symbol of wholeness which can help balance our minds. Religious believers, however, would argue that Christ is more than just a symbol for something else, but rather is important in his own right, as a historical person and the Son of God. Again, then, there is an extra dimension in religious practice which Jung fails to explain.

Freud and Jung held contrasting views on the relationship between religion and mental health.

> ### Link
>
> Remind yourself of Freud's view of religion as a collective neurosis on pp36–37. What similarities did Freud identify between the behaviour of religious people and the behaviour of obsessional neurotics?

Freud's view

Freud associated religion with mental health problems. However he did not focus on the idea that religion *causes* mental illness so much as on his view that, as a collective neurosis, religion is a mental illness. For religion is one of the chief neurotic *symptoms* caused by the repression of the sexual trauma of the Oedipus complex.

Therefore, although Freud argued that religion should be overthrown, his *first* priority towards the goal of mental health should be to enable the psyche to come to terms with the repressed trauma, to prevent the religious neurosis in the first place. Merely attacking religious belief could make matters worse by removing the comfort that it offers, yet leaving the guilt and anguish, resulting in increased anxiety and depression. As a collective neurosis, religion at least helps to prevent people from falling into individual neuroses and psychoses. To this limited extent, Freud's theory should accept that religion can be beneficial to mental health.

Nevertheless, as an obsessional neurosis, religion perpetuates and magnifies the problem, rather than treating its cause. For example, it can heighten the sense of guilt and fear by building up the father into an angry God who can never be satisfied and who threatens a terrifying revenge after death. Religion can also prevent the flourishing of the psyche by encouraging dependency on our beliefs rather than encouraging self-reliance whereby we create our own

Freud and Jung

solutions to the difficulties we face. As a result, Freud's approach tends to regard religion as harmful to mental health.

Jung's view

Jung, by contrast, had a much more positive view of the relationship between religion and mental health. He considered religious belief to be a natural expression of the collective unconscious and argued that if the psyche is to be integrated successfully, we must come to terms with its different components. The images of the God archetype, moreover, are linked with the Self-archetype which drives the whole process of individuation. Religion is thus very important for mental health to the extent that if the religious impulse is repressed, mental health problems are more likely to arise.

Modern interpretations

Given the contrast between the views of Freud and Jung, it is worth considering how modern psychologists interpret this issue. In his introductory chapter to *Religion and Mental Health*, John F. Schumaker writes, 'A large proportion of thinkers take a well reasoned middle ground, maintaining that religion has the *potential* to be either positive or negative in its effects on mental ill health.'

On the positive side, religion can reduce anxiety by explaining and ordering an otherwise chaotic world. It can lead to emotional well-being by giving people a sense of purpose and offering hope. It can satisfy the need to belong to a community, fostering social integration. And it can reduce the shadow cast by the prospect of death.

On the negative side, however, it can foster an unhealthy level of guilt and reduce one's self-esteem through such beliefs as the fundamental sinfulness of humanity. It can lead to dependency on one's God, forcing people to conform rather than to forge their own purpose in life. And it can cause social division as well as fear at the prospect of judgement and punishment.

It may be that the relationship between religion and mental health depends on the many variables including the personality of the individual, the particular religion in question and its role in the believer's life. In addition, Schumaker notes that there is a lack of detailed research, for example into comparisons between the mental health of individuals who have significantly different levels of religious intensity. As a result he warns against the 'tendency to rush towards definitive statements and final conclusions' about the nature of the link between religion and mental health.

■ Conclusion

Even if we accept these psychological theories as true, they cannot prove whether God does or does not exist. Those who are already atheists may cite Freud and Jung in their favour, on the grounds that they offer comprehensive non-religious explanations for religious belief. Religious believers, however, could argue that psychological theories do not tell us anything about God's objective existence. They might even argue that Freud and Jung reveal something about the way in which God makes his presence known to humans. Jung's theory, for example, might demonstrate that God made humankind in his image by placing a blueprint of himself in our minds. Regarding Freud, John Hick (1922–) suggests that 'in his work on the father figure, he may have uncovered

Link

Remind yourself of Jung's view of the role of religion within the process of individuation on p46.

Think about

When you read the results of research in this area, be careful not to jump to conclusions. Suppose an imaginary survey were to claim that religious people are more likely to suffer from a mental health problem. What *entirely different* conclusions might people draw about the relationship between religion and mental health?

■ Activity

Remind yourself of the main features of Freud's and Jung's theories of religion.

■ List all the ways in which their accounts could be seen to challenge religious beliefs.

■ List some weaknesses with their accounts that could prevent them from making a successful challenge.

■ List any ways in which Jung's theory could be seen to support religious belief. To help you, look back at Chapter 2 to find any interpretations of religious experience that Jung's theory might be considered to support.

one of the mechanisms by which God creates an idea of the deity in the human mind.' Hick's conclusion regarding Freud could apply equally effectively to Jung:

> Again, then, it seems that the verdict must be 'not proven' … the Freudian theory of religion may be true but has not been shown to be so.'

John H. Hick, Philosophy of Religion, 1990

Now that you have read this chapter you should be able to:

■ explain the main features of Freud's and Jung's interpretations of religion

■ explain why these views might challenge religious belief and how religion might respond to this challenge

■ evaluate whether God has been explained away by psychology

■ evaluate the strengths and weaknesses of the psychological views of religion

■ assess the relationship between religion and mental health.

4 Atheism and postmodernism

Learning objectives:

- to understand the nature of atheism and how atheism differs from agnosticism

- to understand the reasons for the rise of atheism and the meaning of the slogan 'God is dead'

- to understand religious responses to atheism including a postmodernist view of religion

- to evaluate how successfully religion has responded to the challenges of atheism

- to assess whether religion is in retreat in the modern world.

Key terms

Atheism: the doctrine or belief that there is no God.

Negative atheism: also known as weak atheism. A position that asserts a lack of belief in any God or gods, without a positive denial of the existence of any god or gods.

Positive atheism: also known as strong atheism. A position that asserts that there is no God; the explicit denial of all spiritual powers and supernatural beings.

Agnosticism: a suspension of accepting or rejecting belief in God until there is sufficient data to reach a conclusion. Modern usage has the meaning of regarding God's existence and his non-existence as equally probable.

☑ Atheism and how it differs from agnosticism

The term **atheism** derives from two Greek words: 'a' meaning 'without' and 'theos' meaning 'god'. Atheism thus describes the position of being without a belief in God or gods. There are different interpretations, however, as to what this means.

Types of atheism

Negative atheism is so called because it involves a lack or absence of belief in God. This position could come about simply through never having considered the possibility of God's existence. Thus, a child who had never thought about the concept of God would technically be a negative atheist. However, it may also be the result of informed debate, leading to the conclusion that the belief in God cannot be justified. For example, a negative atheist might have studied the arguments for the existence of God and judged them to be unconvincing, or at least to be outweighed by their criticisms.

Positive atheism incorporates the position of negative atheism but goes a step further, and makes, in the words of Gavin Nyman, 'a definitive metaphysical claim about the non-existence of God.' (General Introduction, *The Cambridge Companion to Atheism*, 2007.) It requires the conscious denial of God's existence, which in turn requires satisfactory reason(s) for this denial, meaning that positive atheism can never come about through lack of thought. In addition to refuting the arguments for the existence of God, the positive atheist must provide further argument(s) against it.

Critics might argue that positive atheism can never be established with certainty, for it is impossible to prove that a thing does not exist. Positive atheists might respond, however, by arguing that the burden of proof always lies with those who seek to prove the existence of something, rather than nothing, for until we are given convincing evidence that God does exist, we must assume that he does not.

Different interpretations of atheism might also arise from considering the question, 'In which God or gods do atheists not believe?' Many atheists do not believe in any gods or goddesses. This interpretation is closer to the original roots of the word, for the Greek 'theos' refers to any type of god. Others, however, might define atheism more narrowly, to mean that there is a specific God or type of god in which they do not believe. One possible candidate is the omnipotent, omniscient and omnibenevolent God of classical theism. An atheist in this narrower sense could thus accept the existence of some other kind of god, such as a deistic one.

Agnosticism

Agnosticism derives from the Greek words for 'without knowledge' and refers to the belief that there is insufficient knowledge to prove or disprove the existence of God. Agnostics neither believe nor disbelieve in God. They do not believe that God exists, nor do they positively believe that he does not, for both positions would require knowledge about God's existence.

Think about

You may well not believe in unicorns or the tooth fairy. Do you consider it reasonable to deny that these exist? How might one attempt to demonstrate or prove their non-existence?

Link

Read Chapter 5, p79, to understand the difference between theism and deism. What type of God do deists believe in?

Activity

Write an explanation of the different understanding of the existence of God/gods between atheists and agnostics.

Link

Read Chapter 6, pp92–6, to find out how the scientific world-view has developed.

Which areas of this development might have posed the greatest challenges to belief in God?

There can be different reasons for adopting agnosticism. Some might do so because they believe that there are no good reasons for adopting a belief in God and no good reasons for rejecting such a belief. One explanation for this view would be the argument used by psychologists like Jung that nothing can ever be known about the world outside our own psychological experiences, because we can never escape from the confines of our mind in order to see what lies beyond. Others, conversely, might accept that there are good reasons for accepting God's existence, but that these are cancelled out by equally good reasons against it.

Agnosticism is often contrasted with atheism. Clearly it is incompatible with positive atheism, for one cannot deny God's existence (positive atheism) at the same time as not deny his existence (agnosticism). Unlike positive atheism, agnosticism can be seen as the 'default position' for those who are not persuaded by the arguments for or against God's existence. However, it has a much closer relationship with negative atheism, in that to be an agnostic, one must not believe in God, which is the position that negative atheists adopt. In other words, agnosticism entails negative atheism. The difference between the two is that whereas negative atheists can go on to deny God's existence, agnostics, as we have seen, cannot.

Reasons for the rise of atheism

It is often considered that atheism as a deliberate rejection of the divine had its origins in ancient Greece. For example, Thales (6th century BC) rejected religious mythological explanations of the world in favour of natural ones. It is further argued that atheism as a self-contained belief system, with an atheistic world-view to challenge the religious one, did not emerge until the 18th century AD. David Berman's work *A History of Atheism in Britain* argues that the first avowedly atheist work is Pierre d'Holbach's *The System of Nature*, published in 1770. Before this rise of atheism, he notes that in Europe belief in God was universal. He refers to 17th-century writers who believed it was not even possible to be genuinely atheist. We will here consider five areas that were influential in the rise of atheism: science, empiricism, evil, the rebellion against moral absolutes and awareness of other faiths.

Science

In *Religion Without God*, Ray Billington describes science as 'the supreme catalyst' for the rise of atheism. It has had this influence because the development of science has provided natural explanations for many of the universe's processes, even its very existence, that were previously seen as miracles that were dependent upon God.

Billington argues that three scientific developments above all others have contributed to this process:

> The first, after the invention of the telescope, followed the astronomical discoveries of Copernicus and Galileo. The cosy picture of the earth as the centre of the universe, with Homo Sapiens as its guardian under God had to go: the solar system could be explained without the hand of God. The second, two centuries later was the biological revolution culminating in Darwin's *The Origin of the Species*. As a result people were now brought face to face with Tennyson's 'nature, red in tooth and claw'; with the realisation that all its manifestations were brought about by trial and error rather than purposiveness. Third, in the early decades of

> the twentieth century, arrived the psychoanalysts with, in particular, Freud's teaching about the unconscious mind, suggesting that the idea of the conscience as the still small voice of God must go, to be replaced by that of an accumulation of experiences and ideas encountered at all stages of any individual person's life.

Ray Billington, Religion Without God, 2002

Billington's account makes it clear how the role for God in a world increasingly explained by science was slowly being squeezed out with each new discovery. God could no longer be associated with the smooth running of the cosmos, nor the creation of human life, nor even our sense of conscience and moral awareness. This gradual relegation of God's activity to explain those things which science still cannot is known as the 'God of the gaps'. This process leads some to conclude that belief in God can now be abandoned entirely, for it is only a matter of time before gaps will be filled and God will be fully redundant.

Empiricism

Empiricism is the view that all that may be known of reality is what can be known through the five senses. It is through sight, hearing, touch, smell and taste that something is proved true or false. An empiricist believes that knowledge can only be gained through experience, e.g. experiments. We can have no knowledge of anything beyond the bounds of sense experience.

Empiricism can, to a large extent, be seen as the basis of the development of science that we have already considered. For the scientific approach reaches its theories and conclusions on the basis of experience in the form of observation and experiments. Even without reference to science, however, the empiricist tradition has supported the development of atheism. Although empiricists such as John Locke tried to justify the belief in God on empirical grounds, Gavin Hyman argues that there is a fundamental difficulty in doing so, for 'according to theological discourse, God is precisely that which is nonempirical'. (Gavin Hyman, 'Atheism in Modern History', in *The Cambridge Companion to Atheism*, 2007.) In other words God cannot be touched, smelt, tasted, seen or heard. This is because God is not a physical object within the world. Therefore events interpreted by believers as religious experiences, perhaps in which God himself is revealed, are not open to empirical proofs, and are often considered to be supernatural.

The implications of empiricism for religious belief were made clear by David Hume. Hume argued that we must draw our conclusions 'merely from the known phenomena', which meant that we must abandon 'every arbitrary supposition or conjecture'. There could be no knowledge except in relation to the physical, and since God was metaphysical (meaning literally 'above the physical') we could have no knowledge about God, and thus no justification for the belief that God exists. In the words of Gavin Hyman, 'Hume saw what Locke had not: that theism was fundamentally incompatible with empiricism.' (*ibid.*)

Empiricism dealt a further blow to theism when it was combined with what the British philosopher A. J. Ayer (1910–89) called the **verification principle**. This was the principle that unless we know in principle how to verify a statement (that is, to prove whether it is true or false), then that statement is meaningless and it is therefore illogical to make it. For example, the statement 'Earth is the only planet in the universe on

Link

Read Chapter 5, p81, to understand the meaning of the phrase 'God of the gaps'.

Activity

Chapter 2 describes religious experiences as 'non-empirical'. Read Chapter 2, pp17–22, and write an explanation of why mystical experiences (as an example of religious experiences) cannot be empirically verified.

Key terms

Verification principle: developed by the school of logical positivism (c. 1920) and claims the only criterion for whether or not a statement is meaningful is to know how that statement may be proved true or false.

■ **Think about**

Why do you think that Ayer considered it so important that we know how to verify a statement? Do you think it would ever be justified to believe something that you would not know how to verify?

which there is life' would be considered meaningful because we know how to prove the statement even if we cannot do it yet, that is to travel to all parts of the universe. However, the statement 'God exists' would be considered meaningless because we do not know how to prove it true or false using our senses, for the reasons stated above.

Ayer accepted the empiricist view that the only way to verify a statement is through empirical evidence, except for those statements that are true by definition because they are tautologies (e.g. 'a bachelor is an unmarried man'). Noting that statements about God cannot be verified by either method, Ayer concluded that they are meaningless. Since we cannot believe in that which is meaningless, we cannot believe that God exists.

The problem of evil

Thomas Aquinas, despite being one of the most influential Christian theologians, was well aware of the threat to belief in God posed by the existence of evil:

> It seems that God does not exist: because if one of two contraries be infinite, the other would be altogether destroyed. But the name of God means that He is infinite goodness. If therefore, God existed, there would be no evil discoverable; but there is evil in the world. Therefore God does not exist.'

Thomas Aquinas, Summa Theologica

Aquinas himself, of course, went on to reject this conclusion, but the problem of evil is nevertheless often presented as one of the most compelling reasons for rejecting the God of classical theism. The argument can be summarised thus:

■ Since God alone created the universe out of nothing, God has total responsibility for everything in it. If God is omnipotent, then God can do anything that is logically possible. This means that God could have created a world free from actual evil and suffering, and free from the possibility of ever going wrong. It also means that, should God have allowed it to come about, God could end all evil and suffering.

■ Being omniscient, God has complete knowledge of everything in the universe, including evil and suffering, and also knows how to stop it.

■ If God is all-loving, however, God would wish to end all evil and suffering. Any loving being, as we understand the term, would wish to stop the multiple horrors heaped upon the millions of innocent people over the years. No all-loving God would allow any creation to suffer physical and mental torment for no reason and to no avail. Being omnipotent, God could immediately step in and stop the suffering.

■ Yet evil and suffering continue to exist, so either (1) God lacks omnipotence or omnibenevolence or (2) he does not exist. By denying one of his essential attributes, even the first alternative entails atheism, with regard to the God of classical theism.

Of course religious believers would reject these conclusions by presenting a variety of arguments to show that God has a sufficiently good reason for allowing evil to continue, whether as a punishment or for some greater good. An atheist, however, might reply that no argument can rescue the belief in an all-loving God. It can be argued that love can never be expressed by allowing any amount of suffering, no matter what the reason. The British philosopher D. Z. Phillips (1934–2006) argued it would never be justifiable to hurt someone in order to help them. When we consider the magnitude of suffering in our world, this problem is all the more serious.

The problem of evil has become much more significant in the 20th century when through the growing use of the media people have had first-hand experience of such evils as the First and Second World Wars, and worldwide famines. Either they have seen the suffering first hand, as for example a soldier on the battlefield of the Somme or in their living rooms when watching the nightly news. This point of view is adopted by Ivan Karamazov in Fyodor Dostoyevsky's novel, *The Brothers Karamazov*. Ivan refuses to believe in a God who allows innocent children to suffer. He emphasises that such suffering can never be justified, even by the promise of eternal compensation in Heaven. Thus the God of classical theism is rejected. Ivan himself adopts a position known as protest atheism, in which he does not deny the existence of a God, but rather refuses to acknowledge him on moral grounds.

The rebellion against moral absolutes

Moral absolutists believe in moral absolutes, arguing that no matter how inconvenient or difficult, they must always be obeyed. Moral relativists rebel against moral absolutes, arguing that what is right or wrong varies, e.g. according to the situation. In the 20th century it is argued that the post-war social scene developed into a rebellion against what had previously been accepted by earlier generations. The 1960s in particular are regarded as a turning point when the 'old' absolutes of sex within marriage began to decline. An unmarried couple living together are no longer regarded as 'living in sin'. Abortion and homosexuality have been legalised and there is a creeping acceptance of euthanasia. The question arises as to whether such 'freedoms' have followed, or influenced, the rise of atheism.

It is probable that social change and the rise in atheism go hand in hand. There is a long tradition in which the belief in moral absolutes has been linked with the belief in God. Some have claimed that the existence of moral absolutes provides a powerful reason to believe in God. Thus, H. P. Owen states, 'It is impossible to think of a command without also thinking of a commander,' and explains such commands 'in terms of a personal God'. In the words of John Henry Newman (1801–90):

> If, as is the case, we feel responsibility, are ashamed, are frightened at transgressing the voice of conscience, this implies that there is One to whom we are responsible, before whom we are ashamed, whose claim upon us we fear ... If the cause of these emotions does not belong to this visible world, the Object to which [our] perception is directed must be Supernatural and Divine.'

J. H. Newman, A Grammar of Assent, ed. C. F. Harold, David McKay and Co., 1947

Immanuel Kant rejected all the rational proofs of God's existence, and emphasised that moral laws are not divine commands, yet nevertheless argued that our experience of the moral law, that sense of unconditional obligation, justifies us in postulating God's existence. God is required in order for the moral law to make sense, to enable us to attain in the afterlife its ultimate demands of perfect goodness combined with perfect happiness.

Cultural relativists go a step further, arguing that what is right and wrong is based on nothing more than the attitude of our culture. In other

Key terms

Moral absolute: unchanging ethical truth.

words, if we live in a culture where the burying of unwanted children is approved, then this is good. The only reason we ourselves consider it wrong is because our culture does not approve of it. This approach to moral relativism removes not only absolute laws but any objective reason why we even need to try to behave morally. If we dislike the morals of our culture, we need simply find a society more conducive to our own ideas. There is no objective basis for judging or condemning any practice, whether genocide or anything else.

There are several ways in which this rebellion against moral absolutes threatens belief in God and contributes to the rise of atheism. First, it undermines the argument that if a society has moral absolutes then it needs a commander (God).

A more serious problem is that since absolute moral commands are such an integral part of many religions, to reject them destroys a large part of the religion itself. For a start, it would destroy trust in the religious texts that command them. For example, moral absolutes including the Ten Commandments are fundamental to the teaching of the Old Testament, which is the basis of Judaism and, to some extent, Christianity. It is seen by these religions as essential evidence of God's existence. But if there are no moral absolutes, then such texts cannot be trusted, which removes a major reason for believing in God.

The rebellion against moral absolutes also destroys an essential part of our actual understanding of God. It rejects God's authority to set absolute laws, challenging both the belief that God is omniscient as to what is objectively right and the belief that God has the power to command people how to live, threatening the concept of omnipotence. It would mean that the statement 'God is good' has no objective meaning, and, indeed, that God could just as easily be considered evil. There would be no objective benchmark that would enable us to judge God 'all-loving', nor the source of all goodness. And if we reject these ideas about God, of course, we embrace atheism; at least with regard to belief in the God of classical theism.

■ Activity

List all the reasons you can think of why our awareness that there are so many widely differing religions might threaten a person's belief in God.

■ Awareness of other faiths

Although contact between different religions is nothing new, it is only since the 20th century that the work of theologians, sociologists and anthropologists, and the greater ease of transport, have promoted increased dialogue between and detailed study of different faiths. John Hick clearly explains the challenge posed by this increase in awareness of other faiths to the belief in God:

> If I had been born in India, I would probably be a Hindu; if in Egypt, probably a Muslim; if in Sri Lanka, probably a Buddhist; but I was born in England and am, predictably, a Christian. These different religions seem to say different and incompatible things about the nature of ultimate reality, about the modes of divine activity, and about the nature and destiny of the human race. Is the divine nature personal or nonpersonal? Does deity become incarnate in the world? Are human beings reborn again and again on earth? ... Is the Bible or the Qur'an or the Bhagavad Gita the Word of God? If what Christianity says in answer to such questions is true, must not what Hinduism says be to a large extent false? If what Buddhism says is true, must not what Islam says be largely false?

John Hick, Philosophy of Religion, 4th ed., 1990

Moreover, the contradictions between religions do not merely question the validity of some of them: 'It is a short step from the thought that the different religions cannot all be true, although they all claim to be, to the thought that in all probability none of them is true.' (John Hick, ibid) This was the position adopted by David Hume in response to the different miracle accounts of different religions.

Hume's claim that 'in religion, whatever is different is contrary' is explained by his view that each religion makes conflicting claims about the objective nature of God and the world. So, for example, miracles like the Resurrection that purport to establish the exclusive validity of Christianity, implicitly destroy that of Islam, Judaism and all faiths that reject the Christian truth claims. These truth claims, in turn, are rejected by those of all the other opposing faiths. The net result, in John Hick's words, is that 'for any particular religion, there will always be far more reason for believing it to be false than for believing it to be true'. If the balance of evidence lies against any particular belief in God, then an obvious conclusion would be to believe in no God at all.

☑ ⓘ The meaning of the slogan 'God is dead'

Friedrich Nietzsche (1844–1900), the son of a Lutheran minister, had become an atheist by the age of 18. However, Nietzsche did not focus on trying to prove that God did not exist. When he wrote his famous slogan 'God is dead', he was expressing his judgement that God was no longer relevant to society. In his work *The Gay Science* the phrase is uttered by a madman, who nevertheless perceives what those around him have failed to realise.

> Have you not heard of that madman who lit a lantern in the bright morning hours, ran to the market place, and cried incessantly, 'I seek God! I seek God! ... Whither is God? ... I will tell you. We have killed him – you and I. All of us are his murderers ... God is dead. God remains dead. And we have killed him.'

Friedrich Nietzsche, Section 25, The Gay Science, 1882

Nietzsche's point, voiced by the madman, was that modern society had made God redundant. Where society had once relied upon God to make sense of the world and maintain order, now it had the developments in science and philosophy, to name but two, to put in his place. As Alister McGrath explains, Nietzsche meant that 'God has ceased to be a presence in Western culture. He has been eliminated; squeezed out.' With deep irony, Nietzsche argued that part of the cause behind this process was the Christian insistence upon seeking the truth. He refers to, 'the awe-inspiring catastrophe of a two thousand year discipline in truth that finally forbids itself the lie involved in belief in God.' (Friedrich Nietzsche, *The Genealogy of Morals* 111:27.)

Nietzsche realised that the 'death' of God had very profound implications for society, not least because it entailed the death of religious ethics. Much of Nietzsche's work represented his coming to terms with this, and presenting an alternative approach to life to the religious one. This included his view that people must create their own values to realise their potential as human beings.

In the 1960s, in the context of a great questioning of accepted values, the concept of the 'death' found its way into the unlikely environment of the Christian church. John Robinson, a Church of England bishop, in his

Think about

Read Chapter 5, p83. How does Hume justify his view that the miracles claimed by the different religions actually count against, rather than for, the validity of these religions?

Activity

Write a 500–600-word essay explaining the reasons for the rise of atheism.

Think about

If Nietzsche proclaimed 'God is dead' in 1882, meaning that society then had no use for God, what do you think he might have proclaimed about God now? Give reasons for your answer.

book *Honest to God*, presented his view that Christians could no longer defend the belief in an objectively existing God. While some considered this to be a blunt statement of atheism, others saw it as the appropriate Christian response to atheism's challenge. Similar ideas to these will be considered in the section on postmodernism.

■ Religious responses to atheism

One way in which religious believers might respond to the challenges of atheism is to reject them completely and withdraw into the fundamental beliefs of their faith. One argument they might use is that the knowledge that comes from God's revelation, in sacred texts like the Bible, is inherently more trustworthy than the human and thereby fallible attempt of scientists and others who seek knowledge by themselves. They might also claim that the arguments of atheists are deliberate attempts to discredit belief in God in order to suit their own purposes. The difficulty with this approach is that it makes no real attempt to engage with and answer the atheistic challenges, instead merely ignoring them.

An alternative response therefore is to examine each of the atheists' challenges in turn in order to judge how serious they are. They offer various ways of overcoming the challenges in order to show that continued belief in God is justifiable. Here we will briefly consider some possible responses to the five challenges we have examined.

Response to science

The challenges from science have been answered by the argument that nothing within these challenges amounts to a proof that God does not exist (a point that Richard Dawkins, among others, would accept) and that scientific theories are entirely compatible *with* belief in God.

A typical argument would be that even if science explains how the world was created and functions, and gives physical reasons for why these events came about, it does not preclude the possibility that God was behind these events, giving them their ultimate purpose, which science cannot reveal. For some, religion explains why the conditions first came about in which these physical laws and events were able to arise.

Stephen Hawking's hesitancy as to the existence of God can be seen as supporting the possibility of God, which then becomes much more than a possibility if believers have reasons beyond science upon which to base their beliefs.

Response to empiricism

There are several ways around the criticisms of empiricists. Ayer's charge that religious language is meaningless can be dismissed on the grounds that the verification principle itself cannot be verified, and on Ayer's definition is therefore meaningless. To the general demand for empirical evidence of God, however, there are several possible responses. As proponents of the cosmological and design arguments would assert, the physical existence of the earth and the level of design within it could be interpreted as empirical evidence for a creator and a designer.

It might be argued that certain kinds of religious experience contain empirical evidence (e.g. stigmata) that, in the absence of a physical explanation, must point to a cause beyond the physical. Others would widen the definition of sense experience beyond the five senses to include such things as intuitive knowledge and a sense of divine presence. Ray

■ **Think about**

Read Chapter 6, pp102–3. How do Young Earth Creationists justify their rejection of geologists' conclusions about the age of the earth? How does this view counter atheism?

■ **Link**

Read Chapter 6, pp99 –105, and Chapter 7, pp115–16, to understand Richard Dawkins's arguments against the existence of God.

■ **Think about**

Read Swinburne's contribution to the design argument, Chapter 7, pp118–20. How do his arguments from temporal and spatial order justify the belief in God even in the context of scientific explanations?

■ **Activity**

Read Chapter 2, pp30–4, and list the evidence used to support the belief in religious experiences as genuine.

Billington, despite his rejection of the existence of God, nonetheless admits that sense experience cannot account for all human beliefs. Consider, for example, our responses to a favourite piece of music compared with a piece we do not know, or the wide variety in emotional responses to pieces of art or scenes of great beauty. In these examples, humans are clearly picking out a level of meaning that is hard to explain merely in terms of the senses of sight or hearing. It might be argued that religious truths can likewise be accessed by an awareness that operates beyond the bounds of the senses.

Response to the problem of evil

The problem of evil has been answered in many different ways, most of them referring to human free will as a sufficient reason for why God allows evil to continue. St Augustine, for example, argued that evil had come about through human misuse of free will, and evil continues as a consequence of that rebellion against God. St Irenaeus (2nd–3rd century) argued that evil is an unavoidable risk if God has given humans free will. Irenaeus focused on the instrumental value of evil as a means to achieve good. This view has been adopted by many philosophers. John Hick, for example, argues that if God wanted humans to be genuinely loving, he could not create them to always do good as they would then just be robots, but had to give them the freedom to develop this quality themselves. Moreover, in a world devoid of the possibility of suffering, no meaningful love or goodness could come about since nothing we could do would ever cause harm. Hick therefore concludes that while our world is not …

> … designed for the maximisation of human pleasure and the minimisation of human pain, it may nevertheless be rather well adapted to the quite different purpose of 'soul making'.

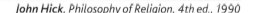

John Hick, Philosophy of Religion, *4th ed., 1990*

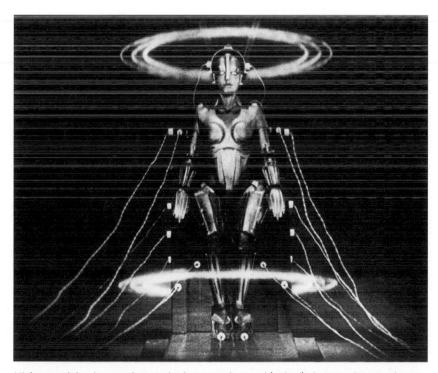

Hick argued that humans have to be free to make good (or bad) choices otherwise they are just robots

Link

Look again at St Thomas Aquinas's challenge on p54. How do you think a religious believer might answer Aquinas's challenge? Think about different views of what God's 'goodness' might mean and why an infinitely good God might allow evil.

Key terms

Situation ethics: Christian ethical theory that was developed in the 1960s by Joseph Fletcher. It states the basic moral principle in any situation is the one in which Christian love is best served.

Religious belief: a strong belief in a supernatural power or powers that control human destiny. It usually relates to a belief in God or gods.

Religious pluralism: describes the world-view that one religion is not the sole and exclusive source of truth, and thus recognises that some level of truth and value exists in at least some other religions.

Activity

For each of the main religious responses to the challenges from atheism, write down how convincing a response you consider it to be. Give reasons for your views.

These approaches show that while the problem of evil may remain a mystery, there are nevertheless ways of explaining how an all-loving and all-powerful God could allow evil. There is certainly no reason why evil would make belief in God literally impossible.

Response to moral absolutes

It can be argued that the rebellion against moral absolutes is not a significant threat to belief in God, unless it is taken to the extremes of moral nihilism, which is the view that there are no objective standards of any kind, so that people can do whatever they want. This, however, is not what many people take relativism to be.

If relativism is simply seen as the rejection of specific moral absolutes, perhaps only in some situations, then it can be seen as compatible with even a traditional belief in God. The American academic Joseph Fletcher (1905–91), for example, argues that God's only absolute command is to 'love your neighbour'. His theory of **situation ethics** interprets this as the need to bring about 'the greatest amount of neighbour welfare for the greatest number of neighbours.' Since we are to bring about the most loving consequences, there are no acts that can always be right or wrong – yet Fletcher considered situational ethics to be a Christian theory.

Moreover, not all atheists reject moral absolutes. Some would argue that certain commands, such as not intentionally killing innocent people, must always be obeyed. This would prevent the problem from arising in the first place. Some would add that the rejection of moral absolutes is more likely to be caused by atheism than to cause atheism.

The challenge of other faiths would immediately be rejected by a substantial number of **religious believers**, who would argue that theirs is the one true faith, and all others are in error. Of course not all religions can be right, but that does not remove the possibility that one of them might be. Individual religions might point to specific reasons within their own tradition as evidence of the supremacy of their faith. For Christians, for example, this might be the Incarnation of God who became a human being in Jesus.

Response to religious pluralism

An alternative approach that removes the difficulty of conflicting claims is **religious pluralism**. John Hick interprets this as the view that all of the major religions are human responses to the transcendent reality that many call God, and that as responses, they are all equally valid and effective. So although key beliefs and practices may be different, these are all symbols of and means of approaching the irreducible truth that in this life cannot be accessed directly by humans. The Sufi thinker Rumi expressed it thus: 'The lamps are different but the light is the same; it comes from beyond.'

While pluralism may be unacceptable to many religious believers, some would argue that it provides the most satisfying answer to the multitude of apparently incompatible traditions. Within Christianity, for example, the Religious Society of Friends lays a particular emphasis on the need for tolerance and acceptance of other faiths.

7 Postmodernist views of religion

Postmodernism, meaning 'after modernism', refers to the cultural era that follows the modernist period. It is both a response to and reaction against modernist values and ideas. These periods may alternatively be known as postmodernity and modernity.

The central feature of modernism was its claim that in all areas of endeavour, whether arts, sciences or philosophy, there is a single Truth that can be discovered through reason and experience. In terms of religion and philosophy, for example, modernists claimed that there is a single correct **meta-narrative**. One modernist approach to religion was to reject all religious claims to knowledge about God and adopt this atheist meta-narrative. An alternative approach was to claim that absolute knowledge of God is, in fact, possible, through, for example, fundamentalist interpretations of the Bible as God's literal Word, or claims that the Pope was infallible.

Postmodernism, by contrast, rejects the trust placed in reason and experience to discover the truth, and indeed rejects all claims to absolute knowledge of what is true, including meta-narratives. As the social critic Os Guinness (1941–) writes:

> Where modernism was a manifesto of human self-congratulation and self-confidence, postmodernism is a confession of modesty, if not despair.

*quoted in **Alister McGrath's** The Twilight of Atheism, 2004*

This clearly presents a challenge to traditional interpretations of religion. In the words of Andrew Wright:

> Theological meta-narratives are ruled out *a priori* by post-modernity. In the post-modern world all ultimate beliefs, meta-narratives and claims to be able to understand the actual structure of reality are deemed invalid. Theological language cannot connect directly with any divine reality; our words simply dissolve into never-ending chains of sign and symbols and are unable to signify any substantial reality beyond themselves.

***Andrew Wright**, Postmodernism and Religion, Dialogue 16, 2001*

It can equally be argued, however, that postmodernism presents a challenge to atheism and atheistic meta-narratives. As John Caputo explains, postmodernism is

> not a particularly friendly environment for atheism…if atheism is a metaphysical or an otherwise fixed and decisive denial of God.

***John Caputo**, 'Atheism, Atheology and the Postmodern Condition', in The Cambridge Companion to Atheism, 2007*

Postmodernism therefore leaves the possibility of some form of religious belief genuinely open, even if its understanding of what is 'religious' might be very different from the way in which many traditional believers use the term.

The following sections examine some features of a postmodernist view of religion. It is important to be aware, however, that postmodernists can vary widely in their responses to religion.

Key terms

Postmodernism: a world-view that emphasises the existence of different world-views and concepts of reality, rather than one 'correct or true' one.

Meta-narrative or grand narrative: an account of reality with an absolute claim to truth. Christians, for example, adopt the meta-narrative that an all-powerful all-loving God created the world and redeemed it through his son Jesus who saves people from their sins.

Activity

Write a definition of postmodernism.

Religions as cultural constructs

The postmodernist rejection of meta-narratives involves the rejection of the absolute truth claims of religions like Judaism, Christianity and Islam. Having rejected these religious claims to the truth then Postmodernists must present an alternative explanation for these beliefs, which they see as the result of **cultural constructs**. The French sociologist Emile Durkheim (1858–1917) argued that religion was the product of the society in which it developed. What is required by the religion results from how the society expects people to behave and to bring the individuals together as one social group. For example, religious symbols, such as the Christian cross, provide a focus for the outpouring of emotion and belief, and religious rituals, such as the Catholic Mass, provide the context for shared experiences with one's community.

Postmodernist thinkers argue that these cultural constructs must be deconstructed. This involves demonstrating that religious claims to absolute truth are unfounded, so that they can then be seen for the relative, subjective accounts they really are. Words cannot give us knowledge of any external reality because they have no meaning beyond referring us to other words, which are after all, created by individuals and their cultures.

The French philosopher Jean-Francois Lyotard (1924–98) argued that beliefs that have been understood as meta-narratives should be seen as local interpretations of the nature of reality, as understood by an individual or a culture. For example, the Hebrew view of a God who cares for and protects his people might well be born out of the experience of escaping from slavery in Egypt, and as a result would have no meaning for people in a different religion and culture who have not had that experience. Such mini-narratives should be seen as relative and thereby compatible interpretations, rather than competing and mutually exclusive absolute claims. This leads to the next aspect of the postmodernist view.

No right or wrong religions

Having rejected all claims to absolute truth, postmodernists would argue that there can therefore be no 'right' or 'wrong' religions. Therefore if there is rejection of absolutes there must also be the rejection of any individual religion's claims to be the exclusive truth. Os Guinness writes:

> There is no truth; only truths. There is no grand reason; only reasons. There is no privileged civilization (or culture, belief, norm and style), only a multiplicity of cultures, beliefs, norms and styles … There is no grand narrative of human progress, only countless stories of where people and their cultures are now.

quoted in **Alister McGrath's** *The Twilight of Atheism, 2004*

This has resulted in the postmodern commitment to religious pluralism and tolerance. The French philosopher Jacques Derrida (1930–2004) stated that: 'Deconstruction is not an enclosure in nothingness but an openness to the other.' What he means is that postmodernism frees people from having to conform to religious or atheistic beliefs. People who do not conform do not have to fear being marginalised or discriminated against because postmodernism accepts different cultures and values, as well as a variety of spiritual and religious ideas.

At the heart of the postmodernist denial of right or wrong religions lies a genuine agnosticism about the existence of God. Many postmodernists, including Derrida, have adopted this view, as to opt for anything more definite would be to move towards meta-narratives and to close oneself to the 'other'. By maintaining a genuine openness, agnosticism enables us to experience a real sense of mystery and spirituality through our awareness as humans.

John Caputo adopts this approach in his book *On Religion* (2001). He promotes what he calls 'religion without religion'; without, that is, the confines of specific dogmas and certainties. For Caputo, 'true religion' refers to 'the "virtue" of being genuinely or truly religious, of genuinely or truly loving God, not the One True Religion, Ours-versus-yours.' Caputo's agnosticism is maintained, despite statements of his belief in God, through the uncertainty as to what God refers, illustrated by his endorsement of St Augustine's confession, 'What do I love when I love my God?' He defines God as love, but immediately questions whether love is our best name for God, or whether God is simply our best name for love. He affirms: 'We do not know what we believe or to whom we are praying.' In relation to the views of different individuals and cultures, Caputo states:

> While faith gives the faithful a way to view things, they are not lifted by the hook of faith above the fray of conflicting points of view.

John Caputo, On Religion, 2001

Religion as personal spiritual search

With no religions that can be seen as right or wrong, it is therefore up to the individual to select their own mini-narrative that most resonates with their own outlook. Some will adopt beliefs and ideas found within traditional religions, though, in keeping with the rejection of absolute truths, such images may need to be interpreted as symbols. In Chapter 3, for example, we have mentioned Jung's emphasis on the symbolic value of the figure of Christ as an image of psychological balance and wholeness. Others will use images from outside the bounds of traditional religion. The wide range of religions from which to choose has been termed the religious supermarket and the process of selecting one's own bespoke religion is called the pick and mix approach. James Beckford, for example, writes:

> At the modern supermarket of faith, the consumer seeks to pick and mix religious items to match their commitment and faith.

James Beckford, 'Why Britain doesn't go to church', BBC news article, 2007

Link

Look back at Chapter 3 pp47-8 and remind yourself of Jung's emphasis on the symbolic figure of Christ.

One example of a faith that appears to be based on this approach is New Age Spirituality, described by Paul Heelas as:

> an eclectic hotchpotch of beliefs, practices and ways of life. Esoteric or mystical Buddhism, Christianity, Hinduism, Islam and Taoism enter the picture. So too do elements from 'pagan' teachings including Celtic, Druidic, Mayan and Native American Indian. An exceedingly wide range of practices – Zen meditations, Wiccan rituals, enlightenment intensive seminars, management trainings, shamanic activities, wilderness events, spiritual therapies, forms of positive thinking – fall under the rubric.

Paul Heelas, The New Age Movement: The Celebration of the Self and the Sacralization of Modernity, 1996

This list illustrates not only the variety of approaches but also the presence of those that many believers would not consider to be religious. This recalls Caputo's concept of 'religion without religion' whereby the distinction between the religious and secular is blurred.

A different understanding of religion as a personal spiritual search is taken by Don Cupitt in his book *Taking Leave of God* (1980). More fundamentally, Cupitt takes a different approach to belief in God from the thoroughgoing agnosticism we considered in the last section. For he presents what has been called an 'atheistic theology', through his adoption of the anti-realist view.

As an anti-realist, Cupitt argued that although God really exists, he exists as an idea within believers, rather than as an external, objective being. For Cupitt, God is the 'unifying symbol that … personifies and represents to us everything that spirituality requires of us'. In other words, God symbolises both the importance of our spiritual life and our spiritual goal of self-perfection. Through living a devoted religious life, we bring ourselves ever closer towards this goal.

Later, however, Cupitt rejected this view, arguing that there is no absolute standard by which to judge even our own self-perfection. In *The Long-legged Fly* (1987) he suggested that the best we can do is to fulfil our desires by exploring imaginatively a wide variety of approaches to the spiritual life.

Living religion rather than intellectual faith

Given the deep agnosticism of many postmodern views of religion, it is not surprising that the emphasis has frequently fallen upon religion as a way of life rather than a system of belief. Caputo affirms that 'the faithful need to concede that they do not cognitively *know* what they *believe* by faith in any epistemologically rigorous kind of a way', meaning that people's religious beliefs are based on faith not fact. Given such uncertainty, it would not even be possible to base religion upon intellectual faith. Caputo instead views religion and God himself as 'a deed, not a thought'. He argues:

> If the question of faith resists an answer, a Big, Final Conclusive Answer, it requires a response, a modest but passionate, humble but heartfelt response … When love calls for action, we had better be ready with something more than a well-formed proposition even if it has been approved by a council. We had better be ready with a deed, not a what but a how, ready to respond and do the truth, to make it happen here and now, for love and justice are required now … Religious truth, being truly religious, is not a formula to recite but a deed to do … The name of God is something to do.

John Caputo, On Religion, 2001

Postmodernist views of Christianity can adopt this emphasis upon deeds rather than creeds. The doctrine of the Trinity, for example, comes to express not an absolute intellectual truth about the nature of God, but the ultimate mystery of a God, at the heart of whom is a loving relationship expressed through the acts of creation, incarnation and self-sacrifice to achieve redemption. Central to this understanding of the Trinity is its power to motivate Christians to live their faith. In the words of Andrew Wright:

> The tradition of 'post-liberal' theology argues that the heart of Christianity is not a set of dogmas and creedal statements which the believer is expected to acknowledge, but rather a transformed

life lived out within the Christian community. Christians are engaged in the experiment of striving to make their personal life stories part of God's own story by immersing themselves in the narrative of creation, incarnation, transformation and salvation.

Andrew Wright, 'Postmodernism and Religion', Dialogue, Issue 16, 2001

Having considered the main features of postmodernist views of religion, our remaining task is to examine whether postmodernism affirms religious belief or whether it presents yet another challenge that threatens religious belief and supports the views of atheists.

Postmodernism and religion

Postmodernism as an affirmation of religion

It is easy to isolate aspects of postmodernism that support or are compatible with traditional religious beliefs. For example, most religions would emphasise the importance of living religion; that is, living out one's faith so that the believer's life is a witness to its religious foundation. Moreover, key religious teachings, such as Jesus's command to 'Love your neighbour', demonstrate the importance of practical actions.

Even the rejection of intellectual knowledge about God could be seen as broadly in line with the approach of the Religious Society of Friends (Quakers). Although Quakers frequently refer to the 'light of God' within the individual, they have no creed of specific religious beliefs and some Quakers do not conceive of God as a personal being.

The traditional religious beliefs that God is omnipotent and, to some extent, transcendent must entail that God cannot be contained within the bounds of human knowledge. This, after all, explains why religions emphasise words like 'faith' and 'belief' rather than 'certainty' and 'knowledge'. It could be argued that these features of religion are broadly in line with the postmodernist rejection of absolute knowledge and its embrace of mystery.

Some religious traditions and practices are particularly well suited to these postmodernist ideas. Christian mysticism, for example, focuses on the encounter with the divine mystery. William James identified ineffability as a key feature of a mystical religious experience. Although he also refers to a knowledge that is gained in such experiences (the 'noetic' quality), he describes this as intuitive, rather than intellectual knowledge. This could be in line with Lyotard's understanding of 'mini-narratives' which are meaningful to individuals without containing universal truth for all. St John of the Cross adopted the *via negative*, which describes God not by saying what he is but by saying what he is not.

A further way in which postmodernism can be seen to affirm religion is the way it exposes atheism as yet another meta-narrative that needs to be deconstructed. Derrida's emphasis on 'openness to the other' preserves the possibility of a religious dimension despite all the arguments used by atheists against the existence of God. By widening the understanding of both religion and God (for example Caputo's 'religion without religion') and preserving a real sense of mystery, postmodernism opens up new possibilities for accepting a religious interpretation of life where otherwise this may be rejected as unjustifiable.

Link

Remind yourself of the definitions of religious experience given by Leuba, James and Happold in Chapter 2.

Activity

List all the ways you can think of in which postmodernism might be seen to affirm religious belief. To help you do this, consider different ideas about what it means to be 'religious'.

Think about

Read the quotation by Nicholas of Cusa on p21. To what extent do you think a postmodernist would accept this interpretation of 'grasping the incomprehensible'? It may help you to reread the explanation of noetic quality on p19.

Activity

List all the ways you can think of in which postmodernism might be seen to challenge or threaten religious belief.

Postmodernism as a threat to religion

Postmodernism can, however, be seen to pose a serious threat to traditional religious belief. Its central claim that we cannot access any universal truth directly contradicts the key teachings of many religions, which present themselves as the only true faith. Consider, for example, the claims of many Christians that Jesus is 'the Way, the Truth and the Life', and the only way to God. Even religious pluralism and other traditions that are tolerant of other faiths generally maintain that there is an ultimate truth and reality behind all of these, and yet it is this that postmodernism questions. The most that postmodernists offer is that they are open to the possibility of God. Many religions would consider such statements of agnosticism as woefully inadequate as the basis for a meaningful 'faith'.

However, postmodernism can come closer to atheism rather than agnosticism. Don Cupitt's anti-realist approach to God would be considered by many believers to be a simple admission of atheism, in all but name. By rejecting the objective existence of God, Cupitt seems to disallow Derrida's open-ended view in this matter.

Despite the frequent emphasis on living religion in the major world faiths, this generally goes hand in hand with certain key intellectual beliefs, so that although practice is important, so too are the truth claims that are seen as the basis for such practice.

Moreover, the rejection of all absolute truth claims that prevents any absolute declaration of faith also makes it difficult to have a specific ethical code of conduct upon which to base one's religious actions. At most, one might be able to justify a rejection of all actions that harm or show intolerance to others, but even this basic principle would be open to doubt as it could be seen as yet another absolute rule based on a meta-narrative of tolerance and respect.

Postmodernism, by allowing so much freedom of thought and action, threatens many traditional understandings of religion, which at their heart contain a strong sense of moral absolutes. Given the importance attached by religions to moral behaviour, a system that challenges the very basis of right and wrong must be seen as a serious threat.

The pick and mix approach to religion allows one to swap and change religious ideas as often as one wishes, and removes any need for being courageous and holding faithfully to one's beliefs and values – and yet many believers would argue that these are central aspects of religion. The very concept of the religious supermarket presents religion as just another commodity, and portrays 'believers' as consumers. Many would reject this view on the grounds that religion is not supposed to be a product that can be bought or rejected but a way of life that commits the believer until death.

Postmodernist methodology

Finally, the methodology of postmodernism has been criticised. Its emphasis that there can be no absolute truth claims can itself be seen as an absolute truth claim, enforcing a relativist outlook upon everyone. So instead of rescuing society from the absolute values of modernity, it simply substitutes a different one in their place.

It can be argued that it would be difficult to interpret postmodernism as an affirmation of traditional religious belief and practice, as these have been conceived, for example, in the mainstream world religions.

AQA Examiner's tip

Avoid the 'here's one I prepared earlier' approach to essay writing. If you use it, you will almost certainly be writing an answer to a different question from the one asked. Even if it is only slightly different it will mean that your answer is not directly relevant or focused.

Activity

Write a 500–600-word essay summarising the main features of the postmodernist view of religion.

Nevertheless, it can be seen to affirm religion when this is interpreted more broadly, and those elements of the major faiths that have most emphasised mystery would be the most likely to identify common ground with postmodernism.

Is religion in retreat in the modern world?

When Friedrich Nietzsche proclaimed 'God is dead' he was clearly sounding the death knell for religion. In the 21st century, there are areas where religion, and specifically conventional religion, is in retreat. A 2004 survey commissioned by the BBC reported that 44 per cent of people in Britain do not believe in God, while Grace Davie reported a 1999 survey which found that in Sweden the figure was as high as 85 per cent. It is frequently reported that church attendance is in decline, and with it, attendance of religious societies. Though the reigning monarch is technically in charge of the Church of England, her role is more symbolic than practical, in both the church and the state. Since the French Revolution, the government of France has been separate from the church. And traditional religious teaching on moral matters, such as that against divorce, has ceased to impact upon current trends of increasing divorce rates and the increasing breakdown in family life.

However, this is only part of the story. Surveys have shown that in large parts of the world things are very different. In Africa, for example, atheism is highly unusual. The 2004 BBC survey, along with a number of others in the previous decade, found that less than 1 per cent of people in no fewer than 33 African countries (e.g. including Ethiopia and Morocco) are atheist, agnostic or non religious. In the USA, church attendance is dramatically higher than in Britain. There, as well as a vigorous representation of conservative Christian beliefs within the administration, there is a stronger emphasis upon traditional Christian morality, which has impacted upon the views of young people as well as old. Consider, for example, the success of The Silver Ring Thing, a charity that promotes the message of sexual abstinence until marriage.

The other part of the argument for the continued significance of religion relates to the increasing variety of ways in which religiosity can be expressed, even in countries like Britain where religion is often assumed to be in decline. The quotation from Paul Heelas (p63) illustrates some of this variety. If the definition of religion is widened to include not only areas such as meditation and astrology but contemplation of art, music

Alisa Baroffio, a member of 'The Silver Ring Thing', studies in class at her high school. In 2005, the USA was divided in its approach to teaching teenagers about sex. The Bush administration favoured an abstinence-only approach. Others felt strongly that sex education was the best and most realistic approach to teaching teenagers about sex.

> ### Activity
>
> If the word 'religion' is understood to include the kinds of experiences to which Leuba, James and Happold referred in Chapter 2, how many human activities can you think of that might be counted as religious? Contemplating a beautiful view might be one example.

Activities

1 List in summary form the main features of a postmodernist view of religion.

2 List different ideas about what it means to be 'religious'. Consider the views of traditional believers as well as philosophers like Leuba, James and Happold.

3 List the reasons why postmodernism might be seen to affirm religious belief.

4 List the reasons why postmodernism might be seen to threaten religious belief.

and nature (witness the massive popularity of walking and wilderness activities), then its centrality to modern culture cannot be overstated.

■ Conclusion

The debate is which will become dominant in the modern world: religion or atheism. Atheists would argue that religion is in retreat in the modern world because of the many factors that have led to a turning away from God such as scientific explanations for natural phenomena that would previously have been explained by reference to God. However, many philosophers would disagree with such a view and argue that atheism is not to be confused with secularization. Society is undergoing a process of transformation as it slowly migrates from close identification with specific religious traditions to an individualization of beliefs. Many people turn away from conventional religion but are not turning away from God.

Many philosophers consider that under the influence of postmodernism, people's religious views are changing. The 'death of God' theology had led to a rethinking of the nature and need for God in modern society rather than a rejection of that need. Postmodernism has resulted in individuals developing their own beliefs rather than follow the beliefs of a religious tradition. Alister McGrath in his essay, *God makes a comeback*, argues that it is atheism that is in decline: 'the atheist case against God has stalled'.

Some philosophers argue the very fact that individuals are rethinking their beliefs but not rejecting God means that traditional religions, such as Christianity, are rethinking their place in the modern world. The changes will strengthen the place of religion in society. Alister McGrath considers that scientific methods have supported beliefs in God rather than undermined them:

> One of the most commonly encountered patterns in scientific development is seeing a pattern of observations and then saying, in order to explain these observations, we propose that there exists something that is as yet unobserved but we can believe that one day will be observed because if it's there, it can explain everything that can be observed. Of course, if you're a Christian you'll see immediately that that same pattern is there in thinking about God. We can't prove there's a God but he makes an awful lot of sense of things and therefore there's a very good reason to suppose that this may, in fact, be right.

Alister McGrath, quoted in 'All's not quiet on the aesthetic front' by Edward Pentin in National Catholic Register, *August 2007.*

Now that you have read this chapter you should be able to:

- explain the nature of atheism and how atheism differs from agnosticism
- explain the reasons for the rise of atheism and the meaning of the slogan 'God is dead'
- explain religious responses to atheism including a postmodernist view of religion
- evaluate how successfully religion has responded to the challenges of atheism
- assess whether religion is in retreat in the modern world.

Philosophy of Religion: summary of key points

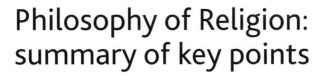

■ Chapter 1: The cosmological argument

The cosmological argument proves the existence of God from the idea that there is a first cause of the universe. Things that exist are caused to exist; the cause of the universe was God.

Proponents of the argument

St Thomas Aquinas seeks to prove the classical version of the cosmological argument through:

- motion and change
- efficient cause
- necessary existence and contingency.

Aquinas argues that things cannot move or cause themselves but does not believe that the movement or cause goes back to infinity, as this would not provide sufficient reason for things existing. Aquinas argues that God is *de re* necessary because if the universe is created by God then, if the universe exists, God must exist too – the nature of the universe demands that God exists.

Aquinas's First Way – the argument from motion/change:

1 Everything in the world is moving or changing from potentiality to actuality.
2 Nothing can move or change by itself.
3 There cannot be an infinite regress of things moving or changing other things.
4 Therefore, there must be a first (prime) mover (changer) which in itself is unmoved.
5 This unmoved mover we call 'God'.

Aquinas's Second Way – the argument from efficient cause:

1 Everything in the world has a cause.
2 Nothing is the cause of itself as this would be illogical.
3 There cannot be an infinite regress of causes.
4 Therefore, there has to be a first cause which in itself is uncaused to start the chain of causes.
5 This first cause we call 'God'.

Aquinas's Third Way – the argument from necessary existence and contingency:

1 Everything in the world is contingent.
2 Given infinite time, there must have been a time when all contingent things did not exist.
3 Nothing can come from nothing yet things exist now.
4 Therefore there must have been a being outside time and space to bring things into existence.

5 This being must in itself have necessary existence.

6 This being with necessary existence we call 'God'.

Frederick Copleston reformulated the cosmological argument in the 1948 radio debate with Bertrand Russell. Copleston concentrated on contingency:

1 There are things in the universe which are contingent; they exist but might have not existed. All things in the universe are like this; nothing in the world is self-explanatory, and everything depends on something else for its existence.

2 Therefore there must be a cause of everything in the universe which is outside time and space.

3 This cause must be a being that that does not depend on anything else and has necessary existence.

4 This being with necessary existence is God.

Challenges to the cosmological argument

David Hume said that we have no experience of universes being made, and so we cannot speak meaningfully about the creation of the universe. To move from 'everything we observe has a cause' to 'the universe has a cause' is too big a leap in logic. Hume argues:

1 There is no evidence for a cause of the universe.

2 Even if there was a cause – there is no evidence that this cause is the God of classical theism.

3 Why does the universe have to have a beginning? It could always have existed and consist of infinite causes.

4 Aquinas contradicts himself by arguing against infinite regression and then argues that God is both unmoved and uncaused, and is an infinite being.

Bertrand Russell put forward his objections in the radio debate with Copleston. Russell argued:

1 There is no evidence of a being with necessary existence.

2 The leap cannot be made from the concept that there are causes of things within the universe to the universe was caused.

3 The universe could just be 'a brute fact' with no explanation. 'It is just there'.

Immanuel Kant argued that we cannot apply evidence based on sense experience to something we have not experienced. We see cause and effect in this world but we cannot transfer that to the creation of the universe that we have not seen.

The steady-state theory is a scientific theory that denies a beginning to the universe. The theory argues for the continuous creation of the universe and therefore denies a creator God.

The Big Bang theory may be used to support or oppose the cosmological argument. It is scientific evidence that the universe began, but was the cause of the Big Bang the God of classical theism?

▮ Chapter 2: Religious experience

A religious experience is a spontaneous or induced mental event over which the recipient has relatively little control. It is often accompanied with the gaining of certain knowledge. The experience is always unique.

Three examples of types of religious experience are:

▮ Visions – e.g. St Bernadette experienced visions of the Virgin Mary

▮ Conversion – e.g. St Paul was converted to Christianity on the road to Damascus

▮ Mystical Experience – e.g. the experiences of the mystic Julian of Norwich.

The argument for God's existence based on religious experience suggests that some people's 'experience' of God is the best evidence that we have that He exists. One of the most important commentators on this subject is William James

James believed that questions relating to religious experience were spiritual judgements which, in turn, were in the family of value judgements – questions concerned with importance, significance and meaning.

James's conclusions are:

▮ It would appear that the physical world is part of something much bigger.

▮ Union with a 'spiritual superior' is our ultimate purpose.

▮ Communication/prayer with this being produces real effects.

Alternative theories regarding religious experience

Sigmund Freud dismissed the notion of a metaphysical side to our existence, suggesting that we were completely material beings. He believed that religious experiences were illusions. In particular, they were the projections of people's most basic and profound ideas (of union with an ultimate 'parent', for example). Freud therefore dismissed the truth of religious claims.

Professor V. S. Ramachandran argues that the cause of religious experience may be temporal lobe epilepsy. However he does not dismiss that this may not be the means by which God communicates with the world.

Dr Michael Persinger argues that religious experiences are no more than the brain responding to external stimuli, and by stimulating the temporal lobes he can artificially induce feelings similar to those of a religious experience.

Richard Swinburne says that a religious experience is an 'experience of God or of some other supernatural thing'. Swinburne's 'Principle of Credulity' suggests that something should be believed (e.g. someone's report that they have 'encountered God'), unless there is evidence to the contrary. His 'Principle of Testimony' suggests that 'we usually believe to have occurred what other people tell us that they perceived occurring'. Swinburne argues that these two principles together can support an argument based on religious experience, particularly when considered cumulatively with other arguments for God's existence (i.e. the design, cosmological, ontological and moral arguments).

Criticism of Swinburne's argument

Caroline Franks Davis suggests that criticisms of Swinburne's argument can be placed into three broad categories:

- Description-related challenges – if the description of the experience given is suspicious, we should reject the experience altogether.
- Subject-related challenges – if the person making the claim is suspicious (e.g. a known liar), we should reject their testimony.
- Object-related challenges – it is obviously impossible to verify or falsify the claims made about the being experienced (i.e. God) in the context of these experiences. This makes it very difficult to accept testimonies of them.

■ Chapter 3: Psychology and religion

Freud's explanation for religion

Religion is an illusion, created by the mind as wish fulfilment (to fulfil its wishes).

Religion as a response to inner psychological conflict

- The developing child undergoes the Oedipus Complex.
- This results in ambivalent feelings towards the father and a powerful sense of guilt.
- These feelings are repressed into the unconscious as a defence mechanism.
- Repression is not completely effective.
- The repressed emotions reappear in dreams and neurotic symptoms.
- As a collective neurosis, religion is the chief neurotic symptom.
- Along with other neuroses, religion causes compulsive attention to detail and produces powerful feelings of guilt when its demands are not met.
- The figure of God is the equivalent to the father figure and is regarded with the same ambivalence.
- Belief in God is the last stage in a series of developments, including animism and polytheism.

Religion as a response to the conflict between our natures and civilisation

It gives a reason for suffering and offers God as the explanation for society's laws. It motivates submission.

Religion as a response to fear of natural forces

It offers protection and comfort against the forces of nature. Religion helps people by calming them down and giving them hope. Religion also helps to remove the fear caused by death by suggesting that natural forces can be controlled through religious devotion.

Freud concluded that religion should be overthrown since it has resulted in conflicts of its own making and has impeded human progress. It should be replaced with science.

Criticisms

- The theory of the primal horde, which explained the development from the Oedipus Complex to religion, has been discredited.
- The Oedipus Complex theory has been discredited.

- Freud's claims depend upon the subjective interpretation of a very narrow selection of evidence.
- Freud's argument for the termination of religion ignored its positive aspects.

Jung's explanation for religion

- Religion stems from the archetypes.
- These are situated in the collective unconscious mind.
- An archetype is part of the structure of the mind which innately generates certain kinds of images. Examples include shadow, animus, anima, God and Self.
- God-images are generated by the God-archetype.
- We can never prove whether or not God exists objectively, outside the mind.

Jung's view of the value of religion

- Religion is a positive force because it helps the individual to maintain mental health through the process of individuation (integration).
- Individuation is the innate drive which integrates and harmonises all the elements of the psyche. It results in a mentally balanced individual, thereby preventing neurotic illness.

Links between religion and individuation

- Individuation is governed by the Self-archetype.
- Any archetypal experience can be termed religious, since Jung's definition of a religious experience is one which alters consciousness and derives from outside the conscious mind.
- The images produced by the self-archetype and which lead to individuation are the same images of God that are generated by the God-archetype.
- Therefore, Jung can affirm that religion is central to individuation.

Criticisms

- Jung's methodology is flawed because he discounts the possibility of there being any empirical evidence to support a religious experience.
- Jung's theory of the archetypes has been attacked.
- Jung's theory of individuation fails to explain the uniqueness of religious experience and the importance of the God-images in their own right.

Chapter 4: Atheism and postmodernism

What is atheism?

- Negative atheism is the lack of a belief in God or gods. A negative atheist does not believe in God or gods.
- Positive atheism is the belief that God or gods do not exist. Positive atheists do not believe in God and go further, affirming that there is/are no God or gods.
- Some atheists do not believe in any gods, while others do not believe in certain types of god, such as the God of classical theism.

■ Agnosticism is the belief that it is not possible to know anything about God's existence. Agnostics do not believe in God or gods, but nor do they deny the possibility that God or gods might exist.

Reasons for the rise of atheism

■ *Science*: the development of scientific knowledge removes the need for God as an explanation for how the world was made and functions. Some scientific theories can challenge belief in God, e.g. the theory of 'survival of the fittest' threatens the belief in a loving God who made a world of peace and harmony. Ray Billington and Richard Dawkins view science as a serious threat to belief in God.

■ *Empiricism*: the view that we can have no knowledge of anything except through sense experience threatens belief in God, for God, as a non-physical, transcendent being, is beyond the bounds of our senses. David Hume therefore rejected belief in God. A. J. Ayer believed that all statements about God are meaningless as they cannot be verified.

■ *Evil*: the existence of evil and suffering in the world threatens the belief in a God who is all-powerful, all-knowing and all-loving. An all-knowing God would know how much people suffer, an all-powerful God would be able to stop all suffering and an all-loving God would want to stop all suffering. D. Z. Phillips argued that evil and suffering are incompatible with God's love, regardless of why God might allow people to suffer.

■ *Rebellion against moral absolutes*: Owen, Newman and Kant argue that our experience of universal moral obligation (moral absolutes) provides good grounds for belief in God. The view that there are no moral absolutes destroys their arguments. It would also mean that religious texts such as the Bible are inaccurate and unreliable. And it would challenge God's power to set absolute laws and would make the view that God is 'all good' nothing more than a personal opinion.

■ *Awareness of other faiths*: John Hick argues that it is not possible to accept all of the different religious beliefs about God, even though they all claim to be true, for many of these are incompatible. Hick argued that it is then but a short step to the view that none of them is true. David Hume argues that the supporting evidence for any individual religion, including its miracle claims, is cancelled out by the far greater evidence supporting all the competing religions put together.

'God is dead'

Friedrich Nietzsche used the slogan 'God is dead' to express his view that society no longer has any need for God, for human advances in areas such as science and philosophy have made God redundant. Since the death of God removed the traditional basis for moral behaviour, Nietzsche argued that it was now up to human beings to imprint their own values upon the world. In the 1960s some Christians adopted the death of God concept, e.g. John Robinson argued that God did not objectively exist.

Religious responses to atheism and postmodernist views of religion

■ Some religious believers completely reject the challenges to belief in God and withdraw into the evidence from their own faith tradition. This can be seen as the fundamentalist approach.

■ Other religious believers tackle the various challenges head-on, finding ways to reject them, so as to defend their traditional beliefs in God. For example, it can be argued that none of the challenges from science actually disproves God and that God is still needed to explain the ultimate purpose of these scientific processes.

- Postmodernists present a radical rethink of the nature of God and of religious belief.

The main features of a postmodernist account of religion

Postmodernists argue that there are no absolute truths that can be found in any field of study, from religion and philosophy to art and culture. Postmodernists reject all meta-narratives. A meta-narrative is any account that claims to explain the ultimate nature of reality. Both religious and atheistic views about God can be considered examples of meta-narratives. Postmodern accounts of religion can vary widely, but the following features are typical:

- Religions are seen as cultural constructs: All religious meta-narratives are seen as different ways of looking at the world that have arisen from the beliefs and attitudes of different cultures. Jacques Derrida argued that these meta-narratives need to be deconstructed, which involves showing them to be the relative accounts they really are.

- There are no right or wrong religions: Jean-Francois Lyotard argued that since all religious beliefs were created by different cultures and individuals, none of them can be seen as right or wrong. Derrida emphasised that deconstruction leads to being open to different views and ideas, which suggests a sense of tolerance and equality. Many postmodernists, including Derrida, are genuinely agnostic about the existence of God. John Caputo accepts belief in God but admits that he has no way of knowing what God is.

- The emphasis falls on a personal spiritual search in which individuals select the religious beliefs which match up best with their own outlook. The wide choice of equally valid religions on offer has given rise to the term the religious supermarket. The approach whereby one borrows ideas from different religions has been called the pick and mix approach, New Age Spirituality being an example of this.

- A different way of seeing religion as a personal spiritual search was adopted by the anti-realist Don Cupitt. Cupitt rejected the idea of an objectively existing God, arguing instead that God is a symbol of human spirituality. By rejecting an objective God, Cupitt's approach differs from Derrida's more open-ended view on this matter.

- The emphasis falls on living religion rather than intellectual faith. Caputo, for example, having rejected the possibility of knowing what God is argues that God is something to do. In other words, religion is to be lived rather than believed. Postmodernist Christians might see the Trinity not as a statement of what they believe about God but as a statement that encourages them to act in the world.

Postmodernism is seen by some as an affirmation of religion. For example, it encourages religious believers to live out their faith, it preserves the possibility of God's existence, and supports the general concept of God as beyond human grasp. Some religious traditions such as mysticism fit particularly well with it, as do some views of religious experience, including those of Leuba, James and Happold. Finally, it preserves the possibility of God's existence and rejects the meta-narrative of atheism.

Postmodernism is seen by others as a serious threat to religion. It rejects the central claim of most religions, that there is a single correct view of God and of how we should behave. It is too vague to be the basis of a meaningful faith, or of practical moral guidance. Its agnosticism fails to inspire religious or moral commitment and Cupitt's anti-realism actually denies God's objective existence. Finally, its absolute rejection of meta-narratives can be seen as a meta-narrative in its own right.

Is religion in retreat in the modern world?

Although in some parts of the world (including Britain) traditional belief in God may have declined, there are other parts of the world, such as the US and many countries in Africa, where this is not the case. Moreover, even in countries like Britain, there are many new expressions of spirituality that some would interpret as religious belief. It could be argued that just as religious beliefs have undergone great changes in the past, so they may continue to do in the future.

AQA Examination-style questions

1 (a) Explain how the cosmological argument tries to prove that there must be a God. *(30 marks)*

(b) Assess the view that the success or failure of the cosmological argument has little relevance for faith. *(15 marks)*

AQA specimen question

2 (a) Explain how a religious experience could be used to support the claim that God exists. *(30 marks)*

(b) 'A religious experience is no more than an ordinary experience that people have misunderstood.'

To what extent would you agree with this claim? *(15 marks)*

3 (a) Explain how religion has been understood by Freud and Jung. *(30 marks)*

(b) 'God has been explained away by psychology.' To what extent is this true? *(15 marks)*

4 (a) Explain the main features of a postmodernist view of religion. *(30 marks)*

(b) 'Postmodernism is not an affirmation of religion.' To what extent is this true? *(15 marks)*

Religion, Philosophy and Science

5   Miracles

Learning objectives:

Learning objectives:

- to understand different interpretations of the term 'miracle'

- to understand the implication of these different interpretations for the way in which God is believed to interact with the world

- to understand difficulties with accepting the existence of miracles, including challenges they may pose to the religious understanding of God

- to evaluate the strengths and weaknesses of these challenges and to consider religious responses to them

- to assess whether the existence of miracles would make it reasonable to believe in God and whether God, if he exists, would intervene to perform miracles.

Key terms

Natural law: in scientific terms these are understandings of the way nature works. Initally they were conceived of in prescriptive terms, i.e. that nature was required to behave in ways prescribed by scientists. In modern times they are conceived of in descriptive terms, i.e. that scientists' understandings merely describe what happens.
In religious terms natural law comes from God and guides human moral behaviours.

What is a miracle?

The concept of the miraculous is perhaps the single feature of religion most vividly able to capture the imagination of the non-religious. Many people use the word in their everyday vocabulary, often to denote nothing more than a very welcome and somewhat surprising event or series of events. It is not unusual to hear recovery from serious illness being described as 'miraculous', though all that is meant is that it is unexpected, against the odds or simply lucky.

Religious believers use the term 'miracle' to refer to something more deeply significant than that which is merely surprising. They argue that miracles provide evidence that God acts within our daily lives. Accordingly, some have used miracles to try to prove the existence of God.

This chapter will examine two important definitions of the term 'miracle':

- a violation of, or exception to, **natural law**
- an event of religious significance.

Upon the first definition, an essential feature of a miracle is the occurrence of something that is not supposed to be possible. It would be difficult, however, entirely to separate this definition from the second. Religious believers would consider such events to have great religious significance – and Richard Swinburne argues that if they did not, they would not be recognised as miraculous.

When taken by itself, however, the distinctive feature of the second definition is that it allows an event to be considered miraculous without any violation of a natural law. The event might be very strange, unexpected or striking in some way – a fortunate coincidence, perhaps – but it does not have to be impossible.

Miracles as a violation of natural law

David Hume states that a miracle may accurately be defined as:

> A **transgression** of a law of nature by a particular volition of the Deity or by the interposition of some invisible agent.
>
> *David Hume*, An Enquiry Concerning Human Understanding, 1748

In other words, a miracle is brought about when some 'invisible agent' affects the working of the universe.

Examples from Swinburne

Richard Swinburne gives some examples of violation of the laws of nature taken from the Bible:

> Levitation resurrection from the dead in full health of a man whose heart has not been beating for twenty four hours and who was dead also by other currently used criteria; water turning into wine without the assistance of chemical apparatus or catalysts; a man getting better from polio in a minute.

Richard Swinburne (ed.), Miracles, 1989

If we break down Swinburne's examples of raising from the dead, a nature miracle and a healing miracle into their individual stages, we find occurrences which happen frequently within nature. Men can recover from illness, and wine can be produced using water as its main ingredient quite naturally, without any questions being raised. It is not the events themselves in Swinburne's examples which make them remarkable, but the timescale and the order in which they occur. They take place without the generally accepted conditions that normally bring about that result. Although, for example, people have frequently recovered from polio, they have not done so 'in a minute'. When water is normally turned into wine, the process does not happen spontaneously, and nor does it take a mere few seconds. These events are therefore considered miraculous because they operate outside the bounds of natural laws. They can be seen either to violate natural laws, or to involve an exception to these laws, whereby the law in question mysteriously does not apply.

Swinburne's view is that the transgression of a natural law is not enough by itself to grant an event the title of a miracle. He argues that miracles need to hold some deeper significance than the transgression itself. That is, they need to point beyond themselves to some underlying plan or reality. Swinburne expresses the point clearly:

> If a god intervened in the natural order to make a feather land here rather than there for no deep ultimate purpose, or to upset a child's box of toys just for spite, these events would not naturally be described as miracles.

Richard Swinburne (ed.), Miracles, 1989

By contrast, a supernatural healing that was believed to be the work of a loving God would be considered miraculous. For it would have the significance of demonstrating God's nature to the world and demonstrating that he has a plan for everyone.

What do miracles tell us about God?

The view that God intervenes in the world to violate natural laws requires a **theistic** understanding of God, as adopted, for example, by Christians, Muslims and Jews. Among theists, however, there are different understandings as to how God interacts with the world. St Thomas Aquinas, for example, distinguished between three different types of interaction. First is God's sustaining activity which does not involve specific actions but refers to the earth's continued dependence upon God for its existence. Second are primary actions which refer to God's specific interventions in human history, where the course of events is changed by God. Examples include the miracles that you have already looked up in the Bible, such as the raising of Lazarus from death to life.

Key terms

Transgress: literally means to pass beyond. A transgression usually refers to a violation of natural law.

Theist: someone who believes that the world was not only made by God but that its existence continues to depend totally on the involvement of its creator. Without God's sustaining power, the world would return to the nothing from whence it came. A deist, by contrast, is someone who believes that, having created the world, God leaves it to run itself, like a machine, governed by natural laws. God has no further interest in the world and makes no further intervention.

Activities

1 Read Richard Swinburne's examples of miracles.

2 List the three different types of apparent violation of natural law.

Think about

Is it possible to rule out a natural and as yet undiscovered explanation for these events?

Activity

Read the following passages from the Bible:
- Luke 8:40–56
- Matthew 9:27–34
- John 11:13–44
- Matthew 14:15–21
- Matthew 14:22–32
- Luke 5:1–11

a Write a description of what occurred in each incident.

b For each incident state the type of apparent violation – raising from the dead, healing or nature miracles.

Third are secondary actions which refer not to God's direct interference in the world but to the way in which God works indirectly through human choices and actions to bring about 'God's will'. Some believe that the entire history of humanity represents the gradual unfolding of God's plan. Others believe that God acts through human beings at particular times, in order to bring about specific events. This understanding of God's interaction with the world is also frequently portrayed in the Bible, such as in the Old Testament book of Judges. Here God punishes or rewards Israel through the actions of the people in Israel and the surrounding nations. For example:

> The people of Israel sinned against the Lord again. Because of this, the Lord made King Eglon of Moab stronger than Israel. Eglon joined the Ammonites and the Amalekites; they defeated Israel and captured Jericho, the city of palm trees. The Israelites were subject to Eglon for eighteen years. Then the Israelites cried out to the Lord, and he sent a man to free them. This was Ehud, a left-handed man, who was the son of Gera from the tribe of Benjamin.

Judges 3:12–15

This passage portrays God's control of events, working through the agency of human beings.

It is worth pointing out that miracles that are violations of nature clearly indicate a God who interferes with the natural workings of the world, rather than one who just works within nature and uses its laws in order to bring about events. Such violations do not indicate that God determines all other events that happen naturally. Indeed the fact that God needs to interfere could be taken to imply that God did not determine everything else.

Does God violate natural laws?

There are religious, scientific and philosophical challenges to the belief that God violates natural laws. These include:

- doubt as to the existence of natural laws
- the argument against miracles from the definition of a natural law
- Hume's critique of miracles
- difficulties with the belief that God intervenes in the world.

Religious believers have also made a number of responses to these challenges. We shall take those challenges and their responses in turn.

Do natural laws exist?

The definition of miracles as breaches of natural laws can only be held if we accept that there are natural laws. Certain theists may not accept this premise.

Theists would argue that every single event in the world is totally dependent upon God. As Brian Davies explains, for such people, 'God is as present in what is not miraculous as he is in the miraculous.' If God is equally present in every action, some theists would argue that it does not make sense to speak of any 'intervention'.

In reality, however, this is not a serious criticism since the majority of theists would accept that it is through natural laws that God continues to sustain the world. In other words, God has put into place a set of natural laws which enable the world to govern itself. One reason for doing so is

■ **Link**

See Chapter 6, pp93–6, for more information about theists and deists.

■ **Activity**

When considering the topic of miracles, it is very useful to have examples of reported miracles. Use the internet and library to find testimonies of miracles.

■ **Think about**

Think about three examples of what you would consider to be miraculous events.

From these examples, what are you taking to be essential features of a miracle?

to give humans a consistent environment, in which we can predict with reasonable accuracy the results of our actions. In this case, it still makes sense to say that in certain exceptional circumstances, God can choose to interrupt the working of God's laws.

The arguments against miracles

It has been argued that our definition of natural laws can preclude the possibility of anything being termed a miracle. John Hick, for example, defines natural laws as, 'generalisations formulated retrospectively to cover whatever has, in fact, happened.' In which case, bearing in mind that a miracle is a breach in a natural law, he argues, 'We can declare *a priori* that there are no miracles.' Upon this basis, the occurrence of an unusual, previously unwitnessed event should make us widen our understanding of the natural law so as to incorporate the possibility of the new event. There would certainly be no grounds for assuming that this new event breaks the law, for the law itself is only established on the basis of empirical evidence.

Scientists might add to this criticism by pointing out that since our understanding of natural laws is incomplete and continually developing, there may one day be a natural explanation for events which at the moment are considered to violate natural laws. In the past, events that could not be explained (e.g. earthquakes) were often understood to be 'acts of God'. Now that these can be explained naturally, there is no need to refer to God. As our knowledge of science develops, there are fewer and fewer events that could be seen to require a divine explanation. This view that religion is simply the explanation for those things that are not understood by science is known as **God of the gaps**. The implication, of course, is that a full understanding of science would explain all apparent miracles and leave religion redundant.

The 'placebo effect' is increasingly being used as an explanation for certain unexpected healings. Doctors are now more aware of the power of the human mind to bring about physical improvements when there is sufficient expectation or faith that this will happen. In the same way that fake pills can 'bring about' recovery because the patient believes them to be genuine, so a belief in God might promote recovery because the patient believes he will act. Many scientists would argue, of course, that in both cases the cause of the recovery is the patient's own mind.

The theory of quantum mechanics is an example of a scientific theory that some might use to account for events that appear quite literally to have no cause. Chapter 8 examines quantum mechanics in more depth, but one of its interpretations is the view that at the level of sub-atomic particles (the smallest building blocks of matter) there is an element of random unpredictability. In other words, there is a level of matter at which the laws of cause and effect do not operate. It is however debatable as to how far this unpredictability affects the larger building blocks of matter, and its significance for 'miracles' is therefore uncertain.

Hick's argument might be considered technically unassailable. Everyone accepts that natural laws must be widened as and when new discoveries are made. What is now considered impossible may one day be common. It may eventually be possible, for example, to communicate with others by thought alone, through the aid of a microchip, implanted in the brain.

Yet this does not mean that certain events might not be found to completely go against our expectations on the basis of all past experience. As a result, we might reasonably look for a cause separate from the normal world of our experience. Swinburne, for example, allows that

Think about

What would happen if you were to drop an expensive glass vase from two metres above a concrete floor?

Upon what basis do you know that this will happen?

Key terms

God of the gaps: the theory that God is the answer to questions and problems that science is otherwise unable to resolve.

When you place a saucepan filled with water on a gas flame, you expect the water to heat up. You know this on the basis of your past experience and the past experience of others. If one day you performed the same action and the water turned instead to ice, would you be surprised?

Upon the basis of Hick's argument, you should simply accept that sometimes the gas flame will cause water to freeze. Why would you not in all probability do this? Why might it be justifiable to suspect the working of a non-human agent?

The second section of this chapter, moreover, considers the view that even if there is no violation of a natural law, religious believers might still consider an event to be a miracle involving God.

David Hume (1711–76) argued that as miracles can never be proved to have happened they can give little support to religion

natural laws are not adequately able to cover every single possible happening everywhere. He believed, however, that they are able to give a generally accurate picture of what we should expect to happen in a given situation. He concluded therefore that an event such as the Resurrection of Jesus could reasonably be considered miraculous since it is totally contrary to the normal results of death and since it would not be expected to happen again in similar circumstances. In practice, then, Hick's comment is more of a technical point about the definition of miracles and natural laws. It does not rule out the possibility of events in which a cause outside the world is involved. For this reason, Hick himself admitted that there are 'unusual and striking events evoking and mediating a vivid awareness of God.'

Hume's critique of miracles

David Hume offered a traditional and comprehensive argument against the occurrence of miracles. Hume's point was not so much that miracles are impossible, but that it would be impossible for us ever to prove that one had happened. He wrote:

> A miracle is a violation of the laws of nature; and as a firm and unalterable experience has established these laws, the proof against a miracle, from the very nature of the fact, is as entire as any argument from experience can be possibly imagined. Why is it more than probable that all men must die; that lead cannot, of itself, remain suspended in the air; that fire consumes wood, and is extinguished by water; unless it be, that these events are found agreeable to the laws of nature, and that there is required a violation of these, or in other words, a miracle to prevent them.

David Hume, An Enquiry Concerning Human Understanding, 1748

Certain miracles, such as the 'feeding of the five thousand', clearly purported to have many witnesses. For Hume, however, this makes no difference:

> No testimony is sufficient to establish a miracle unless the testimony be of such a kind, that its falsehood would be more miraculous, than the fact, which it endeavours to establish; and even in that case there is a mutual destruction of arguments, and the superior only gives us assurance to that degree of force, which remains, after deducting the inferior.

David Hume, An Enquiry Concerning Human Understanding, 1748

Hume's argument is that laws of nature have been supported innumerably over a period of many hundreds of years. There are literally millions of examples to show that humans, once dead, do not return to life; nor that pieces of metal, when dropped, continue to hang in the air. The evidence for an apparent miracle, which contradicts a natural law, would need to outweigh all the evidence which had established the law in the first place. It would always therefore be more probable that the miracle be false than that the evidence in favour of the natural law be proved incorrect. For example, it would be more likely that one was hallucinating than that one was truly witnessing an exception to the law.

Hume went on to give four further reasons why it is certain that no miracle was ever established.

The first is that there has never been:

> ... in all history, any miracle attested by a sufficient number of men, of such unquestioned good-sense, education and learning, as to secure us against all delusion in themselves; of such undoubted integrity, as to place them beyond all suspicion of any design to deceive others; of such credit and reputation in the eyes of mankind, as to have a great deal to lose in case of their being detected in any falsehood; and at the same time, attesting facts performed in such a public manner and in so celebrated a part of the world, as to render the detection unavoidable.

David Hume, An Enquiry Concerning Human Understanding, 1748

Hume's second reason supported his first, and consisted of the claim that those testifying to the miracle will have a natural tendency to suspend their reason and support the claim:

> The passion of surprise and wonder, arising from miracles, being an agreeable emotion, gives a sensible tendency towards the belief of those events, from which it is derived. And this goes so far, that even those who cannot enjoy this pleasure immediately, nor can believe those miraculous events, of which they are informed, yet love to partake of the satisfaction at second-hand, or by rebound, and place a pride and delight in exciting the admiration of others ... A religionist may be an enthusiast, and imagine he sees what has no reality: he may know his narratives to be false, and yet persevere in it, with the best intentions in the world, for the sake of promoting so holy a cause.

David Hume, An Enquiry Concerning Human Understanding, 1748

Hume's third reason made the further claim that: 'It forms a strong presumption against all supernatural and miraculous relations that they are observed chiefly to abound among ignorant and barbarous nations.'

Hume's fourth point argued:

> In matters of religion, whatever is different is contrary ... It is impossible the religions of ancient Rome, of Turkey, of Siam, and of China should, all of them, be established on any solid foundation. Every miracle, therefore, pretended to have been wrought in any of these religions (and all of them abound in miracles), as its direct scope is to establish the particular system to which it is attributed; so has it the same force, though more indirectly, to overthrow every other system. In destroying a rival system, it likewise destroys the credit of those miracles, on which that system was established.

David Hume, An Enquiry Concerning Human Understanding, 1748

This argument rests upon the premise that the different religions are mutually exclusive. As a result, the miracle accounts arising from each religious tradition with the intention of supporting it, cancel each other out.

💡 Critique of Hume's argument

We have now considered Hume's criticisms in some detail because they constitute a grave attack made upon the possibility of the occurrence of miracles. There are however many flaws to his arguments. For this reason, it can be argued that even the cumulative weight of the criticism does not make it impossible to accept the occurrence of a miracle.

Think about

If you were to witness one exception to the law of gravity, what would you expect to happen next time you dropped something?

Why might an exception to a rule not necessarily have to outweigh all those cases which supported a rule?

Think about

Does Hume explain precisely what would constitute a reliable witness?

Why might you find it difficult to identify an actual group of people whose testimony Hume would, in practice, be willing to accept?

Think about

If you want to believe that something is true, will you always be willing to set aside truth and accept a lie?

Why might your desire for truth outweigh your desire to believe what you want?

Activity

1. Write a list of 'supernatural and miraculous' occurrences which have been made, and the nations that have made them.

2. What types of nations are on your list?

3. Is it reasonable to consider them 'ignorant and barbarous' nations?

Think about

If a Christian and a Jew were both, simultaneously, to witness a miracle (as happened in the Bible), what would this say about Hume's argument?

What argument(s) can be used against Hume's fourth criticism?

Let us consider first the criticism that a miracle account would need to outweigh all the evidence in favour of a natural law. This is based on the assumption that there must be a mutually exclusive choice between the generally accepted law on the one hand and the miraculous exception on the other. This assumption is hard to justify. The whole point to a miracle is that it is an exception to the rule. As such, its occurrence in no way challenges the force of the general rule, except upon that one occasion. If Hume's argument were to be accepted, we should need to reject a large proportion of the scientific developments in recent centuries. This is because many of these have forced us to accept as possible things which would once have been considered impossible upon the basis of past experience. Brian Davies provides such an example:

> We might say (though rather oddly) that until someone walked on the moon, people were regularly observed not to walk on the moon. And people, in time, have come to do what earlier generations would rightly have taken to be impossible on the basis of their experience.

Brian Davies, An Introduction to the Philosophy of Religion 2nd ed. 1993.

How strange it would have been if all the people watching the footage of the first men on the moon had, for the reasons that it contradicted previous knowledge, refused to believe what they were seeing. Yet we should need to hold this position if Hume's argument holds true.

Richard Swinburne offers an additional argument against Hume's assumption that natural laws, as scientific evidence, will always outweigh the evidence in favour of miracles, based upon mere testimony.

For Swinburne, there are three types of historical evidence which can be used to support miracles rather than the scientific evidence in the form of scientific laws. These are:

- our apparent memories
- the testimony of others
- the physical traces left by the events in question.

In anticipation to Hume's counter that scientific laws are somehow more objective, Swinburne emphasises that our knowledge of scientific law is in itself based upon these three types of evidence. If such evidence is not sufficient to establish the occurrence of a miracle, neither is it sufficient to establish the certainty of a natural law.

Regarding the four additional reasons against miracles, a good part of the argument is either unclear or unsubstantiated. Hume stated there had never been a sufficient number of men to provide a valid testimony. He did not, however, explain what a 'sufficient number' would be, nor why he considered previous testimonies insufficient. He claimed that miracles 'abound in ignorant and barbarous nations' and are therefore interpreted differently because of their understanding of the world. This argument is hard to accept since just about every nation has provided such claims and all have different world-views. Moreover, the presumption that an eyewitness should require some proof of intelligence before their claim be accepted is objectionable. The fourth objection misses the mark in that it assumed that *all* miracle accounts are the mutually exclusive invention of their own religious tradition. Yet, although clearly the miracles of different traditions cannot support the existence of the whole tradition, there is no reason why the individual miracles themselves may not have occurred objectively, unless they be self-contradictory in themselves.

Difficulties with the belief that God intervenes in the world

Maurice Wiles (1923–2005) argues that the belief that God performs miracles that violate natural laws goes against our understanding of God's relationship with the world. Wiles argues that the world is a single act of God that encompasses the world as a whole. He therefore concludes that miracles do not occur because God does not intervene in events in the world on an individual basis. If miracles did occur then God would undermine the laws of nature and the accepted order of life.

Nelson Pike goes further by claiming that it would not be possible for God to intervene in the world. His argument is based on the view that since God is outside time, with no past, present or future, God would be unable to act at any point in time within the world. Some religious believers might respond to this view by arguing that Pike has misunderstood what it means for God to be outside time, and that timelessness does not prevent God from acting in the world. St Thomas Aquinas, for example, held that while God acts timelessly, the events God brings about are in time.

For religious believers who accept Pike's point about timelessness, the belief that God intervenes through miracles would require them to accept that God exists in time. Richard Swinburne pre-empts the difficulties with this view, arguing that time does not affect God in the same way that it affects humans. For example, he emphasises that time does not harm God. Swinburne accepts, also, that since God is in time, having complete knowledge of every future event would be impossible. He argues, however, that this does not diminish God's omnipotence, since omnipotence only extends to the ability to do whatever is logically possible, and it is not logically possible to know every detail of the future.

There are also significant moral problems with the belief that God intervenes in the world to perform miracles for it raises questions about the continued existence of evil in the world.

Religious responses to the **problem of evil** generally argue that God has a particularly good reason for not intervening to prevent evil. Frequently this involves the argument that free will is of enormous value and that if God prevented evil from happening, this would be interfering with our free will. If there were no possibility of causing anyone any harm, for example, then people would be unable to make a meaningful choice to bring about good, because it would not be possible to do otherwise. One problem with miracles, therefore, is that they can compromise free will. By intervening to rescue the Israelites from Egypt, God was reducing the free will and perhaps responsibility of the Egyptians to make their own decisions.

Moreover, if God sometimes intervenes in the world, it raises the more serious question as to why God does not do so more frequently; why only help some, but not others. Wiles, for example, asks why 'no miraculous intervention prevented Auschwitz or Hiroshima' and yet there are acclaimed miracles that 'seem trivial in comparison'. To the Jews who suffered in the Holocaust, the belief that God had acted to save their ancestors from Egypt, despite the fact that the Bible portrayed these ancestors as sinful, raised some serious questions about God's consistency and justice.

Wiles argues that either God does not intervene in the natural order or has an arbitrary will that results in the intervention to help the plight of some and ignore the need of others. Wiles suggests that a God who chooses to cure an individual of cancer, and yet to ignore the plight of

Think about

For religious believers what are the problems associated with the idea of an interventionist God?

Think about

Consider the possibility that God exists inside time. What problems might this cause for believers in an omnipotent, omniscient God?

Key terms

Problem of evil: the difficulties that the existence of evil and suffering cause for the belief in a God who is both omnipotent and all loving. For, it is argued, an omnipotent God would be able to end all evil and an all-loving God would want to end all evil. The problem of evil has led many to conclude that either God is not omnipotent, or is not all-loving, or does not exist.

Activity

1 Consider God's intervention to prevent the Israelites from being destroyed by the Egyptians. The climax of this story is portrayed in Chapter 14 of the book of Exodus.

2 Read Exodus:14 and list all the ways in which this single intervention has changed human history.

Link

Consider what might be the religious significance of the raising from the dead, the healing miracles and the nature miracles that you looked up in the Bible on p79.

Link

Look at Chapter 2 p24 for the meaning of stigmata.

Activity

The Italian priest Padre Pio (1887–1968) was famous for his experiences of stigmata. Using the internet or a library, find out about their significance for him.

those trapped in the twin towers of New York on 11 September 2001 is not a God who is worthy of worship. Wiles therefore concludes that although God creates and sustains the world, he never acts within it.

Keith Ward recognises these difficulties with the belief in an interventionist God. He points out, for example, that even a minor intervention will have permanent and possibly far-reaching consequences. Ward's solution is to suggest that God intervenes only very occasionally, only when it is for the best and only in order to build up our faith in God. Whereas regular interventions to help some but not others would be unfair, occasional interventions with deep religious significance would not. It could be argued that the Resurrection of Christ or the delivery of the Qu'ran to Muhammad would escape Wiles's criticism because they do not directly bestow favours upon individuals.

💡 Miracles as events of religious significance

Signs

We have already seen that many violations of natural laws would be considered to have great religious significance. Miraculous healings, for example, might be taken as signs that point to the existence of a loving God. This is the approach taken by the author of John's Gospel who uses the word sign instead of miracle. This implies that although Jesus's miracles are important in their own right, their key significance lies in what they reveal about Jesus and God. We have noted (p83) how Richard Swinburne considers that religious significance is an essential element of a miracle, without which the term cannot properly be used.

Unlike, for example, healing miracles, where the religious significance may be of secondary importance to the healing itself, some violations of natural laws appear *only* to have religious significance. To a witness of the Resurrection of Christ, the entire significance of the miracle consists of what it tells of Christ's nature and of God. The phenomenon of stigmata is another example within this category. Stigmata are manifestations of the wounds of Christ on the cross in the bodies of his followers. They do not, in themselves, bring any physical benefit to those who bear them, but they can have a very powerful effect on their faith. Some, for example, might see them as pointing to a deep, spiritual unity with Christ.

One problem with the concept of signs is that it is not always clear exactly what the significance of the experience is supposed to be. As David Hume mentioned, since miraculous healings occur in so many different faiths, it may even be uncertain as to which God the sign is pointing.to.

Amazing coincidences and natural events

The rest of this chapter will consider another category of miracles that may be seen as signs with religious significance. The distinctive feature of these is that they do not even claim to violate natural laws.

R. F. Holland states: 'A coincidence can be taken religiously as a sign and called a miracle.' If, for example, a religious person prayed for the safety of a friend who was known to be in danger, and if a remarkable and unexpected series of events brought about this person's safety, the one who made the prayer would very likely consider the coincidence miraculous. It would be seen as being filled with a sense of divine purpose and significance.

Is this a miracle or just a coincidence?

This second example, provided by Peter Vardy and Julie Arliss, does not even involve prayer, because those concerned were not aware that there was any danger from which they needed to be rescued:

> *Life* magazine reported that all fifteen members of a Church choir in Beatrice, Nebraska, came at least ten minutes too late for their weekly choir practice which was supposed to start at 7.20 p.m. They were astonishingly fortunate because at 7.25 p.m. the building was destroyed by an explosion. The reasons for the delay of each member were fairly commonplace; none of them was marked by the slightest sign of a supernatural cause. However, nothing remotely resembling the situation that all members were prevented from being on time on the same occasion had ever happened before. Furthermore, this singular event took place precisely when it was needed, on the very night when they would otherwise have perished.

Peter Vardy and Julie Arliss, The Thinker's Guide to God, 2003

Unlike some of the violations we considered earlier, a coincidence like this can easily be given a natural explanation. Each member of the choir, for example, could have had a perfectly valid reason for being late. The sense of the miraculous comes from the sheer improbability that the only night when they were all late was on the only night when they all needed to be.

In what sense would a coincidence be miraculous?

It will be useful here to distinguish two different ways in which a coincidence might be seen as a miracle. Despite the possibility of an entirely natural interpretation, some people would attribute this coincidence, like the violations we examined earlier, to God's direct intervention in the events leading up to it. For these people, the only difference between this and the previous violations is that here God's involvement is less obvious, more open to doubt and perhaps closer in line with the normal operation of natural laws. But it is still an intervention to prevent deaths that would otherwise have occurred.

Other people would consider the coincidence to be a truly natural event; that is, an event in which God is not intervening at all, even though he may in some way be believed to be present. Sometimes other natural events that do not even involve a surprising coincidence might be interpreted in the same way. Witnessing a beautiful sunset or the birth of one's child, for example, might evoke a powerful sense of religious significance – of God's 'involvement', even – without any sense that God actually intervened to change the course of events.

How would God act through natural events?

■ Link

Re-read the explanation on pp79–80 of the distinction between deists and theists and the three different ways in which St Thomas Aquinas believed God to interact with the world.

If coincidence miracles are interpreted as interventions by God, we again require a theistic view of God's interaction with the world. In terms of Aquinas's categories, any intervention, along with anything else in existence, requires God's sustaining activity. It also requires either primary or secondary actions, depending on how God is actually understood to bring the coincidence about. In the case of the Nebraska choir, secondary actions would have involved God in working through the desires and the minds of the choristers rather, for example, than interfering with their cars to cause them to break down, which would be a primary intervention. We have already examined some of the difficulties with the idea of an interventionist God.

If coincidence miracles are interpreted as truly natural events with no divine intervention, we at least remove the difficulties with an interventionist God. The problem then becomes how it is possible to see God as being present within them at all; and, more generally, how a God who does not intervene can be said to interact with the world.

The deist argument that God is not present at all would be unacceptable even for this definition of miracles, because, as an event of religious significance, the miracle points towards God's presence rather than a total absence.

Some might argue that despite a lack of intervention, God is fully present in the event because God's will governs everything, in the sense that every human action can be seen as a secondary action of God. Psalm 139:16 expresses the view that God's interaction with the world extends to planning our whole lives: 'All the days ordained for me were written in your [God's] book before one of them came to be.' John Calvin was one influential Christian who accepted the view that human beings are predestined by God, meaning that God decides in advance who will be sent to heaven and hell.

A major problem with this view is the extent to which human free will is threatened. We noticed earlier that God's interventions in the world compromise free will. This is a minor problem compared with the view that the whole of human history is controlled by God's will. There is not only the problem as to how humans can be considered in any meaningful sense to be free. There is also the difficulty that all acts of human evil have been planned by God. And since God is equally present in all events, it would be just as reasonable to deduce the presence of a malicious God in an unfortunate coincidence as to deduce the presence of a loving God from a fortunate one.

Because of these difficulties, those Christians who accept that God determines everything must maintain that human free will is somehow compatible with this. Some, like John Packer, argue that this is a mystery understood only by God. Others might use a view sometimes called soft determinism to argue that although God determines events, humans 'make them their own' through their choices, which are prompted by their desires, which, of course, are determined. But many philosophers argue that soft determinism merely gives us the illusion that we are free.

An alternative approach that avoids this problem is the view that a coincidence is only miraculous because it is interpreted in that way. This, however, is a criticism in itself, because it suggests that the miracle has no objective reality. We shall next examine this criticism and give some responses to it.

Can coincidences and natural events really be miracles?

One difficulty with the view that a coincidence can be miraculous is that unusual and striking coincidences happen all the time. Indeed, every single event in the world can be attributed to a unique and enormously complex set of coincidences. It is not possible therefore to isolate any one of these coincidences and prove that it has been caused by something different from all the others. R.F. Holland himself admits: 'it cannot without confusion be taken as a sign of divine interference with the natural order.'

David Hume, sceptical at the best of times, flatly denies that natural events could be considered miraculous:

> Nothing is esteemed a miracle, if it ever happens in the common course of nature.

David Hume, An Enquiry Concerning Human Understanding, 1748

Quite simply, if an event can be explained naturally, there is no reason why we should look for any deeper significance, and those who do so are merely projecting their own subjective interpretation onto it.

Religious response to this challenge

One response might be that a religious believer does not need any other proof that an event is miraculous because God is being revealed directly to the believer, and our experience is our proof. The miracle would be seen as a personal religious experience through which believers know intuitively that God is present. The issue of religious experience is explored in Chapter 2, which also examines how it might be known to be genuine.

A different response would be given by religious believers who are anti-realists. Anti-realism is a theory of truth. It holds that the truth or falsity of a statement depends not on whether it corresponds to the objective reality of what it describes, but on whether it corresponds to the situation as a person understands it. For example, whether the Nebraska choir incident was a miracle does not depend on what actually physically happened, but on what is *understood* to have happened – which, of course, depends on which person one asks. On this view, a single event can be both a miracle and *not* a miracle at the same time, without any contradiction. The miracle truly exists, but as a concept within the religious community. Of course this admits that our interpretation makes the event a miracle, but argues that our interpretation is all that truly counts.

A third view is given by Paul Tillich, whose understanding of miracles is based on his understanding of God. Tillich describes God as 'being-itself' who is the 'ground of being'. In other words, God is the power who gives existence to everything in the world, and without whom, nothing would exist. Tillich uses the term 'miracle' to describe an event that evokes in the believer a powerful sense of this creative power. We are most likely to sense this in situations like an unexpected healing, in which we are confronted by its power to overcome non-being such as death. In Tillich's words:

Activities

1 List all the coincidences you can think of which have led to your eyes being the colour they are.

2 Why would you not attribute the colour of your eyes to a miracle?

Think about

Why might many religious believers reject anti-realism? Think about what the statement 'God exists' would mean for an anti-realist.

> A genuine miracle is first of all an event which is astonishing, unusual, shaking, without contradicting the rational structure of reality. In the second place, it is an event which points to the mystery of being, expressing its relation to us in a definite way. In the third place, it is an occurrence which is received as a sign-event in an ecstatic experience.

Paul Tillich, Systematic Theology Vol. 1, 1953, p130

■ Think about

How successful do you consider Tillich's response?

Tillich's response to the criticism that an event is only seen as a miracle because we interpret it as such, is that we know that it is a miracle precisely because of our 'ecstatic' response to it, which is an integral part of the miracle.

💡 *What could a miracle prove?*

The final question to consider is what we could actually prove from a miracle, in the sense of a violation of natural law, supposing that one were to occur. Richard Swinburne argues that a miracle would point to the existence of agents other than humans:

> Suppose that E occurs in ways and circumstances otherwise strongly analogous to those in which occur events brought about intentionally by human agents, and that other violations occur in such circumstances. We would then be justified in claiming that E and other such violations are, like effects of human actions, brought about by agents, but agents unlike men in not being material objects. This inference would be justified because, if an analogy between effects is strong enough, we are justified in postulating slight difference in causes to account for slight difference in effects.

Richard Swinburne, The Concept of Miracle, 1970

Suppose, for example, that a tumour afflicting a woman were to disappear overnight. Events similar to this occur frequently in the operating theatres of surgeons, and are attributed to human agents. Swinburne's argument suggests that since our case is strongly analogous, we should reasonably postulate an agent, similar to humans, at work there too. It is justifiable to postulate a non-material cause, however, on account of the 'slight difference' in effects – for example, the fact that no material interference is involved in bringing it about.

Swinburne's argument carries some force; although there is always the possibility that a natural but as yet undiscovered reason might be the cause of the effect. In these cases, there would be no reason to suspect the involvement of non-material beings.

■ Conclusion

Even if we accept Swinburne's conclusion, however, what grounds are there for attributing the miracle to God – and specifically to the omnipotent, all-loving God of classical theism? This depends largely on our prior beliefs. If we already believe in such a God who we know to act through miracles, it seems reasonable to attribute the miracle to this God. The principle of Ockham's razor could be applied here; where a simple and expected cause is the likely explanation for a certain event, it is not justifiable to postulate a more complex explanation, even if it is a possible alternative.

If, however, there is no prior belief in the God of classical theism, the occurrence of a miracle would be insufficient to make us believe in him. For the miracle could be attributed to an angel, to a god who is not omnipotent or all-loving or to some altogether different cause. The occurrence of a miracle would therefore be most likely only to strengthen the beliefs of those who already have a faith in a specific God.

Now that you have read this chapter you should be able to:

- explain the different interpretations of the term 'miracle'

- give examples of each type of miracle

- summarise Hume's arguments against miracles as violations of natural law

- evaluate the strengths and weaknesses of the challenges to miracles and consider the religious responses to them

- assess whether the existence of miracles would make it reasonable to believe in God and whether, if God exists, God would intervene to perform miracles.

Think about

It is claimed by philosophers such as Hume, and many scientists, that miracles do not happen. What evidence could those who reject miracles use to argue that religious believers are trying to support their beliefs by interpreting ordinary events in an extraordinary way?

What evidence could religious believers use to support their view that miracles are real and evidence of God's existence? Consider what the word 'real' might mean in terms of a miracle.

Having evaluated these different claims do you think that miracles make it reasonable to believe that God exists?

6 Creation

Learning objectives:

- to understand the nature and origin of the universe according to religious beliefs and science

- to understand the challenge to religious belief presented by science and the religious responses to these challenges

- to evaluate whether or not science and religion are in conflict, complementary or irrelevant to each other in relation to these issues

- to evaluate whether or not God is simply an answer to unanswered questions, and an explanation for the unexplained

- to evaluate the strengths and weaknesses of religious responses to the challenges posed by scientific views

- to evaluate whether intelligent design is a scientific theory or a religious one.

Key terms

World-view (religious): a belief that an explanation of reality without reference to a supernatural being is an incomplete explanation.

Science and religion share the common purpose of providing a means of research and discussion on the most basic issues regarding:

- how we understand the world in which we live, and our place in that world

- how the traditional concerns and beliefs of religion and philosophy can be related to scientific understanding

- how the joint reflections of scientists, philosophers and believers can contribute to the welfare of humans.

Changing world-views

In the present century, the two disciplines of religion and science are often in opposition to each other in the understanding of these basic issues, and the way in which the truth behind them might be discovered. Modern scientific thought is based on observation and experiment to test out theories and to reach a conclusion as to what is the literal truth. New theories may replace older ones if there is a greater weight of evidence in their favour. Religious thought is usually based on revelation, reflection and abstract ideas, and is concerned with values and beliefs rather than just facts. Religious beliefs are based on faith, and scientific principles may be rejected when there is conflict with the basic tenets of the faith. In the past, religion and science were in much closer agreement with each other, as it was out of the work of theologians and philosophers that science was born. Until the 16th century, the philosophers and theologians were the scientists. The early theologians and philosophers tried to understand the world in which they lived, and asked scientific questions such as:

- How was the world made?
- What holds the world up?
- Why does the Moon not fall down?

The religious and scientific **world-views** agreed with each other because the scientific explanation included reference to God. The beginnings of modern science in the 16th century led to a change in the way in which people understood both God's place in the universe and relationship with humans. This change resulted in a gradual separation of science and religion, so that it became possible to accept scientific principles without reference to God.

Activities

1. List the conflicts that you are aware of between religious belief and science in the modern world.

2. Read and make detailed notes on the biblical account of creation in Genesis 1–3.

3. What are the major differences between the two creation stories?

The medieval world-view

In the Middle Ages, the accepted structure of the universe was based on observation and mathematics. Scholars were aware that planetary movements were erratic when compared to those of the Sun and Moon, but any irregularities observed in the movement of the heavenly bodies were explained away, because any scientific reasoning had to be in line with the Christian faith. Therefore, it was accepted that God created the universe; God controlled everything in the world and was the Prime Mover of all that took place. The accepted world-view was that the Earth was flat and motionless and at the centre of the universe. God had placed humans on Earth, at the centre of creation, with dominance over the animals. God controlled the universe, with a representative on Earth in the Pope. The Christian Church taught that a person's present existence was of little concern. That person's eternal fate after death was all that mattered. The scholars were theologians, who were more concerned with how to achieve Heaven than how the universe functioned. Consequently, there was little interest in finding out more about the world in which people lived. There was no concept of natural laws, since everything that happened was explained in terms of the will and purpose of God. God was the first and final cause of everything, and God's presence was immanent within the world because, at all times, God was commanding things to go to their rightful places. The world-view was seen in religious terms; unlike today, when the world is seen in terms of mechanisms, mathematics and natural causes.

St Thomas Aquinas

Aquinas wrote commentaries on Aristotle, and concluded that Aristotle's 'unmoved mover' was God. However Aquinas rejected Aristotle's assertion that the world was eternal. The God of the Old Testament was much more personal and involved in the creation of the universe than Aristotle's unmoved mover. God had created the universe at a fixed time in the past and, on the sixth day, had placed human life at the centre of creation. The world in which God had placed humans was corruptible and changing, and could be spoilt by sin. Above the Earth was the incorruptible realm of God, in which the heavenly bodies moved in perfect circles.

As attitudes to learning changed, ideas were no longer accepted simply because that was the way it had always been. Through the work of mathematicians and scientists, such as Nicolaus Copernicus (1473–1543) and Tycho Brahe (1546–1601), it was accepted by many that the Sun was at the centre of the universe. In other words, the universe was **heliocentric**: the Earth went round the Sun along with the other planets, and only the Moon revolved around the Earth.

The discoveries of Galileo and Newton

The Italian philosopher Galileo Galilei (1564–1642) was the first astronomer to make systematic observations of the universe through a telescope. He realised that we did not live in a closed, Earth-centred universe, but an immeasurable space. Galileo's

Link

Read Chapter 1 pp3–6 and Chapter 7 p110. How does St Thomas Aquinas's contribution to both the cosmological and the design arguments demonstrate the belief in God as creator?

Link

Look back at Chapter 1, p2, and remind yourself of the meaning of the term 'prime mover'.

Key terms

Heliocentric: model of the universe that has the Sun at the centre, and all of the planets travel around the Sun. A geocentric universe has the earth at the centre and all the planets, stars and the Sun travel around it.

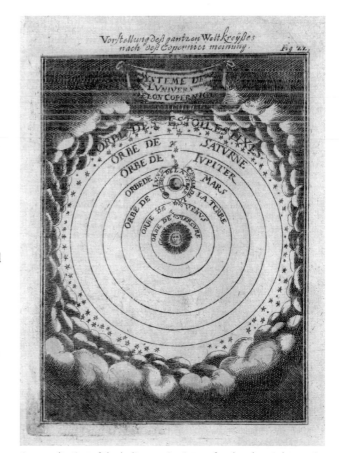

A reproduction of the heliocentric picture for the planets known in the time of Copernicus

Think about

Why would Christians in the Middle Ages have regarded it as important that the Earth was at the centre of the universe?

Why do you think that many Christians in the 16th century could not accept the view that the Earth was not at the centre of the universe?

Think about

Galileo was trying to find out more about God. He did not reject the existence of God or the belief in God as creator, so why do you think the Catholic Church imprisoned Galileo as a heretic and banned his works?

Why did Galileo's books remain banned by the Catholic church until the second half of the 20th century?

Key terms

Universal law of gravity: gravity is one of the universal forces of nature. It is an attractive force between all matter, and is very weak as compared to the other forces of nature. The gravitational force between two objects is dependent on their masses, which is why we can only see gravity in action when at least one of the objects is very large (like the Earth).

Think about

Read the extract from Ivan Peterson's book. According to Peterson how do Newton's laws change the role of God?

observations supported a heliocentric universe in which the heavenly bodies were not made of a substance superior to the Earth. He observed sunspots, which proved that the heavens were not unchanging or infinite. He proved that the movement of the planets was natural and was not the direct result of a Prime Mover. His findings were published in *Dialogue Concerning the Two Chief World Systems* (1632). Galileo continued to distinguish between celestial and terrestrial laws, though Galileo was not anti-Christian. He argued that Scripture must be metaphorical, but still accepted that to study the universe was to find out more about God:

> Philosophy is written in that great book – I mean the universe – that forever stands open before our eyes, but you cannot read it until you have first learned to understand the language and recognise the symbols in which it is written. It is written in the language of mathematics and its symbols are triangles, circles, and other geometrical figures without which one does not understand a word, without which one wanders through a dark labyrinth in vain.

Galileo Galilei, Dialogue Concerning the Two Chief World Systems, 1632

The English natural philosopher Isaac Newton (1642–1727) based his findings on his Christian world-view. He believed that because man was made in the image of God, he had a perception of God's creation. This was why he was able to understand his discoveries of the universal laws of gravity and motion. Newton demonstrated that the same physical laws that we know on Earth are applicable throughout the whole universe. His **universal law of gravity** states that the force of attraction between any two masses, anywhere in the universe, is proportional to the product of the two masses divided by the distance between them:

> With such a fundamental, simple framework in place, it did not take much of a leap for Newton's successors to imagine planets confined forever to totally predictable, orderly orbits around the sun. Such a perpetual clockwork would never need rewinding or adjusting. This mathematical machinery, by encapsulating completely the solar system's past, present and future, in principle seemed to leave no room for the unforeseen.

Ivan Peterson, Newton's Clock: Chaos in the Solar System, 1993

The origin of modern scientific principles

Newton developed a new kind of reflecting telescope, and essentially invented the modern techniques of scientific investigation, in which ideas are tested and refined by comparison with experiments. Science no longer depended on observation alone, and on fitting these observations to the accepted facts. Now, any hypothesis had to be supported by evidence and data as well as observation.

Scientific developments had proved that the planets orbited the Sun according to strict patterns and according to comprehensive laws. This pattern was seen to be a paradigm for the whole universe. Everything seemed to be governed by a set of unbreakable natural laws, which could be discovered by the process of scientific inquiry. If phenomena were investigated in an impartial, open-minded manner, then the truth could be found. Mathematics was an essential investigative tool, and the universal laws could be expressed in mathematical terms. Experiments, rather than philosophy, became the final arbitrator of truth.

Religion and science separate

Many believers were able to accept what became known as the 'New Philosophy' without losing their faith, while others saw the new discoveries as a reason for abandoning religious beliefs and basing their world-view on reason alone. There was a different world-view from that of the medieval period. Religion and science began to separate. Scientific findings were to have some significant consequences for religious belief:

■ The universe was now seen as a 'machine', with all parts working together, rather than as a living creation of God. Each part of this machine affected the behaviour of another part, and resulted in movement. It was no longer necessary to believe that God caused the movements in the universe. The geocentric view had been explicitly religious: the Earth was the stage on which the drama of man's redemption was enacted when God came in the person of Christ. A heliocentric view put man in a different relationship to God. Mankind was no longer the centre of everything, but inhabited a tiny planet that circled the Sun. Human life was no longer regarded as unique, because there was the possibility of other universes and life on other planets. God might have created the world and moved on.

■ Scientists no longer had to refer to God in order to explain the way in which the physical world worked. The Christian faith no longer had control over all branches of knowledge. Kingship, religion and moral order could no longer claim the cosmic backing they had previously. For many, religion now became the explanation for those things that were still not understood by science, a philosophy that became known as 'God of the gaps'.

■ Link

Look at p87 to find out the meaning of 'God of the gaps'.

■ God was no longer regarded as immanent and as the controller of everything. The new scientific world-view developed the acceptance of a world that was a machine that ran itself. The clockwork analogy did not seem to leave room for the spiritual soul. This led to the development of Deism, the belief that once things had been set going, God could not, or did not, intervene in creation. Science dealt with the everyday ticking of the cosmic clock, and religion dealt with first beginnings and last ends. The universe was not a living organism, but consisted of material particles moving in infinite space, in accordance with strict, mathematically precise, universal laws.

■ The medieval world-view had been proved wrong. This resulted in many taking a sceptical approach to Scripture, and viewing the Church as fallible. Many scientists came to dismiss religion altogether. Newton had been unable to explain why two or more planets orbiting the Sun were not upset by the extra gravitational influence and sent tumbling out of their orbits. He had said that the hand of God might be needed from time to time, to nudge the planets back into position. Pierre Laplace (1749–1827), a French mathematician and astronomer, was able to solve this problem, by showing that these lapses are largely self-correcting. When Napoleon commented that there was no reference to God in Laplace's work, Laplace replied, 'I have no need of that hypothesis.' He believed that God was irrelevant. To Laplace, everything in the solar system was determined (caused by previous events). Laplace thought that eventually all the natural laws of the universe would be known and that everything would be explained in scientific terms.

■ Key term

Determinism: for Laplace it was the principle that all information and events embody natural laws. Every event in the universe is caused and controlled by these natural laws.

■ Activity

Write a 500–600-word essay to answer the following question.

'I have no need of that hypothesis.' (Laplace)

Explain what changes occurred in the scientific world-view between the Middle Ages and the 19th century to result in Laplace's comment. Why did Stephen Hawking argue that Laplace's determinism might be wrong?

AQA✓ Examiner's tip

Check part way through your answer that your timing is on track and that you are still answering the question that was asked. If you start each new paragraph with a key point, then by the end of your essay those first sentences will be a summary of your answer.

■ Links

Look back at Chapter 1, p9, to remind yourself of what scientists understand by the Big Bang theory.

■ Think about

Scientists are unable to account for the extreme conditions that existed at the moment of the Big Bang or what caused it to happen.

How do you think a theist would answer the question of what caused the conditions required for the Big Bang?

The physicist Stephen Hawking (1942–) claims that Laplace is wrong in his assumption that there is no need for science to include God in the explanation of the laws of the universe. Hawking argues that:

> In the last 300 years, more and more regularities and laws were discovered. The success of these laws led Laplace at the beginning of the nineteenth century to postulate scientific **determinism**: that is he suggested that there would be a set of laws that would determine the evolution of the universe precisely, given its configuration at one time. Laplace's determinism was incomplete in two ways. It did not say how the laws should be chosen and it did not specify the initial configuration of the universe. These were left to God. God would choose how the universe began and what laws it obeyed, but he would not intervene in the universe once it had started. In effect, God was confined to the area that the nineteenth-century science did not understand.

Stephen Hawking, A Brief History of Time, 1992

⬛ The Big Bang theory

Big Bang theory is an explanation for the origin of the knowable universe and the development of the laws of physics and chemistry. It is thought to have taken place some 10 to 15 billion years ago.

The development of the modern Big Bang theory began in the 1940s with the work of George Gamow (1904–68). The theory is that all matter in the universe was created from a gigantic explosion called the 'Big Bang'. Less than a second after the explosion space and time began.

It is a theory that supports an ever-changing universe because the universe is still evolving. Edwin Hubble (1899–1953) discovered in 1929 that the galaxies are continually moving apart very fast. The universe is continuing to expand from the central point at which it began. By tracing backwards from the outward expansion, Gamow was able to calculate that all the mass of the universe was compressed into a small volume about 10–15 billion years ago. There had then been a tremendous explosion (the Big Bang) which led to the beginning of the universe. The residue radiation from the explosion is still traceable and in fact forms much of the static on a blank television screen.

Scientists argued that seconds after the Big Bang the known laws of physics and chemistry began. These include the forces of gravity and electromagnetism. In the first three minutes protons and neutrons began to form atomic nuclei. After approximately half a million years the temperatures had cooled sufficiently to allow the gases hydrogen and helium to form. It took another billion years before the stars and galaxies began to appear. Many of these stars died before our own sun and its planets were formed in the Milky Way. Some scientists believe it was the death of the early stars that provided the materials needed for life to develop on earth.

The evolutionary model for the origin of life

The Big Bang theory has provided a scientific explanation for the origin of the universe without reference to God. Similarly other **evolutionary** theories have developed to explain the origin of the life on earth without the need for God.

Various theories have been proposed to explain how new species develop. The model for the origin of life based on evolutionary theories accepts that:

- Life has evolved by naturalistic mechanistic processes.
- The first life-form of a single organism arose from inanimate matter.
- All life-forms originated from this simple organism.
- There was a gradual development of increasingly complex life-forms.
- There is unlimited variation in nature, and evolution is continuing.

The two most well-known evolutionary theories were proposed by:

- Jean-Baptiste Lamarck
- Charles Darwin.

The evolutionary ladder

Jean-Baptiste Lamarck (1744–1829) was a significant figure in the development of evolutionary theories. He believed that organisms change to meet their needs according to their changing environment. He believed that organisms were at various stages of evolution. At the bottom of the evolutionary 'ladder' were microscopic organisms and, from these simple organisms, increasingly complex life-forms had developed until, at the top of the 'ladder', human life was reached. Lamarck's theories included the following ideas:

- The organs that a life-form uses increase in size and strength to meet the needs of the species. Those organs that are no longer needed for survival will grow smaller, until they eventually disappear.
- There is an 'inheritance of acquired characteristics' by which individuals acquire characteristics of their ancestors. For example, the long neck of the giraffe was the gradual result of many generations of stretching to reach the leaves high up on trees. Each generation inherited the 'longer' neck of their ancestors.

Natural selection is one way in which evolution is achieved. Natural selection is the mechanism of evolutionary change. Those hereditary characteristics of a member of any species that are for the good for survival and reproduction will lead to more members of the species with those characteristics passing on their genes. Characteristics that help a species to survive will be passed on to each generation until all members of the species have inherited it. In this way, species evolve and change. So, by natural selection, particular variations are favoured and effect a gradual transformation in the appearance and behaviour of any species.

Survival of the fittest

Until Charles Darwin (1809–82) put forward his evolutionary theories, religious thinkers had been able to challenge atheists by asking how chance alone could create such an intricate world – and the atheists had no good answer. Darwin's theory was to provide atheists with a coherent and credible mechanism by which life could conceivably arise without the necessity of a creator or life-giver. Charles Darwin published his

Key terms

Evolution: plant and animal life arising from the earliest and most primitive organisms to reach its present state of development. It means that one species is descended from another species from which it is different. A chain can be established going back through time to trace the origin of each species. Human beings, for example, have descended from a species similar to the apes. The ape species descended from another species of mammal, and in turn the mammal descended from a reptile, before that from a fish, and eventually the chain can be traced back to the origin of all lifeforms, a simple bacterium.

Natural selection: the mechanism of evolutionary change. It involves the differential survival and reproduction of organisms with genetic characteristics that enable them to better utilise environmental resources and survive.

evolutionary theories in *On the Origin of Species by Means of Natural Selection* in 1859. Darwin's observations led him to conclude that organisms produce more offspring than can survive. The offspring are not identical: variations exist within them. Depending on the environment, some of these variations will help some of the offspring to survive better than the others. The offspring that prosper will produce more descendants than those who do not prosper. Over time, this will increase the number of offspring with these particular variations. Therefore, these variations will assist the survival of the species. Darwin described the process:

> As each species tends by its geometrical ratio of reproduction to increase inordinately in number; and as the modified descendants of each species will be enabled to increase by so much the more as they become more diversified in habits and structure, so as to be enabled to seize on many and widely different places in the economy of nature, there will be a constant tendency in natural selection to preserve the most divergent offspring of any one species.
>
> Hence, during a long continued course of modification, the slight differences, characteristic of varieties of the same species, tend to be augmented into the greater differences characteristic of species of the same genus. New and improved varieties will inevitably supplant and exterminate the older, less improved and intermediate varieties; and thus species are rendered to a large extent defined and distinct objects. Dominant species belonging to the larger groups tend to give birth to new and dominant forms, so that each large group tends to become still larger, and at the same time more divergent in character.

Charles Darwin, On the Origin of Species by Means of Natural Selection, 1859

Darwin's effect on creationism

Darwin's theory of evolution undermined the biblical account of creation for a number of reasons:

- ■ He showed how living things developed in small steps, and how this development could be the result of chance. Darwin thus demonstrated that life-forms were not in their final form at the time of creation, and might not be the work of a designer.
- ■ Evolution showed that things changed to fit in with the environment rather than the environment being shaped for their needs. This conflicted with the biblical account that God had created the environment for the benefit of the various life-forms.
- ■ Nature **red in tooth and claw** did not match the idea of a gentle and kind deity, as the exponents of natural theology deemed God to be.

In 1871, Darwin published his findings as to human origins in *The Descent of Man*. He accounted for all human characteristics by natural selection from other life-forms, and concluded that humans descended from apes.

Darwin had attacked the Christian concept that humans were unique and made in 'God's image'. Christians believed that humans had a spiritual soul, which distinguished them from animals. God put the soul there – but if mankind developed from animal origins then where did Darwin's theories leave this idea? Were humans soulless beings like the animals? Darwin had cast further doubt on the biblical account of the Creation, especially the story of Adam and Eve.

■ Key terms

Red in tooth and claw: the ways in which animals kill each other for food.

■ Think about

Why were many Victorians upset by Darwin's suggestion that they had evolved from apes?

Modern evolutionary theories

New evolutionary theories have developed based on those of Darwin. Darwin proposed a gradual change of species, but recent theories have suggested that the process is not gradual.

A theory has developed to suggest that evolution goes through 'jumps', as well as relatively slow changes. These jumps result in sudden changes that happen at certain times, but scientists are unsure why these jumps occur. For example at the normal rate of evolution humanity should not have appeared as yet in its present form.

Religious beliefs about creation

Many scientists accept that the universe began as the result of the Big Bang and following on from this everything has evolved into the universe we see today. However for many theists the Big Bang theory and the theory of evolution conflict with the account of creation in Genesis 1. One reason is because according to Genesis everything was in its final form by Day Six.

The Genesis account of creation

In the beginning God created the heavens and the earth. Now the earth was formless and empty, darkness was over the surface of the deep, and the Spirit of God was hovering over the waters. And God said, 'Let there be light,' and there was light. God saw that the light was good, and he separated the light from the darkness. God called the light day, and the darkness he called night. And there was evening, and there was morning – *the first day*.

And God said, 'Let there be an expanse between the waters to separate water from water.' So God made the expanse and separated the water under the expanse from the water above it. And it was so. God called the expanse 'sky'. And there was evening, and there was morning – *the second day*.

And God said, 'Let the water under the sky be gathered to one place, and let dry ground appear.' And it was so. God called the dry ground 'land', and the gathered waters he called 'seas'. And God saw that it was good. Then God said, 'Let the land produce vegetation: seed-bearing plants and trees on the land that bear fruit with seed in it, according to their various kinds'. And it was so. The land produced vegetation: plants bearing seed according to their kinds and trees bearing fruit with seed in it according to their kinds. And God saw that it was good. And there was evening, and there was morning – *the third day*.

And God said, 'Let there be lights in the expanse of the sky to separate the day from the night, and let them serve as signs to mark seasons and days and years, and let them be lights in the expanse of the sky to give light on the earth.' And it was so. God made two great lights – the greater light to govern the day and the lesser light to govern the night. He also made the stars. God set them in the expanse of the sky to give light on the earth, to govern the day and the night, and to separate light from darkness. And God saw that it was good. And there was evening, and there was morning – *the fourth day*.

And God said, 'Let the water teem with living creatures, and let birds fly above the earth across the expanse of the sky.' So God

Think about

Why might a believer argue that the 'jumps' in evolution occur?

In what ways do the creation model and evolutionary model conflict with each other?

Do you think that it is possible to accept both models?

Link

Look back at p96 to remind yourself of what scientists understand by the Big Bang theory, and the theory of evolution on pp97–9.

created the great creatures of the sea and every living and moving thing with which the water teems, according to their kinds, and every winged bird according to its kind. And God saw that it was good. God blessed them and said, 'Be fruitful and increase in number and fill the water in the seas, and let the birds increase on the earth.' And there was evening, and there was morning – *the fifth day*.

And God said, 'Let the land produce living creatures according to their kinds: livestock, creatures that move along the ground, and wild animals, each according to its kind.' And it was so. God made the wild animals according to their kinds, the livestock according to their kinds, and all the creatures that move along the ground according to their kinds. And God saw that it was good. Then God said, 'Let us make man in our image, in our likeness, and let them rule over the fish of the sea and the birds of the air, over the livestock, over all the earth, and over all the creatures that move along the ground.'

So *God created man in his own image, in the image of God* he created him; male and female he created them. God blessed them and said to them, 'Be fruitful and increase in number; fill the earth and subdue it. Rule over the fish of the sea and the birds of the air and over every living creature that moves on the ground.' Then God said, 'I give you every seed-bearing plant on the face of the whole earth and every tree that has fruit with seed in it. They will be yours for food. And to all the beasts of the earth and all the birds of the air and all the creatures that move on the ground, everything that has the breath of life in it, I give every green plant for food.' And it was so. God saw all that he had made, and it was very good. And there was evening, and there was morning – *the sixth day*.

Thus the heavens and the earth were completed in all their vast array. By the seventh day God had finished the work he had been doing; so on the seventh day he rested from all his work. And God blessed the seventh day and made it holy, because on it he rested from all the work of creating that he had done.

Genesis 1–1:31

Activity

Read the account of creation in Genesis 1:1–31.

Make a list of what happened on each day of creation.

Think about

What appear to be the conflicts between the scientific theories of the Big Bang and evolution and the Genesis account of creation?

What are the major differences between Deism and the 'God of the gaps' philosophy?

Can religion and science agree?

Many believers feel that the conflict between science and religion is over superficial points. If the biblical accounts of the universe are not taken literally, then science is regarded as revealing the laws by which God created the universe. A movement has developed in theology that stresses how God is revealed through nature. The scientific laws prove that the universe is the result of a skilled designer, and this designer is God. In the Middle Ages, if scientific observations conflicted with the biblical account, then it had been accepted that science was wrong, and the laws of science were adjusted accordingly. By the 18th century, however, the opposite was true. If the biblical account was contrary to the findings of science, then it was accepted that the Bible was wrong. The Bible had to be reinterpreted in the light of the scientific world-view. The result was the development of Deism and of the 'God of the gaps' philosophy, which we have referred to in the previous section.

Other believers realise the dangers of adapting religious truths to fit scientific laws. They argue that the Bible as the word of God must contain revelations about God. It came from God and must therefore be perfect. The events in the Bible, they insist, are historical events, events that actually happened, including the account of the Creation. As science progressed, however, it became harder to accept a literal interpretation of the Bible, especially when evolutionary theories were put forward to explain the origin of life on Earth.

God as creator

Judaism and Christianity accept that God is the creator of everything and use Genesis 1–3 in the Old Testament as a basis for this belief. The writer of Genesis does not set out to prove or argue for the existence of God. God is simply assumed to pre-exist before the creation. The opening statement of Genesis – 'In the beginning God created the heavens and the earth.' – has led to discussion as to the exact meaning of this statement. It cannot be doubted that it means God created the cosmos but what form did this creation take. Most Jews and Christians understand this to mean that as prior to the act of creation there was only God, the 'heavens and the earth' were created out of nothing ('creatio ex nihilo'). However there are others who interpret this statement to mean that God created the 'heavens and the earth' out of pre-creation chaos.

Genesis states that prior to creation 'the earth was formless and empty, darkness was over the surface of the deep, and the Spirit of God was hovering over the waters.' (Genesis 2:2) The Spirit of God has become identified with the Wisdom or Word of God. Whatever God commands happens, and on each of the six days of creation the different parts of the universe were created. At the end of the six days the writer clearly intends us to visualise a complete universe: 'God saw all that he had made, and it was very good. And there was evening, and there was morning – the sixth day' (Genesis 1:31). The will of God was all that was required to create the material universe.

In Judaeo-Christian terms, God is the designer and builder of the universe. The fact that the universe exists and that there is evidence of design is regarded by many theists as proof of the existence of God. For example, in the book of Job, the description of the creation of the world compares God with an expert builder:

> Where were you when I laid the foundation of the earth?
> Tell me, if you have understanding.
> Who determined its measurements – surely you know!
> Or who stretched the line upon it?
> On what were its bases sunk
> Or who laid its cornerstone?

Job 38:4–6

☑ Christian responses to scientific theories of creation

Fundamentalist Christians

Fundamentalist Christians believe that the Bible is the inspired Word of God, and is therefore the literal truth. For a fundamentalist Christian any scientific account of creation that conflicts with the Genesis account is

Think about

Ian Barbour has declared 'Creation "out of nothing" is not a biblical concept'. He shares the view of many philosophers and theologians who consider the concept as a defence against the ideas of the religious movement known as Gnosticism. Gnostics believe that the pre-existing matter from which the universe was created was evil or the product of an inferior god. Central to Gnosticism is the belief that humans are divine souls trapped in a world created by an imperfect spirit or god (the demiurge). Some Gnostics believe that the demiurge is an embodiment of evil whereas other Gnostics consider the spirit to be benevolent but imperfect, and therefore limited. Alongside the demiurge there exists a supreme being who is unknowable, remote but the embodiment of all that is good. Humans can only be freed from the inferior material world through spiritual knowledge of their true origins, their essential nature and their ultimate destiny. This knowledge is only available to all through direct experience or knowledge (gnosis) of God. For Christian Gnostics this knowledge was brought by Jesus.

Gnostics are dualists as they accept that something pre-exists creation apart from God and is co-eternal with God. As the majority of Christians believe in only one God, who is good and has absolute sovereignty over His creation, why do you think that the concept of creation ex *nihilo* developed as a defence against Gnosticism?

Activity

Read Psalm 104 in the Old Testament.

a   What description of God as creator is found in this psalm?

b   How does the concept of God as creator in the psalm compare with the concept found in the Genesis account of creation?

wrong. The model for the origin of life based on the Genesis account of the Creation accepts that:

■ Life was created by the actions of a creator.

■ The basic plant and animal species were created with their characteristics complete at the time of creation.

■ Any varieties of species were limited within each kind at the time of creation.

■ There was a sudden appearance of the great variety of life forms found on Earth at the time of creation.

■ The characteristics of each species were complete at the time of creation.

■ Human life was the last form to appear, and human characteristics were complete at the time of creation.

This has led to the development of scientific creationism. Creationism is opposed not only to evolution, but also to the modern scientific explanations for the origins of the universe. Thus most forms of creationism are opposed to the Big Bang theory as well as the theory of evolution. There are several creationist beliefs. The two major divisions are:

■ Young Earth Creationism

■ Old Earth Creationism.

Young Earth Creationism

Young Earth Creationism claims a literal interpretation of the Bible as a basis for its followers' beliefs. They believe that the Earth is 6,000 to 10,000 years old. This figure is arrived at using complicated dating procedures based upon biblical records, much like those used by Bishop James Ussher when he dated the point of creation at 4004 BC. Bishop Ussher used the genealogies and ages of people in the Bible to work back to when Adam was created. Young Earth Creationists believe:

■ All life was created in six 24-hour days.

■ Death and decay came as a result of Adam and Eve's 'Fall'.

■ Geology must be interpreted in terms of Noah's Flood.

However, they accept a spherical earth and heliocentric solar system. A leading Young Earth Creationist is Ken Ham. As with other Young Earth Creationists, Ham has to explain fossil records that would suggest a much older earth that has developed over a period of time. These creationists believe that whatever dating method scientists use is fallible, and only a literal Biblical interpretation is plausible. They argue that God created a completed earth after six days and therefore such an earth would look old.

If the millions of years of the geological ages based on the fossil records is accepted then it destroys the Bible's teaching on death, which clearly indicates that there was no animal death or human death before the Fall so the rock layers that contain these things cannot be millions of years old but must have been deposited after Adam sinned. Noah's Flood, which they believe was a worldwide event, caused the depositing of the remains that have formed the fossils and caused geologists to have the mistaken belief that the rocks they examine are much older.

Young Earth Creationists have developed their own branch of scientific creationism. This teaches the biblical account of creation as found in Genesis and rejects the Big Bang and evolutionary theories. Their reasons for rejecting these scientific theories include:

Activities

1 Using the internet, research the other arguments Young Earth Creationists have for rejecting the evidence put forward by those who accept the earth is 4.5 billion years old and evolution took place.

2 List reasons for accepting and reasons for rejecting Young Earth Creationism.

- In the fossil records that have been found, there are gaps – therefore there is no direct evidence that the evolutionary process took place.
- Natural selection is incapable of advancing an organism to a higher life-form.
- Scientists have never found the evidence of the supposed link between apes and humans.
- There is no reliable evidence of the age of the earth and the erosion caused by Noah's Flood has led geologists to think the world is older than it actually is.

Old Earth Creationism

Old Earth Creationism accepts the great age of the Earth. Some view the creative days in Genesis as starting with an already existing Earth and view the six creative days as six time periods of unstated great length, removing any need for the biblical Flood to have created the entire fossil record in a brief period of time. However, if there is conflict between scientific teaching and the Bible, they will always accept the literal truth of the Bible. There are several branches of Old Earth Creationism. These include:

- Gap Creationism
- Progressive Creationism.

Gap Creationism

Gap Creationism is willing to allow for an older earth. Adherents believe that science has proved the Earth is in fact far older than can be accounted for by merely adding up the ages of Biblical patriarchs, as given in the Book of Genesis. Genesis is therefore referring not to six 24-hour days but six periods of time which could be millions of years in length. Also to ensure the Genesis account is maintained, while also accepting scientific evidence that the Earth is extremely ancient, Gap Creationists suppose that certain facts about both the human past and the age of the Earth have been omitted from the Biblical account rather than mythologised by it. For example, between the six days of Creation and the Fall of Man, there must have been a 'gap' in the Biblical account that lasted perhaps tens of thousands or even millions or billions of years.

Progressive Creationism

Progressive Creationism accepts the scientific estimate for the age of the Earth, but that new species of plants and animals that have appeared since the creation are evidence that God directly intervenes to create those new species by methods that science cannot explain. Progressive Creationists generally reject one species evolving from another species.

Conservative Christians

Conservative Christians argue that although scripture was written by humans it was divinely inspired, and in some way God spoke through their words. They believe in the **inerrancy** of the Bible. These Christians would argue that the biblical accounts were of the writer's time and may be outdated. In the Bible there are spiritual truths in scripture but parts of it need to be reinterpreted in the light of new discoveries such as the Big Bang and evolutionary theories. In this way their belief that God inspired the writers of the Bible is kept. The Bible is still the word of God and conveys God as creator and God's will.

Activities

1. Using the internet, research the other arguments the Old Earth Creationists have for rejecting the evidence put forward by those who accept the earth is 4.5 billion years old and evolution took place.

2. List reasons for accepting and reasons for rejecting Old Earth Creationism.

Think about

Would you find it easier to accept Young Earth Creationism or Old Earth Creationism?

What are your reasons for your opinion?

■ Key terms

Liberal Christians: they accept freedom of thought and belief in the interpretation of the Bible. The Bible is not the literal truth but a collection of the writings in which the human authors' beliefs and feelings about God at the time of its writing are expressed. The writings are therefore influenced by the time in which they were written. Reading the Bible helps the individual to discover their own understanding of their relationship to God.

Liberal Christians

Liberal Christians argue the creation accounts are not literally true but contain religious truths, and sometimes the writers used myth to convey the message. The Bible was written by individuals who were influenced by the time and culture in which they lived. This meant that in their writings they promoted spiritual beliefs as they were understood at their period of history. These writers would lack scientific knowledge and therefore were likely to make mistakes in their writings and as a result do not always convey the will of God. This means that they reject much of the teaching on creation and evolution in favour of scientific theories. For example, Genesis teaches that God is creator but God may not have created in exactly the way described in Genesis. Indeed scholars have argued that there are two different creation accounts in Genesis 1:1–2:3, and 2:4–25. It is possible to accept both the Genesis account, which contains the religious truth that God is creator, and the scientific account of the Big Bang as the way in which God created.

Many Christians believe that it is possible to accept evolutionary theories without rejecting their faith. They believe that evolution is the mechanism through which God's creation took place. They see the Bible's account of creation as:

> … a form of narrative, but one in which truth is put across in a symbolic way, because it was dealing with the big questions of life – the questions of meaning and purpose. I think these are more powerfully put across in story form.

> *Ernest Lucas*, former biochemist, in Russell Stannard's book, *Science and Wonders*, 1996

■ Think about

What do you think Ernest Lucas meant in the statement quoted above?

■ Activity

'The creation stories in the Bible are pure invention.'

Write a 500–600-word essay discussing this statement.

■ Think about

Do you think it is possible to accept both evolutionary theories and the belief that God created the world?

The French philosopher Pierre Teilhard de Chardin (1881–1955) accepted that evolution was part of God's plan. He put forward his theories in *The Phenomenon of Man*, which he claimed was 'a scientific treatise'. The work begins with a description of the creation of the Earth, and of the evolution of life-forms, culminating in the emergence of humans. The first life-form developed from a single-celled organism, and each life-form in turn has been increasingly complex, until the higher life-form of humans developed. The higher the life-form, the more intelligent it is, and on a higher level of consciousness. Evolution has not ended, and humans are evolving on to higher levels of achievement and understanding. At some future time, which Teilhard de Chardin refers to as the Omega Point, everything will become integrated with Christ. Evolution is part of God's plan for the ultimate fate of mankind.

⚡ The theory of intelligent design

Intelligent design is the claim that certain features of the universe and of living things are best explained by an intelligent cause, not an undirected process such as natural selection. Not all those who accept this theory would specify the nature or identity of the designer as God. Although they do not state that God is the designer, the designer is often implicitly hypothesised to have intervened in a way that only a god could intervene, and the principal advocates of the theory are Christian.

> The theory of intelligent design holds that there are tell-tale features of living systems and the universe that are best explained by an intelligent cause. The theory does not challenge the idea of evolution defined as change over time, or even common ancestry, but it does dispute Darwin's idea that the cause of biological change

is wholly blind and undirected. Either life arose as the result of purely undirected material processes or a guiding intelligence played a role. Design theorists favour the latter option and argue that living organisms look designed because they really were designed.

Stephen C Meyer's article, 'Not by Chance', National Post of Canada, 1 December 2005

If evolution is taken to simply mean 'change over time', or even that living things are related by common ancestry, then there is no inherent conflict between evolutionary theory and intelligent design theory. However, if as the evolutionary biologist Richard Dawkins argues evolution is driven by natural selection acting on random mutations, and is an unpredictable and purposeless process that has no discernable direction or goal, then there is incompatibility. As evidence for intelligent design supporters refer to the 'jumps' in the evolutionary process that occur at certain times but cannot be explained. These jumps are termed **punctuated equilibrium**. DNA is also seen as too complex to be the result of random chance.

The biochemist Michael Behe argues that some structures at the biochemical level are too complex to be adequately explained by evolution alone. Several structures needed to develop at the same time for the development to have taken place and could not therefore be the result of natural selection. Behe calls this development irreducible complexity. Behe believes that an intelligent designer is therefore the only explanation for these complex structures.

By *irreducibly complex* I mean a single system composed of several well-matched, interacting parts that contribute to the basic function, wherein the removal of any one of the parts causes the system to effectively cease functioning. An irreducibly complex system cannot be produced directly (that is, by continuously improving the initial function, which continues to work by the same mechanism) by slight, successive modifications of a precursor system, because any precursor to an irreducibly complex system that is missing a part is by definition nonfunctional. An irreducibly complex biological system, if there is such a thing, would be a powerful challenge to Darwinian evolution.

Michael Behe, Darwin's Black Box: The Biochemical Challenge to Evolution, 1996

God as 'sustainer'

If God is transcendent then God is separate and superior to the physical, material world. Yet most Jews and Christians believe that God is active in the world. Christians accept that God came into the world in the form of Jesus. God is for most Christians both transcendent and immanent. God is wholly involved in his creation as both 'Creator' and 'Sustainer' of all things.

God as creator but not sustainer

Deists argue that the act of creation was a single event when God started off the process of creation, after which God left the universe to evolve on its own without any interference. Deists assert that God does not interfere with human life and the laws of the universe. They can accept

Key terms

Punctuated equilibrium: the evolutionary process involving long periods without change that is punctuated by short periods of rapid species development.

Think about

Does the discovery of punctuated equilibrium and DNA support or oppose the idea of a divine creator?

How is the theory of intelligent design different from scientific creationism?

Activity

Read Michael Behe's quote opposite.

In your own words explain Behe's reasons for believing in intelligent design.

Activity

Read the section in Chapter 7, pp115–16, outlining Richard Dawkins's scientific reasons for rejecting the idea of intelligent design.

a List the strengths and weaknesses of his arguments.

b Do you find Dawkins's argument convincing? Think of the reasons for your view.

Links

Look at Chapter 1, p2, to be clear of the attributes of the God of classical theism.

Look at Chapter 5, pp79–80, to be clear of St Thomas Aquinas's understanding of God's interaction in the world.

Look back at p79 and remind yourself of meaning of deism.

Activity

Many believers argue that miracles are evidence of God's intervention in the world.

Read Chapter 5, pp85–6. Why does Maurice Wiles think that it would be wrong for God to intervene to perform miracles?

Think about

Do you find all/any of these models for God as Sustainer acceptable?

What are the reasons for your opinion?

The Anthropic principle outlined in Chapter 7 pp116–17 can be taken as important support for the idea that God not only created the universe but also sustains it. List the reasons why this principle supports this idea.

the Big Bang as the means by which God started the process of creation: similarly the order and complexity found in nature coupled with our rational experiences of nature leads to a belief in God as the creator. However, for a deist, God is *not* the sustainer of the universe.

Activities

1. What examples do you think a believer would use as evidence that God is the sustainer of the world?

2. Read Psalm 104.

3. List the evidence that could be used by a believer to demonstrate that God sustains creation.

4. What evidence might a deist produce to demonstrate that God is not involved in the process of continual creation?

God's continuing involvement

However, for the majority of Christians, God continues to be involved with creation. What this means is that, from moment to moment, all that exists only does so because God wills it to exist. Should God stop willing the existence of anything or everything, then that existence would instantly end. St Augustine said: 'Let us therefore believe that God works constantly, so that all created things would perish, if his working were withdrawn.'

Christians who accept the theory of evolution are divided as to how God sustains creation and directs the creation to certain desired ends. Various models for God's action have been proposed. These are not mutually exclusive, so individuals may hold more than one. These models include:

- God is involved in the world and nothing happens except at the will of God.
- God gave, and continues to give, being to a creation gifted with all the capabilities to bring forth all the forms, processes and events willed by God.
- Creation responds to God's will as our bodies respond to ours. However, God's being is not embodied in creation but is transcendent over it.
- God acts to determine the inherent indeterminacies of physical events, at the micro level of quantum phenomena and at the macro level of chaotic systems. The physical universe is not deterministic, but rather is an inherently open causal system.

One supporter of the idea that God is still involved with creation is the scientist and theologian John Polkinghorne (1930–). Polkinghorne argues that God acts as the sustainer of the physical world in which we live. He argues it is not a God of the gaps used to explain the currently scientifically inexplicable, but a God whose act of creation is a continuing act. Polkinghorne argues that no experiment can prove this point and to believe God is the sustainer and upholder of the world is a matter of faith. However this faith can be supported by insights provided by science. This is because, Polkinghorne argues, that the universe is an 'open' and 'flexible' system, where patterns can be seen to exist, and the beauty of these patterns such as those found in mathematics is more than random chance or one act of creation.

7 The Big Crunch

The **Big Crunch** is a developing theory that the universe will collapse into the same state that it began and then another Big Bang will occur to start off a new universe. In this way the universe would last forever but would continually go through these phases of expansion and contraction: Big Bang and Big Crunch, and so on. Paul J. Steinhardt is a theoretical physicist who helped to develop this theory and he summarises the cyclic universe model as follows:

- Space and time exist forever.
- The Big Bang is not the beginning of time; rather, it is a bridge to a pre-existing contracting era.
- The universe undergoes an endless sequence of cycles in which it contracts in a Big Crunch and re-emerges in an expanding Big Bang, with trillions of years of evolution in between.
- The temperature and density of the universe do not become infinite at any point in the cycle; indeed, they never exceed a finite bound (about a trillion trillion degrees).
- No inflation has taken place since the Big Bang; the current homogeneity and flatness were created by events that occurred before the most recent Big Bang.
- The seeds for galaxy formation were created by instabilities arising as the universe was collapsing towards a Big Crunch, prior to our Big Bang.

Paul J. Steinhardt , The Endless Universe: Introduction to the Cyclic Universe, 2002

The Big Crunch would be an acceptable theory to those who believe in the biblical accounts of God bringing the world to an end and a Day of Judgement. However, scientists who accept the theory of the Big Crunch are left with a dilemma as they cannot explain what would make the universe bounce back with another Big Bang. Again, the believer would answer that this is the work of God. Some believers argue the endless cycle of universes causes a problem, however, in that it threatens the biblical view that God created one world, in which human history unfolds, before bringing this to a close and sending people to eternal life or punishment.

Religious believers and scientists seek to answer the question, 'Why do we and the universe exist?' Antony Flew raises the point that even 'if the universe was and/or is caused to exist by something outside itself', that still does not prove that it is the God of classical theism. Perhaps it is something that can never be proved as:

> If we discover a complete theory, it should in time be understandable by everyone, not just by a few scientists. Then we shall all, philosophers, scientists and just ordinary people, be able to take part in the discussion of the question of why it is that we and the universe exist. If we find the answer to that, it would be the ultimate triumph of human reason – for then we should know the mind of God.

Stephen Hawking, The Mind of God, 1996

Key terms

Big Crunch: the scientific theory that the universe will begin contracting and will end in a cataclysmic way: the reverse of its beginnings.

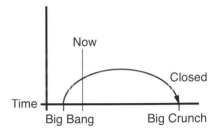

A closed universe

Think about

If on the other hand the universe is endlessly expanding and there is no end to it does this mean that the Bible is wrong and there will not be a Day of Judgement?

What answer do you think a believer would give in response to this question?

■ Conclusion

Many scientists have no problem in accepting both the scientific Big Bang and evolutionary theories and God as Creator and Sustainer. This is because they do not think there is conflict between religion and science. They believe that religion and science serve different functions. Science is seeking to prove how things happen and religion wants to know why. For theists the answer to the how and why is God. The physicist Robert Kaita says that he is:

> ... perfectly comfortable in saying that our universe is all the work of a creator. Everyone would have to agree, however, that a person can hold either position and still be a good scientist. It takes just as much faith to claim that there is no creator behind what I just described as to believe that there is one.

Robert Kaita, Apologetics Science, 2007

Think about

How is Kaita suggesting that Genesis 8:22 supports his argument?

Kaita quotes Genesis 8:22 to support his argument.

> As long as the earth endures,
> seedtime and harvest,
> cold and heat,
> summer and winter,
> day and night
> will never cease.

■ Activity

List the strengths and weakness of the following arguments:

■ There are gaps in scientific knowledge: therefore, the things in this gap are best explained as acts of God. For example God is the cause of the Big Bang or the development of human life.

■ The universe is far too complex to have come into existence by random chance.

■ The Genesis account of creation is the literal truth and all scientific theories that differ from this account are wrong.

Evaluate these strengths and weaknesses and decide which you feel are the strongest. You need to be able to justify your point of view.

Now that you have read this chapter you should be able to:

■ explain the nature and origin of the universe according to religious beliefs and science

■ demonstrate the challenge to religious belief presented by science and the religious responses to these challenges

■ evaluate whether or not science and religion are in conflict, complementary or irrelevant to each other in relation to these issues

■ assess whether or not God is simply an answer to unanswered questions, and an explanation for the unexplained

■ evaluate the strengths and weaknesses of religious responses to the challenges posed by the scientific view

■ assess whether intelligent design is a scientific theory or a religious one.

7 The design argument for the existence of God

Learning objectives:

- to understand the design argument as presented by St Thomas Aquinas and William Paley

- to understand the philosophical and scientific arguments against the Deism argument

- to understand responses to these challenges, including Swinburne's interpretation of the design argument

- to evaluate the strength and weakness of the argument

- to evaluate how far Swinburne's design argument successfully meets the challenges of philosophy and science

- to evaluate how far the argument makes it reasonable to believe in God.

Key terms

Qua: Latin word meaning 'as relating to'.

The design argument for the existence of God is also called the teleological argument. *Teleos* is a Greek word meaning 'end' or 'purpose'. The design argument is an *a posteriori* argument because it is an argument based on external evidence. Supporters of the argument use observation of apparent order, regularity and purpose in the universe and natural world to conclude that the universe is not the result of mere chance but of design and the designer is God. 'With such signs of forethought in the design of living creatures, can you doubt they are the work of choice or design?' (Socrates)

The classical argument for design

The basic argument for design states:

- The universe has order, regularity and purpose.
- The complexity of the universe shows evidence of design.
- Such design implies a designer.
- The designer of the universe is God.

The argument makes the basic assumption that there is order and design in the universe, and that all things function to fulfil a specific purpose. For example, the changing seasons, the lifestyles of animals and birds, the intricate organism of the human body and the perfect adaptation of its parts to the whole, appear to provide the evidence that the universe was designed.

The classical version of the design argument is in two parts:

- design *qua* regularity
- design *qua* purpose.

Activity

With a partner list on paper the evidence that a religious believer might put forward to prove the world is designed by God. One of you is partner A and the other partner B. When the list is complete each B partner moves to a new A partner. Discuss your two lists and add any missing ideas from previous lists. Continue to move round as many times as is useful to develop a detailed list of arguments.

Design *qua* regularity

This aspect looks at design in relation to the order and regularity in the universe. Philosophers who support the argument consider the order and regularity evident in the universe is evidence of a designer at work. Just as a formal garden shows evidence of a gardener because of the order, a lack of weeds, and the regularity in the arrangement of the flowers in the borders, so there is order and regularity evident in the universe, for example the rotation of the planets and the natural laws. Philosophers conclude that just as the formal garden did not come about by chance but through the work of a gardener, so the order in the universe can only have occurred by design.

■ *Aquinas's Five Ways*

The design argument forms the fifth of Thomas Aquinas's Five Ways, 'from the governance of things.' Aquinas argued from design qua regularity. He stated that everything is directed towards an end and as inanimate objects have no rational powers then they must be directed to this purpose by some external power. He identified that the way in which 'natural bodies' act in a regular fashion to accomplish their end provides the evidence for the existence of an intelligent being, and concluded that this being must be God.

> Hence it is plain that they achieve their end, not fortuitously, but designedly. Now whatever lacks knowledge cannot move towards an end, unless it be directed by some being endowed with knowledge and intelligence; as the arrow is directed by the archer. Therefore some intelligent being exists by whom all natural things are directed to their end; and this being we call God.
>
> *St Thomas Aquinas, Summa Theologica*

Design *qua* purpose

This aspect of the argument looks at design in relation to the ways in which the parts of the universe appear to fit together for some purpose. The universe is compared to a man-made machine in which a designer fits all the parts together for a specific function. For example, the parts of a television are fitted together in such a way as to receive pictures and sound. If the parts were fitted together in a random manner then the television would not function. Similarly, there are complex arrangements within nature that have been fitted together by a designer for special purposes.

Design *qua* purpose developed in the 17th century in response to the new, mechanistic physics. Scientific developments had proved that the planets orbited the Sun according to strict patterns and according to comprehensive laws. Isaac Newton discovered the universal laws of gravity and motion, and demonstrated that the same physical laws that we know on Earth are applicable throughout the whole universe. Many scientists began to see the universe as a 'machine', with all the parts working together as perpetual clockwork that never needed rewinding.

■ *The analogy of a watch*

In response to the mechanical analogy, William Paley (1743–1805) put forward the most famous form of the design argument in his book, *Natural Theology*:

> In crossing a heath, suppose I pitched my foot against a stone, and were asked how the stone came to be there, I might possibly answer, that for any thing I knew to the contrary it had lain there for ever; nor would it, perhaps be very easy to show the absurdity of this answer. But suppose I had found a watch upon the ground, and it should be inquired how the watch happened to be in that place, I should hardly think of the answer which I had before given, that for any thing I knew the watch might have always been there. Yet why should not this answer serve for the watch as well as for the stone; why is it not as admissible in the second case as in the first? For this reason, and for no other, namely, that when we come to inspect the watch, we perceive – what we could not discover in the stone – that its several parts are framed and put together for a purpose, e.g. that they are so formed and adjusted as to produce motion, and

that motion so regulated as to point out the hour of the day; that if the different parts had been differently shaped from what they are, or placed after any other manner or in any other order than that in which they are placed, either no motion at all would have been carried on in the machine, or none which would have answered the use that is now served by it.

William Paley, Natural Theology, 1802

Paley's first argument

The first part of Paley's argument was design *qua* purpose. Paley put forward the argument for design in the form of a simple **analogy**. If we came across a watch, we would conclude that all the parts fitted together for a purpose and did not come into existence by chance. An intelligent person would infer a designer of the watch. In the same way, if we look at the world we can infer a design because of the way in which things fit together for a purpose. For example, Paley thought that a similar conclusion might be drawn from the intricate mechanisms of the human body.

■ Key terms

Analogy: a comparison between two things, when a similarity between two things is suggested by the use of the same word. In the phrases a 'clean house' and a 'clean break', the word 'clean' is not used in the same way but there is a similarity between the way in which it is used and so there is understanding of the meaning behind the words.

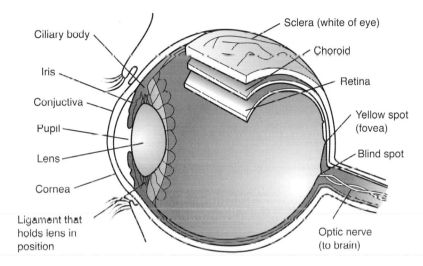

The structure of the eye

◪ Evidence for a designer

Paley used the example of the eye and the way in which it is adapted for sight. Its various parts cooperate in complex ways to produce sight. He believed that the eye was designed for the specific purpose of seeing, and this complex design suggests an intelligent designer. He adds to this example the adaptations of animals that aid survival: a bird's wings for flight, or a fish's fins for swimming. Another example he used was the lacteal system:

The lacteal system is a constant wonder; and it adds to other causes of our admiration, that the number of the teats or paps in each species is found to bear a proportion to the number of the young. In the sow, the bitch, the rabbit, the cat, the rat, which have numerous litters, the paps are numerous, and are disposed along the whole length of the belly: in the cow and the mare, they are few. The most simple account of this, is to refer it to a designing creator.

William Paley, Natural Theology, 1802

Mammals which have numerous litters have the appropriate number of teats in the right place to feed the many offspring

Think about

Read Paley's quote from *Natural Theology*. Paley is explaining that any minor change in the laws of nature would have led to things not developing in the world. How do you think for Paley this proves the existence of design?

Activity

Write a 500–600-word essay outlining the design arguments of Aquinas and Paley.

Think about

There is a hole forming in the ozone layer. Give reasons why this hole might undermine Brown's argument for design *qua* purpose.

Such evidence, Paley argued, could only be the result of a 'designing creator', which for Paley was God.

Paley's second argument

The second part of Paley's argument for the existence of God is design *qua* regularity. Paley used evidence from astronomy and Newton's laws of motion and gravity to prove design in the universe. Paley pointed to the rotation of the planets in the solar system, and how they obey the same universal laws, and hold their orbits because of gravity. This could not have come about by chance. He concluded an external agent must have imposed order on the universe as a whole, and on its many parts, and this agent must be God. He noted that even slight differences or irregularities within the system would have resulted in chaos:

> While the possible laws of variations were infinite, the admissible laws, or the compatible laws compatible with the system, lie within narrow limits. If the attracting forces had varied according to any direct law of the distance, let it have been what it would, great destruction and confusion would have taken place. The direct simple proportion of the distance would, it is true, have produced an ellipse; but the perturbing forces would have acted with so much advantage, as to be continually changing the dimensions of the ellipse, in a manner inconsistent with our terrestrial creation.

William Paley, Natural Theology, 1802

In the 20th century, Arthur Brown supported the argument for design based on astronomy. Brown pointed to the ozone layer as evidence of design. He argued that the ozone layer's purpose, to filter out the ultraviolet rays to protect life, could not have happened by chance. Brown argued,

> The ozone gas layer is a mighty proof of the creator's forethought. Could anyone possibly attribute this device to a chance evolutionary process? A wall which prevents death to every living thing, just the right thickness and exactly the correct defence gives every evidence of a plan.

Arthur Brown, Footprints of God, 1943

Evidence against the existence of God

Pierre Laplace argued against the existence of God to fill in the gaps that science could not understand. It was no longer necessary to believe that God caused the movements in the universe. Scientists no longer had to refer to God in order to explain the way in which the physical world worked. Laplace argued that the universe was like a machine in which each part of the machine affected the behaviour of another part and resulted in movement. Laplace concluded that everything in the solar system was determined (caused). Laplace thought that eventually all the natural laws of the universe would be known and that everything would be explained in scientific terms.

💡 David Hume's challenge to the design argument

David Hume was a major opponent of the design argument in his work *Dialogues Concerning Natural Religion* (1779). Hume asked why we must conclude that the universe had to have a beginning: 'How can anything that exists from eternity have a cause, since the relation implies a priority in time and in a beginning of existence?'

Even if it were possible to discern order and purpose in the universe it would still not be evidence that it was the work of the God of classical theism. The design could have been the work of several lesser gods, or alternatively, an apprentice god who has moved on to create bigger and better worlds. The evidence of flaws in the design such as suffering and death would be more supportive of a designer that was not an infinite, perfect Being.

> This world, for all he knows, is very faulty and imperfect, compared to a superior standard; and was only the first rude essay of some infant deity who afterwards abandoned it.

David Hume, Dialogues concerning Natural Religion, 1779

Hume's main reasons for opposing the argument fall into two categories. Hume challenges the argument to design and the argument from design.

Challenges to the argument for design

Hume's challenge to the argument to design includes:

- Humans do not have sufficient knowledge and experience of the creation of the world to conclude that there is only one designer. Humans have only the experience of the things they design and create. Humans can only recognise human-designed objects, for example a ship. This limited experience is not sufficient to come to similar conclusions about the creation and design of the world. For in order to point to a designed world, we would need to have experience of a range of different worlds. As we only experience the one the analogy cannot be applied.

- Hume does not think that it is a good analogy to liken the universe to a vast machine. The universe is more like a vegetable or inert animal; something that grows of its own accord, rather than something made by hand.

- Hume argues that to try to discuss the design of the universe in human terms was not an acceptable analogy because God transcends human understanding. If we are going to use an analogy

Link

Look back at Chapter 6, p96, for the definition of determinism.

Think about

Look at Chapter 6, p95. Why did Laplace believe that he did not need reference to God in his work?

How might Laplace's opinion be applied to the design argument for the existence of God?

Link

Look back to Chapter 6, p105 and remind yourself of Michael Behe and his work on intelligent design.

of manufactured objects then it is more usual for a machine to be designed and made by many hands. This analogy would suggest many gods rather than one God.

Challenges to the argument from design

Hume's challenge to the argument from design includes:

■ Even if the world is designed it still cannot prove that the designer is God. The conclusion could easily be reached that the universe's configuration is the result of some morally ambiguous, possibly unintelligent agent or agents whose method bears only a remote similarity to human design.

■ Hume argues that if the world is ordered then this is either because of chance or because of design. The 'Epicurean hypothesis' demonstrates how it would be possible for the universe to appear ordered yet be the result of random chance.

The Epicurean hypothesis

Hume's Epicurean hypothesis argued that at the time of creation, the universe consisted of particles in random motion. This initial state was chaotic but gradually the natural forces evolved into an ordered system. The universe is eternal, and in this unlimited time it was inevitable that a constantly ordered state would develop. The stability and order is not the result of a divine designer but of random particles coming together through time to form the current stable universe.

■ Does evidence of design prove the existence of God?

John Stuart Mill (1806–73) was an empiricist and for him knowledge had to be grounded in experience. He challenged the idea that evidence of design in the world proves the existence of the God of classical theism because evidence supported either the non-existence of God or a god that did not have the attributes accepted by Christians. He argued that because there is evil and suffering in the world then the designer cannot have been all-powerful, all-knowing and all-loving. If the designer were all-loving then the suffering of humanity would not have been included in the design. As it is, then, at least one of these three attributes must be missing.

How can the world be designed when natural disasters such as the tsunami on Boxing Day 2004 occur?

Think about

Do you agree with Hume or Paley? Do you think the way in which all parts of the universe appear to function together is the result of design or random chance? Justify the reasons for your view with examples.

Think about

If the world is designed what are the reasons for natural disasters?

Activity

Write a 500–600-word essay to explain the philosophical challenges of Hume and Mill against the design argument.

Think about

Epicurus (341–270 BC) was a Greek philosopher who maintained that the universe was only made up of atoms and space, nothing else. The atoms are eternal, but they move and change. All physical objects are a combination of atoms. How might such an idea result in the appearance of design?

The challenge from Darwinism

In Chapter 6 we considered how the work of Charles Darwin challenged the Genesis account of creation. Darwin's evolutionary theories also challenge the design argument.

Darwin's evolutionary theory appeals to a mechanistic self-ordering process in nature. His work *On the Origin of the Species by Means of Natural Selection* challenged the argument for design as it revolutionised thinking about the way in which species, including humans, developed. The theory proposes that certain species have become extinct and new species emerge over time. Darwin provided an alternative explanation for the design of the world without reference to creation by God. Darwin offered a mechanical explanation for the development of life on earth in which natural selection took place. Herbert Spencer coined the phrase 'the survival of the fittest' to explain part of the process. Darwin argued that random variations, which gave the best advantage to a plant or animal in the struggle for survival, resulted in the survival of the fittest member of that species.

> In order to make it clear how, as I believe, natural selection acts, I must beg permission to give one or two imaginary illustrations. Let us take the case of a wolf, which preys on various animals, securing some by craft, some by strength, and some by fleetness, and let us suppose that the fleetest prey, a deer for instance, had from any change in the country increased in numbers, or that other prey had decreased in numbers, during that season of the year when the wolf was hardest pressed for food. Under such circumstances the swiftest and slimmest wolves would have the best chance of surviving and so be preserved or selected, provided always that they retained strength to master their prey at this or some other period of the year, when they were compelled to prey on other animals. I can see no more reason to doubt that this would be the result, than that man should be able to improve the fleetness of his greyhounds by careful and methodical selection.
>
> *Charles Darwin, The Origin of Species, 1859*

🔲 An appearance of design

The Origin of Species led many people to claim that a belief in God was no longer necessary to explain the way in which the natural world had developed. More recently, evolutionary biologist Richard Dawkins has written several books to support Darwinian evolution and reject God. Dawkins argues that natural selection gave the appearance of design, and that this led to the mistaken belief that there was a designer. He rejects any design in the world, and argues that the variations in the world were caused by random mistakes in the DNA molecules of any life-form. Any human action that appears to have altruistic motives is in reality behaviour motivated by the need of the human genes to survive. Humans are no more than DNA carriers that will ensure the survival of the species.

> The true utility function of life, that which is being maximized in the natural world, is DNA survival. But DNA is not floating free; it is locked up in living bodies, and it has to make the most of the levers of power at its disposal. Genetic sequences that find themselves in cheetah bodies maximize their survival by causing those bodies to kill gazelles. Sequences that find themselves in

AQA Examiner's tip

Know your 'experts' and make sure you can refer to their views or use their arguments in your answer. If you want to comment on the exact words someone has written, then quotes can be useful, but the key to success is being able to understand and explain their ideas.

Link

Look back at Chapter 6, p97, and remind yourself of what is meant by evolution and natural selection.

Think about

How do you think that evolution and natural selection challenge the argument of design as evidence of God's existence?

How do you think that evolution and natural selection support the argument of design as evidence of God's existence?

Link

Look at the arguments in Chapter 6 pp99–108. What links between creation and design can you see?

> gazelle bodies increase their chance of survival by promoting opposite ends. But the same utility function – the survival of DNA – explains the 'purpose' of both the cheetah and the gazelle.

Richard Dawkins, article in Scientific American, November 1995

⟁ Memes

In his book *The Selfish Gene* Dawkins argues that genes-molecules of DNA are the fundamental units of natural selection, the 'replicators'. Organisms, including human organisms, are no more than the 'vehicles', or packaging, for the 'replicators'. The success or failure of replicators is based on their ability to build successful vehicles. Dawkins considers the family, or the social group, to be no more than the environment that animals create to ensure survival of the genes. Dawkins takes a Darwinian view of culture, and refers to the **memes**, a term he has invented to refer to the unit of cultural inheritance; memes are essentially ideas, and they, too, are operated on by natural selection. It is for this reason Dawkins argues that humans appear to have an appreciation of beauty but it is no more than part of the survival mechanism.

Activity

Read either Dawkins's *Blind Watchmaker* or *The God Delusion*. Make detailed notes on why Dawkins attacks the religious interpretation of the data.

> Nightingale songs, pheasant tails, firefly flashes and the rainbow scales of tropical reef fish are all maximizing aesthetic beauty, but it is not – or is only incidentally – beauty for human delectation. If we enjoy the spectacle it is a bonus, a by-product. Genes that make males attractive to females automatically find themselves passed down the digital river to the future. There is only one utility function that makes sense of these beauties; it is the same one that explains elephant-seal sex ratios, cheetahs and antelopes running superficially futile races against each other, cuckoos and lice, eyes and ears and windpipes, sterile worker ants and superfertile queens. The great universal Utility Function, the quantity that is being diligently maximized in every cranny of the living world is, in every case, the survival of the DNA responsible for the feature you are trying to explain. Peacocks are burdened with finery so heavy and cumbersome that it would gravely hamper their efforts to do useful work, even if they felt inclined to do useful work – which, on the whole, they don't. Male songbirds use dangerous amounts of time and energy singing. This certainly imperils them, not only because it attracts predators but because it drains energy and uses time that could be spent replenishing that energy. A student of wren biology claimed that one of his wild males sang itself literally to death. Any utility function that had the long-term welfare of the species at heart, even the long-term survival of this particular individual male, would cut down on the amount of singing, the amount of displaying, the amount of fighting among males. Yet, because what is really being maximized is DNA survival, nothing can stop the spread of DNA that has no beneficial effect other than making males beautiful to females. Beauty is not an absolute virtue in itself. But inevitably, if some genes do confer on males whatever qualities the females of the species happen to find desirable, those genes, willy-nilly, will survive.

Richard Dawkins, article in Scientific American, November 1995

⟁ The anthropic principle

Not all scientists agree with Richard Dawkins. Some accept that the universe came about through the work of God. The physicist and priest

John Polkinghorne uses the **anthropic principle** to support his belief that chance alone is an unlikely theory to explain why the exact conditions occurred in the universe to develop intelligent life. Polkinghorne considers Dawkins and his supporters to have missed the point that all that was required for life was available in our universe, and this could only have been the result of a designer (creator), but the creator of that universe has stood back and given creation the freedom to be itself.

> Evolutionary history seems to unfold through the interplay of two contrasting tendencies: 'chance' (by which is meant the particularity of historical contingency, that this happens rather than that) and 'necessity' (by which is meant the generality of the lawfully regular environment within which the process is played out, the reliability of the world).

John Polkinghorne, The God of Hope and the End of the World, 2002

The anthropic principle is a recent development of the teleological argument. The argument claims that the cosmos is constructed for the development of intelligent life. If there had been just a minute change in the values of, for instance, the strong nuclear force or the charge of the electron, then intelligent life, or any form of life at all, would have been unlikely to develop on earth.

The 'new' design argument denies any claim that there is a chain of coincidences that led to the evolution of human life. Supporters of the argument go on to make the further claim that the best explanation is the existence of a designer, and this designer is God.

Natural evidence for a designer

F. R. Tennant (1866–1957) developed the anthropic principle in his book *Philosophical Theology*, (1930). Tennant believed that there were three types of natural evidence in the world in favour of a divine designer:

- the fact that the world can be analysed in a rational manner
- the way in which the inorganic world has provided the basic necessities required for sustaining life
- the progress of evolution towards the emergence of intelligent human life.

Tennant believed that it would be possible to imagine a chaotic universe in which no rules applied. However, the universe is evidently not chaotic and was designed in such a way that the evolutionary process would create an environment in which intelligent life could exist. This led Tennant to conclude that human life is either the culmination of God's plan or at least the current stage in God's plan.

> The forcibleness of Nature's suggestion that she is the outcome of intelligent design lies not in particular cases of adaptedness in the world, nor even in the multiplicity of them ... it consists rather in the **conspiration** of innumerable causes to produce, by either united and reciprocal action, and to maintain, a general order of Nature. Narrower kinds of teleological arguments, based on surveys of restricted spheres of fact, are much more precarious than that for which the name of 'the wider teleology' may be appropriate in that the comprehensive design-argument is the outcome of synopsis or **conspection** of the knowable world.

F. R. Tennant, Philosophical Theology, 1930

Key terms

Anthropic: to be linked to the science and study of mankind.

Think about

Where does Tennant believe the evidence for design can be found in Nature?

Key terms

Conspiration: to join together, to combine.

Conspection: a survey or observation of events.

Think about

What does Tennant mean when he states that: 'beauty seems to be superfluous and to have little survival value?'

Why does Tennant regard the appreciation of beauty as evidence of design?

Charles Darwin saw the process of natural selection as gradual and ongoing: the result of natural and random processes rather than the work of a divine being. The Origin of Species led many people to claim as Dawkins does that it is part of the survival mechanism.

With which view do you agree and why do you hold that view?

Think about

Why do you think that philosophers such as F. R. Tennant were able to accept Darwin's theory of evolution as part of God's design for the universe whereas scientists such as Richard Dawkins use Darwin's theory as evidence that God does not exist?

The aesthetic argument

Tennant developed the argument further by concluding that the universe is not only ordered but moreover appears to be beautiful at all levels. This part of Tennant's argument is often called the aesthetic argument to prove God's existence. Tennant argued that humans possess the ability to appreciate the beauty of their surroundings, to enjoy art, music and literature. Yet such an appreciation is not necessary for survival or the development of life, and is therefore evidence of a divine creator. It cannot therefore be the result of natural selection alone.

> Nature is not just beautiful in places, it is saturated with beauty – on the telescopic and microscopic scale. Our scientific knowledge brings us no nearer to understanding the beauty of music. From an intelligibility point of view, beauty seems to be superfluous and to have little survival value …
>
> *F. R. Tennant*, Philosophical Theology, 1930

Two forms of anthropic principle

In recent times two forms of the anthropic principle have developed: the strong anthropic principle which argues that the conditions for the development of human life were intrinsic to the Big Bang and the expansion of the universe. It was the purpose of the design that life would develop on earth. The weaker version of the anthropic principle does not accept that life on earth was inevitable from the beginning but just happened to have occurred.

The anthropic principle accepts both Darwin's evolutionary process and the existence of God. The principle claims that evolution is part of God's plan for the development of intelligent life. Nature produces living beings but without the 'fine tuning' that is found in the universe, life could just as easily have not developed on earth. Supporters of the principle suggest that Nature may be compared to a machine that makes other machines, and like all machines, it needed an intelligent designer.

A reformulation of the design argument

Richard Swinburne accepts that Darwin's theory of evolution undercuts the classic design argument that living things are intricately constructed to serve a purpose and that a divine creator deliberately created them. For Darwin offered a scientific explanation of apparent purpose in nature, and eliminated the need to attribute it all to a creator God and as Swinburne states it was Darwin's data that 'added to the probability of his theory of the evolution of the species by natural selection of variations'. It's not that animals and plants have been fashioned by a divine designer and given what they need to serve the purposes of survival. It's just that over long periods of time new kinds of living things have come into existence as a result of random genetic variations. Those new variants which happened to be better adapted to their environment survived, and those that weren't died out. Swinburne does not believe that this rules out the possibility of God as designer, only that the design argument needs to be reformulated bearing in mind the theory of evolution. Swinburne has developed two versions of the design argument to meet these challenges from modern science.

A reformulation from temporal order

Swinburne calls the first version of his argument the argument from temporal order. Swinburne accepts the anthropic principle and that the universe is law-governed. He recognises that the universe could just as easily have been chaotic, but the fact that it is not suggests design rather than chance. Swinburne argues that everything in the universe takes place with predictable regularity in accordance with scientific laws. Evolutionary theory, like any other scientific explanation, explains particular events by discovering scientific laws which make them intelligible and show them to be instances of some regular pattern. However science cannot explain itself why these things happen. Swinburne considered that it came down to **probabilities**. Is what we see around us the result of design or random chance? Which is the most probable reason for order in the universe: random chance or design? To explain his point, Swinburne uses the analogy of a card-shuffling machine:

> Suppose that a madman kidnaps a victim and shuts him in a room with a card-shuffling machine. The machine shuffles ten packs of cards simultaneously and then draws a card from each pack and exhibits simultaneously the ten cards. The kidnapper tells the victim that he will shortly set the machine to work and it will exhibit its first draw, but that unless the draw consists of an ace of hearts from each pack, the machine will simultaneously set off an explosion which will kill the victim, in consequence of which he will not see which cards the machine drew. The machine is then set to work, and to the amazement and relief of the victim the machine exhibits an ace of hearts drawn from each pack. The victim thinks that this extraordinary fact needs an explanation in terms of the machine having been rigged in some way. But the kidnapper, who now reappears, casts doubt on this suggestion. 'It is hardly surprising', he says, 'that the machine draws only aces of hearts. You could not possibly see anything else. For you would not be here to see anything at all, if any other cards had been drawn.' But of course the victim is right and the kidnapper is wrong. There is indeed something extraordinary in need of explanation in ten aces of hearts being drawn. The fact that this peculiar order is a necessary condition of the draw being perceived at all makes what is perceived no less extraordinary and in need of explanation. The teleologist's starting-point is not that we perceive order rather than disorder, but that order rather than disorder is there. Maybe only if order is there can we know what is there, but that makes what is there no less extraordinary and in need of explanation.

Richard Swinburne, The Existence of God, 1979

Swinburne is arguing that the sheer complexity of the universe makes it unlikely that the universe would just 'happen' to be the way it is, so Swinburne accepted that it is more probable that there is design. If there is design, then he concluded that God is the simplest explanation.

The argument from spatial order

Swinburne calls the second version of his design argument the argument from spatial order. Swinburne accepts that the existence of plants and animals and humans, intricately constructed and adapted to their environment, can be explained by the theory of evolution through natural selection, but this process occurred only because the initial conditions were right. There had to be a planet like ours with just the right kind of atmosphere, the right amount of oxygen and water and so on, and for the universe to evolve in such a way as to produce such a planet, the initial conditions of the 'Big Bang', which began our universe 15 billion years ago, had to be just right to lead to the development of human life (the anthropic principle).

> So I suggest that the order of the world is evidence of the existence of God both because its occurrence would be very improbable *a priori* and also because, in virtue of his postulated character, he has very good, apparently overriding, reason for making an orderly universe, if he makes a universe at all.

Richard Swinburne, The Existence of God, 1979

Immanuel Kant anticipated that developments in science would prompt new versions of the teleological argument. Kant emphasised that the design argument depends on the assumption that there is design in the universe. The design must be the independent work of a designer who imposed order on the universe. The argument is based on the assumption that there is regularity, order and purpose in the universe. Kant argued that the universe may be in chaos but because of the way in which our minds organise our experiences, the world around us appears ordered. We impose the design on the world ourselves, and cannot be certain of the reality of the situation.

■ Conclusion

Whether or not there is design in the universe comes down to probabilities. Hume accepted that it was more probable that the universe was designed and there was a designer, but there was no proof that the designer was God.

The physicist Paul Davies (1946–) accepts that there is a reason for the organisation of universe, and that someone designed it. According to Davies, this someone might be God.

> It's certainly consistent with that. This is really a question of your threshold of conviction. As the philosopher John Lesley has remarked, if every time we turned a rock over we saw the message Made by God stamped on it, then I guess everybody would have to assume that we did live in a universe of his design. It has to be a matter of personal taste whether you regard the accumulated evidence as compelling enough to want to make that leap. But inevitably it's outside the scope of science as such. Science deals with the facts of the world, religion deals with the interpretation of those facts.

Paul Davies in R. Stannard's, Science and Wonders, 1996

■ Think about

Do you think that it is more or less probable that there is design in the universe?

If there is design in the universe, do you think that it is probable that the designer is God?

What similarities do you think there are between the thinking of Kant and Dawkins with regard to the possibility of design in the universe?

■ Think about

Thomas McPherson said: 'How can we talk sensibly of the existence of a world independent of order, when to talk at all is to impose order.'

What do you think he meant by this statement?

How might the statement be applied to the design argument for the existence of God?

Activities

1 List the key ideas in the design argument of Aquinas and Paley.

2 List the key ideas in the evolutionary theories of Darwin.

3 List the key objections of Richard Dawkins to the design argument.

4 List the key ideas of the counter-arguments of Swinburne and those who support the Anthropic Principle that scientific theories are a description of God at work.

5 Assess the strengths and weakness of the arguments for and against the design argument.

6 Evaluate whether or not science has made the design argument a failure.

Now that you have read this chapter you should be able to:

- explain the design argument as presented by Aquinas and Paley

- explain the philosophical and scientific arguments against the Deism argument

- explain the responses to these challenges, including Swinburne's interpretation of the design argument

- evaluate the strength and weakness of the argument

- evaluate how far Swinburne's design argument successfully meets the challenges of philosophy and science

- assess how far the argument makes it reasonable to believe in God.

8 Quantum mechanics and a religious world-view

Learning objectives:

- to understand the world-view of quantum mechanics including: quanta, light as a wave and a particle, the nature of the electron, and the role of the observer in resolving uncertainty

- to understand the implication of the world-view of quantum mechanics for the way in which God is believed to interact with the world

- to understand parallels between quantum mechanics and mystical insights in the Eastern traditions into the nature of reality

- to evaluate whether science can be 'religious'

- to assess whether science has discovered something that mystics knew all along.

Quantum theory is the set of physical laws that apply primarily on the very small microscopic scale, for entities the size of atoms or smaller. At the heart of quantum theory lie the linked concepts of uncertainty and wave–particle duality. In the quantum world, every entity has a mixture of properties that we are used to thinking of as distinctly different: such as **waves** and **particles**. For example, light, which is often regarded as an electromagnetic wave, behaves under some circumstances as if it was composed of a stream of particles, called photons.

John Gibbin, Companion to the Cosmos, 1996

An atom was originally thought to be the smallest particle that could not be cut into smaller parts. Modern science uses the term 'atom' to refer to the composition of various subatomic particles, including:

- electrons that have a negative charge, and a physical size which is so small as to be currently immeasurable
- protons that have a positive charge
- neutrons that have no charge.

Both protons and neutrons are themselves now thought to be composed of even more elementary particles: quarks.

Quantum mechanics

Newton was a Christian who was convinced that he would find order in the universe, and indeed he did. Newton believed that the laws of gravity and motion were part of God's design; however, other scientists became convinced that his laws gave science the certainty that it would be possible to discover all the laws of nature and predict all events without any need to refer to God. As we will see in this chapter, quantum theory has brought into question some of this certainty.

The understanding of Newtonian physics was that bodies obeyed fixed laws, and that it was possible to predict their behaviour in every situation. Matter was considered to be solid and predictable, and all the laws of the universe would be discovered eventually. There would be no need for reference to God, as science could provide all the answers. This certainty was lost with the development of quantum mechanics because of its unpredictability.

What is quantum mechanics?

Quantum mechanics is the study of the behaviour of **matter** and **energy** at the molecular, atomic, nuclear, and subatomic particle level. The word 'quantum' means a definite but small amount. In the early 20th century, it was discovered that the laws governing **macroscopic** objects do not function the same in such small realms. Because it is not possible directly to experience objects on this scale, many aspects of quantum behaviour seem strange and even paradoxical. A good explanation of the quantum behaviour was provided by the physicist Paul Dirac. He

Link

Read Chapter 6 pp92–96, to understand how the scientific world-view has developed.

Think about

How has the scientific world-view changed the relationship between religion and science in the 21st century?

took a piece of chalk and broke it in two. He put one piece at one side of the lectern from which he was speaking and the other piece on the other side. Dirac said that the one piece of chalk could be referred to as 'here' and the other piece as 'there'. These are the only two possible positions for the chalk. Dirac went on to say that at the quantum level there is not only here and there but 'a whole host of other states that are mixtures of those possibilities – a bit of "here" and a bit of "there" added together'. Although there is a high degree of precision in aspects of quantum physics, such as quantum electrodynamics, such theories are in a mathematical framework and therefore trying to interpret the theory in plain language has proved controversial.

The history of quantum mechanics

Quantum mechanics developed in the early 20th century after the German physicist Max Planck (1858–1947) discovered that **radiation** was not produced in a continuous stream, as originally thought by Newton, but in packets of energy of a definite size (quanta). Planck specified that the energy content of one of these quanta would be in proportion to the frequency of the radiation. This constant proportionality was taken to be a universal constant of nature and is now known as Planck's constant. This constant is known as h and is equal to 6.626069×10^{-34} Joule-seconds.

Wave-particle duality

Newton had inclined to the view that a beam of light was made up of a stream of tiny particles. However, in 1801 the English scientist Thomas Young presented very convincing evidence to support the idea that light had the character of wave motion. It became clear through experiments that light functions as both a particle and a wave, depending on how the experiment is conducted and when observations are made. Scientists call this the principle of wave-particle duality. Just like light, matter exhibits both wave and particle properties under the right circumstances, and for small objects, the wavelength can be observable and significant. Scientists were able to use the discovery of quanta to explain this previously unexplainable phenomena as to whether light is a wave or a particle. Light is neither wave nor particle, and it depends on what the light is doing as to what is observed – wave or particle.

The central problem is as follows. Light is usually thought of as a wave, and as such exhibits typical wave phenomena like interference and diffraction. However, it sometimes behaves in ways that can only be explained if light was a particle: for example, the photoelectric effect, whose successful explanation led to Einstein receiving the Nobel prize. Meanwhile, electrons usually behave like particles – that is, like tiny billiard balls – but occasionally behave in ways that can only be explained if they are waves as well: for example, electron diffraction.

Why does a stick appear bent when submerged in water?

Key terms

Quantum theory: the physical laws applying to the microscopic level.

Waves: the behaviour of phenomena such as light or other sub-atomic particles.

Particles: any part of reality smaller than an atom.

Matter: any substance that has mass and occupies space. All physical objects are composed of matter, in the form of atoms, which are in turn composed of protons, neutrons, and electrons.

Energy: the capacity of a physical system to perform work. Energy exists in several forms such as heat, kinetic or mechanical energy, light, potential energy, electricity, or other forms.

Macroscopic: physical objects that are measurable and observable by the naked eye; microscopic being those smaller.

Radiation: as used in physics it is light or energy in the form of waves or particles.

Think about

Have you ever half submerged a straight stick into water? What appears to happen to the stick because the wave of light is being refracted at the water/air surface?

How would light as a particle be different? Here is a clue – light as a particle is called a photon. The Starship Enterprise uses photon torpedoes to destroy its enemies.

The photoelectric effect

The next important developments in quantum mechanics were the work of Albert Einstein (1879–1955). He used Planck's concept of the quantum to explain certain properties of the **photoelectric effect**. The theory had been that the energy, as measured by the voltage of the emitted electrons, should be proportional to the intensity of the radiation. It was found, however, that the energy of the electrons was independent of the intensity of radiation, which determined only the number of electrons emitted. This depended solely on the frequency of the radiation. The higher the frequency of the incident radiation, the greater is the electron energy; below a certain critical frequency no electrons are emitted. Einstein explained these facts by assuming that a single quantum of radiant energy ejects a single electron from the metal. The energy of the quantum is proportional to the frequency, and so the energy of the electron depends on the frequency.

Matter can exhibit wave-particle duality

The French physicist Louis de Broglie (1892–1987) suggested in 1922 that if energy could behave as both particles and waves, perhaps matter could also. He produced the mathematics and predicted that under the right conditions a beam of electrons (clearly matter made of particles) might show wave properties, and when the experiment was performed, a beam of electrons was found to diffract just like a wave would have done. He had shown that both energy and matter could both exhibit wave-particle duality. It appeared that a moving particle had a wavelength.

Like a photon, an electron can therefore be both a wave and a particle, but it cannot be both a wave and a particle at the same time. There are two puzzling questions here:

■ The electron seems to behave as a wave or a particle according to the experiment being performed. Thus, is it the electron's interaction with the experimental set-up that makes the difference – or the role of the person observing what happens? It is easier to explain this mathematically – but interpreting the theories remains controversial!

■ Even more fundamentally, what exactly is the wave when it refers to a single electron? Despite the extraordinary success of the mathematics of the theory, understanding what the wave actually is remains open to debate.

🔍 The problem of probability

Two important physicists who sought to solve the problem of probability were:

■ Erwin Schrödinger (1887–1961)

■ Werner Heisenberg (1901–76).

In 1926, Erwin Schrödinger realised that he could use the mathematics of wave mechanics, a normal branch of classical physics, and adapt it to the quantum world. This introduced the concept of the **wave function**. Heisenberg's matrix mechanics (1927) provided an alternative mathematical framework but it is essentially consistent with Schrödinger's theory. The German physicist Max Born suggested in 1928 that the wave function should be related to probability: that is, the probability of an electron being in a particular place depended on its wave function. The wave itself is thus pictured as a 'probability wave', within whose constraints the electron may be said to move randomly.

Heisenberg relied on what can be observed, namely the light emitted and absorbed by the atoms, to predict the action of particles. Heisenberg concluded you could measure the position of an electron (or other

■ **Link**

Remind yourself of the belief in deism in Chapter 6, p79.

■ **Think about**

Why do you think the quantum theory appears to undermine deism?

particle) *or* you could measure its momentum precisely, but in either case precision in one would lead to greater uncertainty in the other. This is because the more precisely you measure one property, the more you throw the other off.

> The more precisely the position is determined, the less precisely the momentum is known in this instant, and vice versa.

Werner Heisenberg, Uncertainty paper, 1927

As a result of his observations Heisenberg developed his uncertainty principle and this theory is the essence of quantum theory. He demonstrated that everything that can be observed or measured, including the smallest component parts of matter, are subject to unpredictable fluctuations. These fluctuations appear to be spontaneous events that cannot be predicted or explained.

The effect of the uncertainty principle

While many scientists resisted Heisenberg's uncertainty principle, it is now accepted as a fundamental law of nature. The uncertainty principle has limited the scientists' power of prediction. If the mechanical processes are not as predictable as once thought, then the concept of Deism is undermined because science cannot predict things with certainty as was once thought. This leaves the way open for the belief that God is still involved with creation and did not set the universe going like a mechanical clock and leave it to its own devices. Pierre-Simon Laplace had argued that he had no need of the hypothesis of God as soon all the laws would be discovered and explained by science. Science would no longer agree with Laplace and therefore there is still room for God to explain what science cannot.

Heisenberg realised that the uncertainty had profound implications. First, if we accept Heisenberg's argument that every concept has a meaning only in terms of the experiments used to measure it, we must agree that things that cannot be measured really have no meaning in physics. Thus, for instance, the path of a particle has no meaning beyond the precision with which it is observed. But a basic assumption of physics since Newton has been that a 'real world' exists independently of us, regardless of whether or not we observe it. (This assumption did not go unchallenged, however, by some philosophers.) Heisenberg now argued that such concepts as orbits of electrons do not exist in nature unless and until we observe them: 'What we observe is not nature itself, but nature exposed to our method of questioning.'

Think about

Quantum theory raises the following question: Was the origin of the universe a spontaneous quantum event and not the action of a divine being that planned the development of the universe?

Think about

Was God responsible for setting up the laws of physics so that the universe began?

We are not at the centre of the universe, but we circle round an insignificant star in a spiral galaxy similar to the one in this picture

The Copenhagen interpretation

One interpretation of quantum theory's implications for the nature of reality is the Copenhagen interpretation. The Danish physicist Niels Bohr (1885–1962) proposed the Copenhagen interpretation of quantum theory when he asserted that an electron is both a wave and a particle until the act of experimental measurement, or some other interaction, forces it to be one or the other. Bohr said, 'Everything we call real is made of things that cannot be regarded as real.' Bohr wanted to discover what exactly is objectively real. For example, is it the wave? The particle? The wave function? Or is the only objective reality the measurement or observable? Asking such questions is not to deny objective reality but to ask in what it actually lies. Bohr believed in the reality of objects, such as electrons, but was not inclined to ascribe objective reality to theoretical interpretations, which he believed to be mathematical conveniences. This was in the vein of the philosophical debates that were circulating at the time, and is one that tends to be revisited periodically. This translates to a principle called **superposition**, which claims that while we do not know what the state of any object is, it is actually in all possible states simultaneously, as long as we don't look to check. Erwin Schrödinger developed a hypothetical experiment known as 'Schrödinger's Cat' to explain this principle of superposition. His aim was to demonstrate the apparent conflict between what quantum theory tells us is true about the nature and behaviour of matter on the microscopic level, and what we observe to be true about the nature and behaviour of matter on the macroscopic level. It is important to realise that Schrödinger was seeking to ridicule the Copenhagen interpretation.

⁊ *Schrödinger's Cat*

Remember this is a theoretical experiment. Schrödinger said to imagine that a live cat is placed into a steel box which contains a test tube of hydrocyanic acid. In the box there is also a small amount of a radioactive substance. If even a single atom of the substance decays during the test period, a relay mechanism will trip a hammer, which will, in turn, break the vial and kill the cat. It is not possible to know whether or not an atom of the substance has decayed, and consequently, whether the vial has been broken, the hydrocyanic acid released, and the cat killed. As we do not know the answer until the box is opened then the cat is both dead and alive according to quantum law, in a superposition of states. It is only when the box is opened that the condition of the cat can be known.

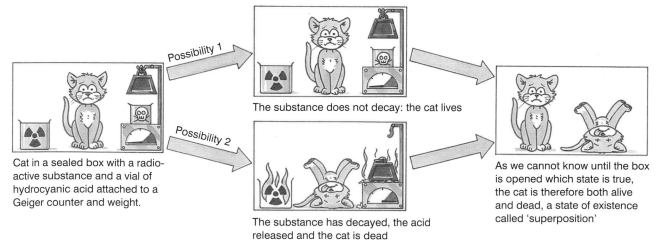

Possibility 1

Possibility 2

The substance does not decay: the cat lives

Cat in a sealed box with a radioactive substance and a vial of hydrocyanic acid attached to a Geiger counter and weight.

The substance has decayed, the acid released and the cat is dead

As we cannot know until the box is opened which state is true, the cat is therefore both alive and dead, a state of existence called 'superposition'

The Schrödinger's Cat experiment

The superposition is lost because the cat is one or the other (dead or alive). It is the observation or measurement itself that affects an outcome, so that the outcome as such does not exist unless the measurement is made.

It is known that superposition actually occurs at the subatomic level, because there are observable effects of interference, in which a single particle is demonstrated to be in multiple locations simultaneously. What that fact implies about the nature of reality on the observable, macroscopic level is one of the areas of quantum physics that is most difficult to prove.

God does not play dice

Albert Einstein was unhappy with the probabilities interpretation of quantum theory. He was willing to see it as a successful mathematical description, but felt that there were likely to be hidden variables which, once discovered, would enable quantum physics to become deterministic again. This is the origin of Einstein's famous quote that 'God does not play dice with the universe'. Although Einstein lost the argument at the time, it is one that is still ongoing. For example Gerard 't Hooft (Nobel Prize 1999 for developments in the theory of quantum physics) is trying to develop a new formulation for quantum mechanics that is deterministic: the apparent uncertainties that Heisenberg pointed out are due to information loss.

There is a multiplicity of interpretations of quantum physics. The online reference tool Wikipedia lists twelve interpretations. The second well-known interpretation is the Bohm pilot-wave theory (1952) which developed an idea from de Broglie, and is also deterministic. The fact that there are so many interpretations of the theory shows the problems of explaining and understanding the theory. This is one of the factors that sets it apart from classical theories like Newtonian mechanics, Maxwell's electromagnetism and Einstein's relativity.

The many-worlds interpretation

The second interpretation of quantum theory is the many-worlds (or multiverse) theory proposed by the American physicist Hugh Everett in 1957. According to this interpretation, whenever numerous viable possibilities exist, the world splits into many **worlds**, that is one world for each different possibility. In each of these worlds, everything is identical, except for that one difference; and as the result of that one difference from that point on, each world develops independently, and no communication is possible between them. The people living in each of those worlds, and splitting along with them, may have no idea that this is going on. The worlds branch endlessly as all the possibilities occur. We might think we are in the present but this could be the past of an unaccountably or immeasurably huge number of different futures. The theory is that everything that *can* or *could* happen, does, somewhere.

The many-worlds interpretation is an interpretation of quantum mechanics, but it also has implications for macroscopic systems. It would mean, for example, that there would be an infinite number of versions of every human, who have all split off at some time in the past from the path they are now following. These versions could have split off at any point in an individual's life when a choice had to be made and could result in an immeasurable number of possible outcomes.

It may be possible to observe experimentally one of the predicted effects of the many worlds: quantum interference between adjacent worlds. It has even been suggested that the 'Heisenberg Uncertainty Principle' derives from this quantum interference as, after a measurement that

■ Think about

Albert Einstein, when speaking of quantum physics, said: 'God does not play dice with the universe.' Although what Einstein meant by 'God' is often debated, what do you think Einstein meant by this statement in relation to quantum mechanics?

■ Activity

Using Wikipedia find out more about these different interpretations. Write an explanation of the Bohm pilot-wave theory.

■ Think about

There was a television programme called *Sliders* in which university student Quinn Mallory invents a device known as the 'timer' where he is able to slide between parallel universes through wormholes in time. He is always in the same city but through one minor change a different possibility of Los Angeles occurs. For example, if the American War of Independence had not taken place then the city would still be under British rule, or disease would be prevalent if penicillin had not been discovered. Think of all the possibilities of how your life could be different from how it is now if you had achieved different GCSE grades.

■ Key terms

Worlds: in this context the term refers to what most people would call 'universes'.

■ Think about

What are the major differences between the many-worlds interpretation and the Copenhagen interpretation?

What influences your choices?

Is there any choice you know you would never make? What would your reasons be for not making that choice?

■ **Key terms**

Ockham's razor: William of Ockham was a 14th century English friar and scholar who stated that, 'All things being equal, the simplest solution tends to be the right one.' This maxim has become known as Ockham's razor.

■ **Activity**

Write an essay of 500–600-words to explain the major features of quantum mechanics.

The traditional symbol representing the forces of yin and yang.

■ **Key terms**

Metaphysics: the branch of philosophy that investigates principles of reality transcending those of any particular science, and includes cosmology. Metaphysics is also concerned with explaining the ultimate nature of being and the world.

Tao: means path. Taoism is a Chinese system of philosophical and religious traditions and concepts. The philosophy emphasises the link between people and nature, and by following the path a better understanding of the world can be achieved.

splits the world has been made, it is not possible to be certain about the subsequent state of the observed system, because it is not possible to be sure which world you are in. Stephen Hawking is among the scientists who have expressed a preference for the many-worlds theory.

The advantage of the many-worlds interpretation is that it is deterministic; the disadvantage is that, at every point in space and time, an infinite number of new universes are sprouting up that are thereafter disconnected from each other. This seems like a blatant violation of a concept that has been dear to scientists down the centuries known as **Ockham's razor**; an infinity of universes has, until recently, seemed to most people so self-evidently absurd, and the opposite of the elegant simplicity that physicists strive for, that it was of little more than academic interest. It's an interesting reflection of the changing culture in which we live that Ockham's razor is less obviously a correct principle, whereas the many-worlds interpretation is more in tune with modern thinking.

ⓘ Mystical insights into the nature of reality

For those who follow the Eastern mystical traditions, there is a belief that at the moment of connection to a higher source, understanding of the nature of reality is gained, and that there is an underlying unity of things. For some mystics a link is seen between a 'mystical' view and the insights of quantum mechanics. Heisenberg himself was well aware of these parallels, as was Niels Bohr. Heisenberg believed that an understanding of the mysticism of India had helped him in his understanding of the problems raised by quantum mechanics, especially the role of the observer in creating what is observed. A modern physicist who shares this belief in a link between physics and metaphysics is Fritjof Capra.

☑ Do quantum variables have definite values?

Fritjof Capra (1939–) has carried out research in particle physics and systems theory. He has also written books on the links between physics and **metaphysics**, particularly Eastern mysticism. His most famous work is *The Tao of Physics*, subtitled *An Exploration of the Parallels between Modern Physics and Eastern Mysticism*. In the book, Capra examines how Eastern mysticism and contemporary scientific findings relate, and how Eastern mysticism might also have answers to some of today's scientific challenges.

> The most important characteristic of the Eastern world-view – one could almost say the essence of it – is the awareness of the unity and mutual interrelation of all things and events, the experience of all phenomena in the world as manifestations of a basic oneness. All things are seen as interdependent and inseparable parts of this cosmic whole; as different manifestations of the same ultimate reality.

Fritjof Capra, The Tao of Physics, 1975

Capra argues that quantum mechanics makes similar claims about the wholeness of reality to Eastern mysticism. He believes that both consider the role of the observer and that observer and observation are inseparable. Capra points to the fact that paradoxes in quantum mechanics such as the wave-particle duality may be compared to the **yin/yang** polarity in **Taoism**. Capra believed that what we observe in nature is nothing more than the 'creations of our measuring and categorizing minds', and the same is true of quantum variables as they have no definite values until human observation and thought intervenes.

The universe as a web

Capra points to the fact that for Eastern mystics the universe is an 'inseparable web, whose interconnections are dynamic and not static'. For these mystics the universe moves, grows and changes continually. Eastern religions believe that life is transitory as existence is impermanent and in continual motion. Similarly Capra points to the fact that modern physics also accepts a timeless realm, and the universe is seen as an intrinsically dynamic web.

> The dynamic aspect of matter arises in quantum theory as a consequence of the wave-nature of subatomic particles, and is even more essential in relativity theory, where the unification of space and time implies that the being of matter cannot be separated from its activity. The properties of subatomic particles can therefore only be understood in a dynamic context; in terms of movement, interaction and transformation.

Fritjof Capra, The Tao of Physics, 1975

☑ Challenges to Capra

Ian Barbour is an eminent scholar in the field of science and religion. He argues that Capra has emphasised the similarities between Eastern mysticism and quantum mechanics at the expense of the differences. For example the mystic speaks of a universe that is an undifferentiated structureless unity, whereas in physics there is a unity that is highly differentiated, within which there is 'organized interaction and cooperative behaviour of higher-level wholes'.

Barbour also believes that there is a difference in the understanding of time and timelessness. Quantum mechanics is considering temporal change and impermanence whereas Eastern mysticism considers the temporal world as illusory, and it is the ultimate reality that is timeless and unchanging. Also the goals of science and religion are different as science seeks to explain the nature of the world whereas a mystic seeks understanding of the ultimate reality. The argument could be levelled back at Barbour that surely the goals of science and religion are not different, and they are both seeking to explain the nature of the world and ultimate reality.

The implications of quantum mechanics for religion

Physicists have not as yet gained a full understanding of all that is implied by quantum mechanics. However, what has been discovered to date raises questions for the religious believer about the relationship between the hidden atomic and subatomic world of quantum mechanics and the macroscopic world in which we can observe and measure things.

Determinism and randomness

Previously scientists had assumed that there was determinism in the natural laws and this challenged God's involvement in the world. Newtonian physics depicts a universe in which objects move in perfectly determinative ways, and gives predictions that in many areas check out as completely perfectible, to the accuracy of measurement. Quantum mechanics does not have this certainty as there is the randomness of observable events within a range of probable values, and it has revealed previously concealed aspects of events.

Key terms

Yin/yang: the two primal opposing but complementary principles or cosmic forces said to be found in all non-static objects and processes in the universe. Yin (dark) is often symbolised by water and air, while yang (light) is symbolised by fire and earth. All forces in nature can be seen as having yin and yang states, and the two are in constant movement rather than held in absolute stasis.

Link

Look back at Chapter 2, pp17–22, to find out about the major features of a mystical experience.

Activities

1 Find out more about Taoism.

2 List the similarities you can think of between quantum mechanics and yin/yang.

AQA Examiner's tip

Remember that all the examiner knows about how knowledgeable you are, and how skilled in applying information to the question set and in arguing a case, is what you have shown through your answers. Your aim is to impress and the exam is your opportunity to do that.

Activities

1 Using the internet find out more about Barbour's challenges to Capra. Make a list of Barbour's challenges.

2 Do you agree with Barbour's challenges to Capra? What are the reasons for your view?

Link

Look back at Chapter 6, p96, and remind yourself of the meaning of determinism.

■ **Think about**

If quantum mechanics is deterministic how might that influence beliefs about God?

■ **Link**

Look back at Richard Swinburne's design argument based on probabilities in Chapter 7, pp118–20.

Some scientists argue that in addition to observation and the rules that can be deduced there are hidden factors or hidden variables that determine the course of the universe. Humans are screened from knowledge of the determinative factors and therefore it only appears that things proceed in a merely probabilistically determinative way. Actually, they proceed in an absolutely determinative way.

The level of control

However quantum mechanics could still argue against God having control of the world. What it has demonstrated are the limitations in human knowledge about the reality of the world in which we live, and that it may be that science and religion are not totally unrelated and independent.

Some religious believers have suggested that God controls the world at the atomic level, and that it is God who decides the actual value within the probability distribution. Quantum theory has therefore supported the involvement of God within creation at all levels and this is why the physicist cannot find a natural cause; for example why there is no definite position for an electron in a superposition of states, because God is the cause. One small change by God at the atomic level can result in large-scale changes at the macroscopic level. It is by controlling quantum events that God has affected events in both evolutionary and human history.

Ian Barbour in *When Science Meets Religion* (2000) rejects the idea that God is the hidden variable with quantum mechanics because:

■ Such a belief suggests total control over all events and supports predestination. Such a belief is 'incompatible with human freedom and the reality of evil'. It also removes any possibility of chance. However not all believers would reject predestination and therefore for them such an argument would not be valid.

■ To accept God's involvement would mean that God's will is achieved through 'the unlawful rather than the lawful aspects of nature'. Barbour feels that this may argue against Deism is but is still a one-sided argument as he is suggesting that God is not involved in the world where there are consistent scientific laws, and God is only involved where no predictable law can be established.

■ Such a belief is reducing God's actions to the molecular level and does not allow for God directly influencing the macroscopic level, which would include God not influencing humanity. However if God has given humans free will then it could be argued that God would not be expected to influence humanity's actions.

In contrast to Barbour's arguments Robert Russell accepts that God may influence certain events at the quantum level but also at the higher level. In this way it would be possible for chance events, natural laws and God's action in the world to co-exist. This removes the suggestion that all events are determined directly by God and still allows for freedom of choice.

Evidence for and against God

Physicists and philosophers of science have argued about how to understand quantum mechanics' probabilistic description of reality. This is because the different interpretations of the same evidence have led to the multiplicity of interpretations of quantum physics.

The Copenhagen interpretation that the act of observing causes the outcome to be determined has led to some believers suggesting that the implication of quantum mechanics is that the universe only functions because it is continually observed by God.

■ **Think about**

Look back at the Copenhagen interpretation on p126. What philosophical problems does it pose about the existence of God or the nature of God?

Activities

Read the following quotation from Albert Einstein. Einstein doubted the theory of quantum mechanics.

'Scientific research is based on the idea that everything that takes place is determined by laws of nature, and therefore this holds for the actions of people. For this reason, a research scientist will hardly be inclined to believe that events could be influenced by prayer, i.e. by a wish addressed to a supernatural Being. However, it must be admitted that our actual knowledge of these laws is only imperfect and fragmentary, so that, actually the belief in the existence of basic all-embracing laws in nature also rests on a sort of faith. All the same this faith has been largely justified so far by the success of scientific research. But, on the other hand, everyone who is seriously involved in the pursuit of science becomes convinced that a spirit is manifest in the laws of the universe – a spirit vastly superior to that of man, and one in the face of which we with our modest powers must feel humble. In this way the pursuit of science leads to a religious feeling of a special sort, which is indeed quite different from the religiosity of someone more naive.'

Write an explanation of what you think Einstein believed were the links between science and religion.

Stephen Hawking takes the random nature of the quantum mechanics universe as evidence that the universe lacks purpose and design. Hawking argues that quantum mechanics shows that if there is a God at all, this God cannot be purposeful or act deliberately in the world. This is because the randomness and irrationality of quantum mechanics makes it impossible for even God to foresee or govern the future.

The physicist and theologian John Polkinghorne sees the beauty of the mathematics involved in quantum mechanics as evidence of the divine and human free will. Mathematics, he argues, has the enduring ability to accurately describe the physical world and our brains have the capacity to understand these abstract concepts, such as quantum superposition, and this cannot have happened as the result of evolution. It is the work of God who has made us in his own image and at the same time given us freedom of choice. The omniscience of God is self-limited so that we have genuine free will. For Polkinghorne, the universe is not a universe of clockwork determinism and he rejects Deism. Quantum mechanics demonstrates that it is a universe in which the interplay of chance and necessity is so constructed that God can act personally within it and yet allow human beings to exercise their free will within it, and in the natural order things can evolve. Polkinghorne believes that a study of quantum mechanics is not a challenge to belief in God. Polkinghorne believes that 'All science can do is provide a vague notion of God as some sort of divine mathematician or supreme designer, and there is a great deal more to God than that.'

Activity

Compare and contrast how the religious world-views of Capra and Polkinghorne have influenced their perception of reality.

Can science be religious?

Richard Dawkins would argue that it is not possible for science to be religious as science must be based on empirical evidence whereas religion is based on faith which has no such basis. Science requires reason and observation and according to Dawkins' 'verifiable evidence'. However it could be argued that quantum mechanics has demonstrated that there are some aspects of science which have similar problems to religion. There are things that cannot be verified and there has to be acceptance of probabilities. Richard Swinburne argued for the design argument to prove the existence of God based on probabilities and so it could be argued a scientist at times has to have faith in what they believe to be true when there is no empirical evidence to support this belief. In quantum mechanics much of the findings for example are dependent on probabilities. Similarly Dawkins's conviction that the theory of evolution is true could be regarded as faith. Dawkins argues that it is not faith that makes him believe in the theory but evidence that anyone can examine and this is not true of faith as faith is subjective and is not open to examination. But for others Dawkins's conviction that it is true goes beyond mere acceptance of evidence to faith.

For many science is seen as a religion because it is seeking the reasons for the origin of life and the universe and these are religious questions. Modern science has even been described as the 'new religion' as it is only another way by which humans are trying to find the meaning to life.

For some believers science and religion can be of mutual benefit to each other. They argue that science can provide evidence to support religious teaching, for example the Big Bang theory may be used to support a beginning to the universe and for religion this beginning is caused by God. These believers consider that in the modern scientific age when atheism is growing it is important for religion to accept such support from science to stop people turning away from God. The evidence from science may be so overwhelming that if religion does not adapt to the new scientific findings then there is a risk that religious teachings will be rejected. For example the theory of evolution can be regarded as the work of God as the most important religious teaching is that God is the creator of life. Evolutionary theories do not threaten such beliefs. Science is not rejecting the existence of God, it is just not looking for God in its research. Most Muslims argue that the more discoveries made by science then the more evidence there is to prove the existence of God as only God could have created the complicated universe discovered by science.

On the other hand there are believers such as Fundamentalist Christians who argue that when science does not agree with a literal interpretation of the Bible it is important to stress that it is science that is wrong. When science conflicts, for example, with the biblical account of creation there can be no agreement with science, the argument being that once you begin to reject any part of the Bible in favour of science then where do you stop? Once one part is questioned then you are in danger of rejecting all of the Bible and with it the moral code it contains, and then the basis of faith is undermined.

The link between religion and science

How important for religion is agreement with science depends very much on how literally a believer takes their religious writings and teachings to be. In the following quotation the Reverend Ricky Hoyt argues why he believes religion does need to be in agreement with science:

> Religion needs science, because, although the sphere of morals, values, meanings, and purpose, belong to religion, uniquely (that is they aren't part of science), morals, values, meanings, and purpose are not the only elements of religion. Religion also contains a description of the world the way the world is in all its particulars, both the physical and the non-physical. The religious world is not only peace, love and justice, the stuff that science could leave alone to it, the religious world is also people and plants and rocks and sky. The religious world is human bodies, as well as human souls. The religious world is compassionate relationships, and biochemical relationships. The

religious world is both the weak and the strong, and the weak and the strong electromagnetic forces. Religion begins with a statement of beliefs. And what beliefs are is a description of the world, the same thing that science gives us. A complete description of the world isn't limited merely to such obviously religious subjects as whether or not angels exist, or whether or not there is an objective source for morality, a complete description of the world also includes whether or not the sun exists, whether we get our personality traits from a soul injected into the womb or from our genes, or from the way we were raised as infants. A complete description of the world includes how old it is: 4.5 billion years, or 6,000.

Reverend Ricky Hoyt, Archived Sermon, 2007

■ Conclusion

The development of quantum theory has demonstrated that space, time, energy and matter are interconnected. The universe is more complex than scientists of the 18th and 19th centuries thought. Quantum mechanics has shown that Laplace's hopes of determinism are not realistic, as sought-after universal theories may well remain beyond the scope of human understanding. Modern science is able to begin to describe the *what* of the universe, but it is not able to answer the *why* of the universe. The why could be God.

The main aim of modern physics is to find a complete unified theory, which will link the laws of space, time, matter and energy together. When Einstein said that 'God does not play dice with the universe', he meant that there are unifying laws in nature, rather than a series of random, chance events. Those laws still have to be found.

> However, if we do discover a complete theory, it should in time be understandable in broad principle by everyone, not just a few scientists. Then we shall all, philosophers, scientists, and just ordinary people, be able to take part in the discussion of the question of why it is that we and the universe exist. If we find the answer to that, it would be the ultimate triumph of human reason – for then we would know the mind of God.

Stephen Hawking, A Brief History of Time, 1992

Now that you have read this chapter you should be able to:

■ explain the world-view of quantum mechanics

■ explain the parallels between quantum mechanics and mystical insights in the Eastern traditions into the nature of reality

■ evaluate whether science can be 'religious'

■ assess whether science has discovered something that mystics knew all along.

Activities

1 Summarise the major features of quantum mechanics including: the quanta, light as both wave and particle, the nature of the electron, and the role of the observer in resolving uncertainty.

2 List the major similarities and differences between the insights of quantum mechanics and a 'mystical' view of the universe.

3 Assess the strengths and weaknesses of the argument that there is a similarity between the insights of quantum mechanics and a 'mystical' view of the universe.

4 Evaluate whether or not quantum mechanics is in any sense 'mystical'.

5 Evaluate whether or not quantum mechanics is a modelling based on empirical observation or an intuitive insight into the nature of things.

Religion, Philosophy and Science: summary of key points

■ Chapter 5: Miracles

What is a Miracle?

A miracle can be interpreted as:

- ■ an event in which a natural law is violated or does not apply
- ■ an event of religious significance.

Violations of natural laws

- ■ Examples of these are found in the Bible and include raising from the dead, healing and nature miracles.
- ■ David Hume took this definition of a miracle.
- ■ Richard Swinburne argued that to be considered a miracle, an event must not only violate a natural law but also have religious significance.

What does this definition of a miracle tell us about how God interacts with the world?

- ■ It means that God directly intervenes in the world to change the natural course of events.
- ■ This requires a theistic understanding of God, as adopted by Christians, Muslims and Jews, rather than the deistic view that God leaves the world to govern itself.
- ■ A miraculous violation might be understood in terms of Thomas Aquinas' explanation of God's primary actions in the world.

Arguments against the existence of miracles as violations of natural law

1 Certain theists argue that everything depends on God, whether violation or not. Most, however, argue that God governs the world through regular laws.

2 Hick argued that any apparent violation of a natural law could be explained through an exception to that law. However, Swinburne suggested that events can be unexpected enough to be considered violations of what we would normally expect to happen.

3 Hume argued:
- ■ It is always more likely that the testimony of a miracle is incorrect.
- ■ Such testimony is generally unreliable.
- ■ Natural laws have been observed to function an uncountable number of times.
- ■ Evidence for a miracle would have to outweigh all the evidence for the natural law.
- ■ Miracle accounts from different religions cancel each other out.

Criticisms of Hume

- ■ Swinburne argued that natural laws are based on the same kind of testimonies as miracles.
- ■ Since miracles are exceptions they do not have to outweigh the natural law.

- Miracle accounts from different religions may cancel out the religions, but not always the miracles.
4 Difficulties with the belief that God intervenes in the world.
    - Nelson Pyke argues that God cannot intervene in the world as God is outside time.
    - Maurice Wiles argues that it raises serious moral problems. It raises the question why God does not intervene more frequently and presents an inconsistent God. For example, if God violated natural laws to save the Hebrews from Egypt, why did he not do the same to prevent the Holocaust? Wiles argues that a God who intervenes selectively would not be worthy of worship.
    - It also threatens human free will.
    - The moral problems and threat to free will make the problem of evil even harder to solve.

Miracles as events of religious significance

These can be understood in different ways:

- Miraculous violations are often seen to have great religious significance. The author of John's Gospel calls such events signs. This emphasises their importance for telling us about the nature of Jesus as the Son of God.
- Some miraculous violations appear only to have religious significance, e.g. stigmata.
- Certain events have been considered to have religious significance as miracles, even though they included no violation of natural laws. These include amazing coincidences and natural events.

What does this definition of a miracle tell us about how God interacts with the world?

- The implications of miraculous violations have already been considered.
- If miracles are defined as truly natural events, including natural coincidences, the problems of an interventionist God are removed but they are replaced by the difficulty of how to see God as being present and interacting with the world through the natural event.
- If God is understood to be present through the miracle, a theistic view of God is still required.
- Some would argue that such miracles, like all other events, are determined by God. All human actions could be seen as secondary actions of God. The arguments of soft determinists might be used to explain how we can still be free. But many critics would argue that our free will is altogether removed if God determines us.
- Others argue that such events are only miracles because they are interpreted in that way. Upon this view there are three ways in which God might be understood to be present:
1 Some would see the miracle as a private religious experience which communicates a sense of God's presence.
2 Anti-realists would say that the event is only a miracle that communicates God's presence for those who see it that way, meaning that God is not objectively present.
3 Paul Tillich argued that such events can communicate a powerful experience of God as the 'ground of being'.

The main problem with seeing a natural event as a miracle is that there is no reason why one needs to do so. David Hume, for example, denied that any natural event should be seen as miraculous.

What could miraculous violations prove, if they were to occur?

■ They could be attributed to psychic or other natural powers about which, as yet, we know little.

■ They could be attributed to a non-material personal being or beings (Swinburne).

■ They may or may not be performed by the God of Classical Theism.

■ Chapter 6: Creation

Religious beliefs and the creation of the world

The God of classical theism is believed to have created the universe and all that is within it. For Jews and Christians an account of God's creation can be found in Genesis 1–3. Christians do not agree as to whether this account is to be taken literally.

God is believed not only to have created the world but also to be sustaining the world.

Science and the creation of the world

Scientists have different theories about the origin of the universe and the way in which the world has developed.

The Big Bang theory

■ The universe originated with a 'big bang'.

■ Time began when the Big Bang occurred.

The Big Crunch theory

Some scientists believe that the universe will reverse its direction and begin to collapse under its own weight.

The steady-state theory

■ The universe has no beginning or end.

■ The universe is a process of continuous creation.

The evolutionary theory

We are the consequence of chemical/biological events which were/ are inevitable, and which are not controlled by anyone/anything but themselves. This view is supported by Richard Dawkins.

The challenge of scientific theories to religious beliefs

■ 'God of the gaps' – God is used to explain what science cannot.

■ Deism – a clockwork universe which God set going and left.

■ There is no beginning to the universe and it is continually being created.

■ The beginning of the universe was no more than a random explosion.

■ Humans are no more than the result of natural selection over a period of time.

Religious responses to these challenges

■ There is evidence of intelligent design that best explains the features of the universe and living things.

- The anthropic principle demonstrates that humans are more than the product of natural selection.
- Evolution is part of God's plan.
- Science cannot explain everything such as why the Big Bang happened – God is the explanation.
- The Big Crunch is supported by the belief in the end of time and a Day of Judgement.

Chapter 7: The design argument for the existence of God

The design argument

The design (teleological) argument proves the existence of God from the idea that:

- There is evidence of design, order and purpose in the universe.
- If there is design then there must have been a designer.
- The designer is God.

There are two forms of the design argument:

- Design *qua* regularity seeks to prove design through the evidence of regularity and order in the universe.
- Design *qua* purpose seeks to prove design through the evidence of order for a specific purpose.

St Thomas Aquinas sought to prove the design argument through the way in which there is regularity and order in the universe. For example the regularity of the rotation of the planets, Sun and stars must be the result of design. The designer is God.

William Paley used evidence from nature to prove the argument from design *qua* purpose. He argued that the way in which things fit together for a specific purpose cannot have happened by chance. For example, a bird's wings for flight or the eye for sight are evidence of design. The designer is God.

Paley used Newton's discovery of gravity to prove the argument from design *qua* regularity. The movement of the heavenly bodies obeying universal laws of movement could not be by chance but by design. The designer is God.

The anthropic principle considers that there is evidence that there is design in the universe and world for the specific purpose of the development of intelligent life. Natural selection could be part of this design. The designer is God.

Richard Swinburne support the anthropic principle from temporal order and spatial order. Swinburne's argument from temporal order accepts that the universe is law governed. What we see around us could be the result of design or random chance but Swinburne argues that the sheer complexity of the universe makes it unlikely that the order in the universe happened by chance and it is more probable that there is design. Swinburne's second argument related to the spatial order of the universe develops in such a way that they were just right for the evolutionary development of plants, animals and humans. He argues that it is improbable that these conditions would have been right without the existence of God.

Criticisms of the argument

David Hume was a major critic of the argument. He argued that:

■ There may be design, but this does not prove it is God. The universe could be the work of many designers, or of an apprentice designer.

■ We do not know enough about the world to conclude that it is the work of one designer. Human experience would demonstrate that complicated projects are the result of many designers – not just one.

■ The flaws in the design of the world, such as death and disease, would suggest that the design was not a good one. This counts against the benevolent God of classical theism.

The Epicurean hypothesis argued that given sufficient time, the random particles that make up the universe would come together to give the appearance of design. Random chance caused the universe and world to exist in its present form, not design.

John Stuart Mill challenged the idea that the world was designed by the God of classical theism because of the existence of evil and suffering.

Charles Darwin's publication *The Origin of the Species by Means of Natural Selection* (1859) demonstrated why there appeared to be design in the world. Life has developed as the result of evolution. The survival of the fittest and natural selection have given the appearance of design.

Evolutionary biologist Richard Dawkins argues against the anthropic principle and the design argument in general. Dawkins argues that humans appear to have an appreciation of beauty but it is no more than part of the survival mechanism. Humans are no more than the result of natural selection.

■ Chapter 8: Quantum mechanics and a religious world-view

Quantum mechanics is the branch of theoretical physics explaining the behaviour of matter at atomic and subatomic levels.

Key ideas in quantum mechanics

Matter is made up of atoms. Atoms are composed of three types of particles: protons, neutrons and electrons.

When an atom changes its state, it absorbs or emits an amount of energy just sufficient to bring it to another state. This is the quantum of energy. Max Planck showed that light energy must be emitted and absorbed in discrete 'quanta' to explain black body radiation. 'Planck's constant' is used to describe the sizes of quanta. An electron is a negatively charged atomic particle which rotates around the nucleus of the atom. The electrons give off light and other electromagnetic radiation. Light can function as both a particle and a wave.

Heisenberg's uncertainty principle demonstrated that the more precisely you know the position of the electron the less accurately you can measure its speed. He concluded that orbits of electrons do not exist in nature unless and until we observe them. It is only the probability of the electron's location at a certain time that can be predicted.

Niels Bohr proposed the Copenhagen interpretation of quantum theory when he asserted that an electron is a wave or a particle according to what it is measured to be, that is a wave or a particle, but that it cannot be assumed to have specific properties, or even to exist, until it is measured.

Erwin Schrödinger argued that we can observe things at the macroscopic level but that does not mean things behave in the same way at the microscopic level. Therefore you cannot tell what is happening at the microscopic level, but only predict the probabilities of what is happening. At the quantum level things are in more than one state at once, called superposition. One way to overcome this, Schrödinger argued, is to forget the particle and only seek to measure the wave.

Hugh Everett developed the many-worlds interpretation, arguing that in addition to the world we are aware of directly, there are many other similar worlds which exist in parallel at the same space and time. The existence of the other worlds makes it possible to remove randomness and action at a distance from quantum theory and thus from all physics.

Parallels between quantum mechanics and mystical insights into the nature of reality

The parallels between quantum mechanics and mystical insights into the nature of reality include:

- a similarity between the role of the observer in creating what is observed
- an awareness of a oneness in the world giving unity to all things and events
- similarity of wave-particle duality and the yin-yang polarity
- both see not a static world but a timeless realm that is forever growing and changing though movement, interaction and transformation.

The implications of quantum mechanics for religion

The implications of quantum mechanics for religion include:

- Quantum mechanics has brought uncertainty back into science and as with religion there are questions that cannot be answered solely by observation and measurement. It may be God who controls the world at the atomic level, and decides the actual value within the probability distribution. This counters Deism.
- There appear to be hidden variables that stop humans gaining knowledge of the determinative factors so humans can only proceed using probabilities. This may mean that God wants humans to have free will.
- Quantum mechanics has demonstrated the limitations in human knowledge about the reality of the world and that it may be that science and religion are not totally unrelated and independent.
- Ian Barbour rejects the idea that God is the hidden variable with quantum mechanics because:

1 It removes any possibility of chance, and so limits human freedom.
2 God's will is achieved through 'the unlawful rather than the lawful aspects of nature'. Barbour feels this may argue against Deism but it is still a one-sided argument.
3 Such a belief is reducing God's actions to the molecular level and does not allow for God directly influencing the macroscopic level, which would include God not influencing humanity.

Robert Russell accepts that God may influence certain events at the quantum level but also at the higher level. In this way it would be possible for chance events, natural laws and God's actions in the world to co-exist. This removes the suggestion that all events are determined directly by God and still allows for freedom of choice.

AQA Examination-style questions

5   (a)   'A miracle is a violation of natural law.'
          (i)   Explain the meaning of this statement.
         (ii)   Explain why some religious believers would claim that God does not perform such miracles.   *(30 marks)*
       (b)   Assess the view that miracles are only ordinary events interpreted in an extraordinary way.   *(15 marks)*

AQA specimen question

6   (a)   Explain how religion and science can offer contrasting answers to the question, 'what happened at the beginning of time'?   *(30 marks)*
       (b)   How far is it true that there is no room for God in a scientific view of the origin of the universe?   *(15 Marks)*

AQA specimen question

7   (a)   Explain the key ideas in the design argument for the existence of God.   *(30 marks)*
       (b)   Assess the view that science has made the design argument a failure.   *(15 marks)*

AQA specimen question

8   (a)   Explain the main features of the world-view of quantum mechanics.   *(30 marks)*
       (b)   'Quantum mechanics leads to a mystical view of the nature of reality.' To what extent is this true?   *(15 marks)*

AQA specimen question

Index